GIRL SHOCK!

*I dressed as a girl for Halloween
but then she took over my life!*

BY MARIA KONNER

Published by Under the Golden Gate Media
www.underthegoldengate.com

First Edition, First Printing
ISBN: 978-1-7367461-0-3

Photos marked "Credit: David Steinberg" in Chapters 1, 2, 10, 11:
© 2008–2020 David Steinberg, All Rights Reserved.
For additional photos by David Steinberg, see www.davidsteinberg.com.

Artwork concepts by Maria Konner, drawn by:

Cover art and final painting at end:
DIEGO GOMEZ

Preface cartoons and chapter drawings:
DIEGO SANDOVAL

Drawings San Francisco day & night, Power Exchange:
DAVID LAWRENCE HAWKINS

DEDICATED TO SAN FRANCISCO:

May she always remain a village for love of diversity, love of Earth, and radical inclusion of all people and all species, throughout the ebbs and flows of time, no matter what new forms she may take.

I never thought I'd find in me such fabulosity,
until I started living as a girl . . .

MARIA KONNER

AUTHOR'S NOTE

Hi! Thanks for coming into my world! I wanted to write a quick note before we get started.

This is a true story about my personal experiences and my observations, feelings, and opinions after leaving my straight suburban life and discovering a trans life in San Francisco—while also living within the various subcultures in the queer and alternative communities of this great city. I also share opinions and experiences from friends, acquaintances, and those I interviewed on my show http://underthegoldengate.com.

This includes a period of my life when I was also discovering an active, party-oriented sex life. Many other trans folks live a different lifestyle and have different opinions than I do. I also go into how I saw some of the subcultures in the community—both as a member and as an outsider. I am trying to explain something that is hard for someone to understand without experiencing it. The best I can do is to just describe how I experienced it, and what I was thinking and feeling from my own unique and limited point of view.

Since I was fortunate to have had the opportunity to have an such a wondrous time, it is my pleasure to share these intimate, exciting, and profound set of experiences with you!

I'm NOT an expert on trans and LGBT issues, alternative lifestyles, etc. Please consider exploring other sources to learn more about these issues.

Some names have been changed to protect the privacy of individuals. Thanks again, and welcome! XOXXOO

MARIA

www.mariakonner.com
www.underthegoldengate.com

CONTENTS

PART 6: SEX CHANGE?!

GIRL
SHOCK!

I CAN'T BELIEVE I'M DOING THIS!

"Fuck yea!" I screamed.

A few weeks ago, I was a straight, boring, married dude living in the burbs outside San Francisco. Now I'm at Divas, *the* transsexual bar of San Francisco[1], staring at a hot woman in the mirror...me.

When my marriage crumbled, I didn't just get separated from my wife, I got separated from my life. I got separated from the American Dream, which, in my case, was a failed marriage of five years with the wrong person due to my desperation to not be alone in my beautiful house on the golf course with the swimming pool in the East Bay burbs of San Francisco.

Every man getting divorced has his own way of coping. Some dive into work, some get on a motorcycle for a few months, some do nothing but drink and watch TV. When my American Dream turned into a nightmare, I pulled the ripcord and landed on the edge of the seedy Tenderloin neighborhood of San Francisco, rejoicing in the skank and diversity. I moved into an apartment two blocks from a transsexual bar. I wanted to get as far away from married life as I could, wanting nothing to do with the straight world for a while. I had no children, and now I wanted to live a life free of expectations, relationships, responsibilities, and the

---

1. Divas was the only transsexual bar in San Francisco. Asia SF featured transsexual performers and waitresses, but it was not a bar in the sense of a place to hang out and meet and hook up with t-girls. If you wanted to meet a t-girl, you went to Divas. You might run across us in other bars, but Divas was the only place in the city dedicated to t-girls. Diva's closed in early 2019 due to the declining alternative night life scene in SF.

suburban castle. I worked in Tech, and other than putting in the time to take their money, I no longer wanted anything to do with that world, either. Something in my life wasn't adding up. Something was missing, and I needed to find it. But I wondered . . . was I just running away from reality, or was I running toward something more real? Was I entering a den of debauchery, or was I finally finding my people?

Then this mystery superwoman Maria appeared and somehow became my ticket to a whole new life.

The year was 2006, and the neighborhood was the Polk Gulch, wedged between the dirty, drug- and prostitute-filled Tenderloin neighborhood of San Francisco, the emerging SoMa Tech Industry neighborhood, and the ultra-wealthy Nob Hill and Russian Hill neighborhoods. These areas of the city were separated by only a handful of blocks. And Divas was on Post at Polk, right on the boundary between the sleaze and the upscale. Just the place for me—the intersection of two very different worlds resulting in a lot of cultural eddies and strangeness.

When you walked into Divas, you would first be shocked by the smoking hot women. Eventually, you'd be hit with a secondary and much stronger shock when you realized there were very few if any genetic girls[2] in the place—these girls were born male. Many of them had invested in surgery to sculpt and transform their bodies into beautiful women. Going to Divas was *literally* a jaw-dropping experience for the many thousands who visited it over its 31-year history.

Divas was a sort of trans town square, where locals and visitors alike went to meet trans women and their lovers and admirers in *real life*. The patrons spanned the spectrum—t-girls (trans women)[3], blue collar guys, white collar guys, curious straight tourists, curious straight couples, LGBT couples, and a potpourri of the *authentically* weird and fun underground San Francisco community. Some were looking to get laid or experiment, some were looking to mingle with friends old and new, some were there for the drag show, and some just wanted to hang out and see all the glorious colors. Back then, people in the city met mostly in person, not online. And how glorious that way of living was.

---

2. Born women. We referred to them as GG's. There are many other terms for this.
3. I refer to Male-to-Female transgendered girls using several different names (e.g. gurls, t-girls, trans women). There are a variety of terms/labels that people use, often meaning something different to different people.

I stood in a narcissistic haze on the third floor of Divas—the dance floor—an orgy of mirrors, dance music, booze, trans women, and, of course, those who love us trans women. Just the right kind of place to disappear for a time while recovering from the trauma of getting divorced and questioning a lot of decisions I made in the past.

The mirrors on the dance floor reflected from every wall and every angle, so I could see my butt, the back of my bra, my big boobs from the side, and my front all at the same time—just like in a Macy's dressing room! Yeah! I could make this woman strike any pose I wanted. It was totally surreal, seeing this hot woman staring back at me. *Look at those insanely hot legs covered in shiny black nylons, gurl! Damn those shoes look great on me. Who is that girl? That's not really me, is it?!*

I can't explain what being there as a woman unleashed in me. It reached into my soul and pulled out pure fun and joy. I found it intoxicating and empowering. It put a big smile on my face and let me live in the moment and find my soul. This wasn't some fake TV show! Fuck yea! I had no idea what it felt like to be so fabulous! *Guys, you have to try it. I know so many of you think about it—you've told me. The things that come out at a transsexual bar—the honesty, the sleaze . . . I love it. Little else in our adult world is so authentic and pure. It is truly beautiful.*

I looked at the other gurls and noticed they were admiring themselves in the mirror, too. I loved watching the working girls grabbing their large breasts (implants). I tried to imagine myself being one of them. Was this some kind of sick addiction, or was this a beautiful thing where a man can become a woman and appreciate the gift of being unshackled from a limiting male persona? I wondered, *wouldn't it be crazy to get breast implants like that?* I couldn't help it. I didn't expect to actually do it, but the fantasy allowed me to be in the moment, and all my thoughts and troubles melted away. Perverted addiction or gift and spiritual awakening? This nagging question would persist for many years.

The Bee Gees' "Stayin Alive" came on. I hated disco. I hated that song. I had hated it from the first time I heard it when I was *forced* to watch *Saturday Night Fever* when I was a young man. I loathed disco—as a man. This time, the music grabbed my spirit, and I jumped up to the mirror and started dancing like a mad woman. I didn't have time to think how much **The Dude** (that's what I call my guy self) hated the song, because the girl, **Maria** (that's me), had apparently been waiting decades to do this. *Fuck him.* Dancing to "Staying Alive," I was more alive than ever before. *What is happening to me?! Look at that red leather mini-skirt. Stop it! Stop dancing! I can't. What's wrong with me? I don't even feel ashamed, I just fucking love it. I love feeling so sexy on my own terms. I'm ready for something new.*

A muscle guy came up to me from behind and I felt his cock pressing up against my ass. It was like nothing I'd ever felt before. Someone *taking* me. It was repulsive at first, but it was exciting—I guess because it was different. I looked at us in the mirror and thought, *wow, I just got separated from my wife, and a few days later, I'm getting all sexed and roughed up. This is so fucking easy—unlike being an average guy where it takes years before I get any kind of action.*

I decided to see where this would go. I was sexy! Wow, new rules! But I was also scared, because as our bodies started moving with the rhythm of the music, and I allowed myself to feel sexy, I went weak and felt goosebumps as I succumbed to his domination. *Oh shit, this is actually pretty hot! Am I really enjoying receiving such sexual attention from a guy, or is it the alcohol and weed?*

This is so weird. He clearly didn't know I wasn't really this fabulous woman . . . that I was really some lame ass dude. Or was I? I let him lunge into me a bit more. I wanted more. I wanted sex, and I didn't care what kind. I wanted to have fun after years of unhappy, boring misery. I wasn't gay—I just wanted some action. One of the beautiful things about Divas was nobody cared if you wanted to experiment, because it was everywhere. In fact, you might have looked weird if you *weren't* getting some kinky thing on.

I was fueled by a trifecta of cross-dressing, alcohol/weed, and now a whole new category of easy fun sex. I got scared. I told my suitor I needed a drink and escaped to the bar. It was just too weird for me, too fast. He followed me to the bar and bought me a drink. *Wow, nice perk. Are there rules regarding how long I should flirt with him after he bought me a drink?* I wasn't really interested in him or what he had to say. This was about me getting some action and attention. He was just another guy to me. Right or wrong, this was one of my first nights out, so give me a break! Plus, it was just too weird having a guy hit on me. The dancing thing was physical, but at the bar, he wanted to chat with me, and that was way too much. Not only was it weird, I felt like a fraud.

Then I did something to him that always pissed off The Dude when he interacted with girls. I said, "Gotta find my friends" and just took off.

Yes, it was a lie. I was alone that night. The Dude hated when girls acted like this. I supposed that was probably rude, but what did I know? I was just starting to learn this new playing field and my new power. I had never thought about all the things girls had to deal with until I was one. There was definitely a lot to learn.

I dashed outside, which was always a fun scene as the ultra-smoking-hot t-girls who worked the streets around Divas would often stop to chat and get a smoke. One of the t-girls outside offered me a cigarette. Her oversized breasts and lips excited and confused me, and her smoky eyes mesmerized me. Did my excitement show? I don't smoke cigarettes, but the social act of another t-girl giving me a cigarette was part of my indoctrination into being a member of this new sister club. I liked the new kind of connection. It wasn't about impressing with cleverness or power, it was just sharing what we were feeling. *This is what it's like to be a girl? Cool. Very easy, very honest. Not what I expected!*

As I smoked the cigarette without really inhaling and awkwardly pretending I knew how to handle it, I wondered if she knew I was a newbie. This night was turning out to be amazeballs. I was one of the sought-after sexy people this time, not one of the nondescript dudes clawing for some attention. I liked this, and I was just getting started in my gurl life. My new friend dropped her cigarette, put it out with her stiletto heel, and dashed into Divas while several more t-girls came out.

The sidewalk outside Divas was a revolving door of a variety of t-girls— White, Hispanic, Asian, Black, and a few Middle Easterners, who were the hottest in my book. Talk about a perfect and confusing blend of hard-core male and female. Some slender, some with huge breasts popping out of their lacy outfits, some with oversized huge hips. It was fun seeing all the different guys coming to Divas—old/young, black/white/yellow/ brown, clean-cut/disheveled and how they would act. Some knew the girls and would immediately flirt with them. Many clearly hadn't been there before. They would cautiously walk up to the door, hesitate, and go in. Others would boldly walk up to the door and rigorously grab the handle and enter the promised land. Many walked by Divas multiple times, finally mustering the courage to go in, while some hesitated, chickened out and took off. And often if it was a larger group of guys, some would go in and others would argue and then chicken out. I would just watch, amused, because I knew how they felt. That could have been me.

It was also really fun to see so many groups of guys just walking by on their way elsewhere. Most of them took a peek, and many of the younger guys clearly didn't want their friends to notice. The Dude in me understands. And some of these passersby would make derogatory comments about us gurls to their friends, "Fucking faggots," "That's a fucking dude," "What the fuck is that?" The irony? Many of those same obnoxious guys often came back later by themselves after their friends disbanded for the night. This was so common that it was an ongoing joke, and some of them probably ran into each other!

DIVAS WAS A PLACE WHERE FANTASIES COLLAPSED INTO REALITY EVERY NIGHT.

I enjoyed just standing there, smoking, watching, and chatting. I never felt awkward in those moments alone at Divas like I often did when I went somewhere as The Dude. I would either quietly savor this insane scene or easily start flirting with somebody. I didn't have to feel like I was a loser just standing there by myself. *Yes, the new rules!*

After taking in this variety for a while, I looked down at my awesome strappy shoes and sexy shiny legs, stroked the nylons I could feel through my skirt, and again thought about how I couldn't believe I was doing this. *Get the fuck out of here, this is so rad! I'm a sex creature!* I wondered again what they thought of me. *Do they see a hot woman, or do they see some kinky dude getting off on dressing up as a girl?* And that guy at the bar, didn't he see that I was a dude? It was hard for me to accept he could think of me as feminine and sexy, but when I walked past a mirror and took a glance, I would be shocked. I often forgot how hot I looked. This was going to take a lot of getting used to.

I then took a pause and reflected on my walking away from that guy. I wondered, *is this really something I'm not interested in or am I just afraid? Afraid of getting physically hurt? Afraid of what others might think? Did I just blow the opportunity to have a fun night?* But I already could tell hooking up as a woman was going to be so easy. I was getting some action in my first few times out as a girl and there was clearly a lot more where that came from. So, nothing to worry about.

My plan was to go out a few times before Halloween, which was six weeks away. I wanted to hone my new fashion skills and figure out the best clubs to go to during the Halloween weekend. Then I'd have a big cross-dressing Halloween bash and go back to my normal straight dude life.

THE BEST LAID PLANS...
NEVER IN A MILLION YEARS WOULD I HAVE THOUGHT...

Unbeknownst to me, I was stirring up a demon who was going down a *slippery slope*. This was just the beginning of a very long, colorful, fun, and enlightening journey. I blew past my Halloween weekend like it was tissue paper commissioned to hold back a fifty-ton bulldozer. It wasn't long before I found myself waking up in the morning next to a muscular ex-convict, still wearing my bra, garter belt, and stockings, with my chiffon blouse and leather skirt on the floor and thinking, *how did I end up here*? And then finding myself getting tied up and whipped on a horse by a female rock star at the Kink.com[4] headquarters at the San Francisco Armory.

Life just kept getting better as I started rewarding myself for hard work weeks by lots of easy flirting and lots of sex—picking up guys, and, occasionally, women, at various clubs throughout the city—instead of being some nondescript guy standing alone at a bar or party, or sitting at home ordering pizza or Indian food and watching TV on a Friday night. It was so much more fun being a gurl getting fucked on a swing in a cage at the Power Exchange sex club while people watched and jerked off... or having lesbian sex with a hot genetic female stripper from the famous Mitchell Brothers O'Farrell Theater ... or supervising a transsexual orgy at Burning Man ... or singing and playing guitar in a band on the main stage at the Folsom Street Leather Fair. In my previous life, I hated parties and events like New Year's Eve, but now I loved them, as I was no longer invisible. I was the sexy one! I now had fun on a consistent basis because I was now as fabulous on the outside as I was on the inside.

I didn't even feel gay or queer. I just felt sexy for a change. It was **so** much more fun going out as a girl than as a dude—and **so** much easier to get attention. Almost every night was epic in stark contrast to my life as The Dude, where an epic night would happen about once a decade. *Uh oh, am I in big trouble? How am I going to control myself?* Instead of a great weekend being a rarity, a quiet weekend had now become the rarity. I was exhausted most of the time. I started looking forward to going to work in

---

4. The largest BDSM website in the world. It used to be located in the heart of San Francisco's Mission District and was located literally in a castle, which was originally an US Army armory and arsenal.

order to get some rest. At first, I went out as Maria for something new to do and to have little fun, but soon I was going out just to get some sex.

But I wasn't equipped to deal with this new power. I didn't understand how this weird dork social loser was suddenly transformed overnight into this cool queen loved by even the trendiest of queers. I felt like a fraud at first. I had never experienced easy sex and fun. I was like a horny adolescent in a sex store the size of a city, and most everything was free—except of course the clothes. I tried dating women as The Dude during these early years, but the contrast in power and action between the boy and the gurl was too drastic. I wasn't ready to go back to being a social loser, just another average guy.

This new power was pervading my whole life. One night I'd be out walking on the street like a hooker, getting constant whistles and guys pulling up to me in cars, and then walk straight into a club as an instant VIP despite the line around the block. And the next morning, I'd be at some tech company in Silicon Valley talking to a bunch of geeks and managers about cryptographic protocols with supreme confidence, chuckling to myself about what I'd been doing the night before. I was slowly becoming immune to the frustrated victim disease so many of us have when we have to deal with life's bullshit. Over the years of being battered around as The Dude, I had slowly found myself dissolving into the background. But no more. New rules, new game!

I had the keys to the city and there was *a lot* to explore. Eventually, I found myself producing and hosting a web channel *Under the Golden Gate*, resulting in over seven hundred videos about underground San Francisco.

We interviewed many local people across the Alt and LGBT spectrum and even some celebrities, but our most popular topic by far was learning what kink was *really like* and about those who lived such lives.

There were so many great places to visit in this small, yet big city— the street fairs, the shops, the sex clubs, really colorful private parties, and the Kink.com Armory, which hosted many of the shows we produced. This was ground-zero for probably the sexiest, kinkiest, most open city in the world. I met so many wonderfully unique, weird, and diverse people. I giggle with joy to this day just thinking about it. This was an antidote to the decades of negative energy I had absorbed living in a culture that tried to control everybody by putting them in a defined box, telling them who they are and selling them constant junk—consumer

Filming our variety/talk show at the Kink.com San Francisco Armory. I'm on the couch on the right. This Highlights video provides a flavor.
Credit: https://photosbygooch.com

products, fashion, fake entertainment, mediocre education, and *stories* of great political leaders.

I was so fascinated by all these San Francisco people whose lives were so different from my previous life, and who had such color, joy, authenticity, and variety, that I wanted to learn about them. I was lucky to be here, and also lucky to capture some of it through our high-quality video show.

Note: The videos contained herein are from underthegoldengate.com. More on Under the Golden Gate later.

The biggest, most joyful surprise of all was my relationship with women *as a woman*. The sisterhood is so different. I was now immersed in all that wonderful, positive female energy that's largely unavailable to The Dude because of all the cultural bullshit and barriers around us. It wasn't about sex; it was about seeing a different way of being that I was totally unaware of—the true beauty and spirit of the feminine. This had been gravely squashed in me and in so many other men and women . . . and ultimately squashed in our whole culture by mysterious forces. Seeing the beauty of the feminine as an outsider is very different from *being* it. Another unexpected bonus of my new vantage point was talking with women about sex. Wow! Did I learn a few things! And *yet another* surprise was seeing men from this female perspective and thinking about my attitude and behavior when I was The Dude. That was embarrassing.

After coming to the Emerald City, I quickly discovered the fabulousness that had been hidden inside me all my life. It all happened so fast, going from a suburban social loser to a fabulous t-girl of San Francisco who tore up almost any place she walked into. And dare I say, encouraged the fabulousness to come out in others I ran into.

HOW THE HECK DID MY BIGGEST KINK BECOME THE PART OF ME THAT EVERYBODY LOVED THE MOST?

So many people loved this alternative world—straight couples, gay folks, straight women, lesbians, and especially straight guys excited and curious to discover what it's like to just talk with or have sex with a t-girl for the first time. I've always loved it when different worlds collide. In this city, that happened all the time, and I could be part of it.

I discovered these secret powers, but I had nobody to help guide me through learning how to use it and live with it[5]. I had no restraint. I was in big trouble! Maria started taking over my life and spending my money. I thought I might need to stop. It was too much. But I had to first explore this new power and freedom from the box, so I forged ahead and figured I'd discover what it all meant later. Damn the torpedoes. Maybe it was time to be the center of attention for a little while.

How the heck did I end up here? I was a regular American kid, but with a little twist. I was lucky to visit and live in some really magical places when I was very young, the kind of places people with money might go to only when they are retired. I guess I had thought the world was magical. And maybe it is, but adult life often takes you on too straight a path, and you miss the really good stuff our souls crave.

It wasn't until I moved to San Francisco that I found the magic again, revisiting a life hijacked and twisted by an evil villain. I felt like I was living my life in reverse, as sometimes we find ourselves going backwards to take another look at those things that shaped our being. And if we give ourselves the opportunity to shake those deep parts of ourselves

---

5. There were many t-girls in the community that were helpful, but often we have to discover our unique perspectives ourselves. Mine was unusual even for strange alternative San Francisco.

around a little, we might find a joy, fascination, and freedom we never imagined, or we suspected was crying and screaming from within.

Prepare yourself for a bumpy ride as I take you through my transformation into fabulosity. No holds barred. Only the brave dare enter Maria's World.

All aboard!

Note

This story is not for the tame. The most real and most important things in life are buried amid our darkest feelings and secrets, and there we will find gold. If you want to be spared some of the dirtiest stuff, yet still get the story, skip the sections marked:

SORDID DETAILS

HOW DID I GET HERE?

We all have a story. We may be missing half of it, but that's the way we saw the world at the time . . . .

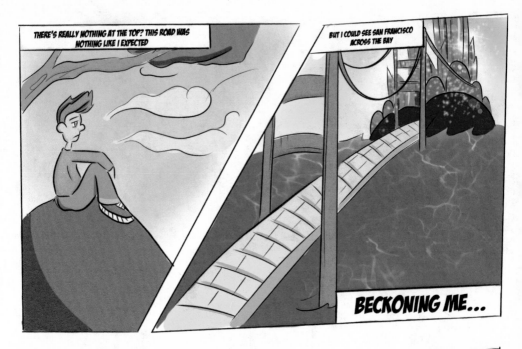

PART 1

THE ROAD TO THE RAINBOW

CHAPTER 1

GETTING ON THE T-GIRL TRAIN TO SAN FRANCISCO

Where do I start?

After my pursuit of the suburban American dream ended up in the gar-
bage dump, and my spiritual quest ended with me puzzled and alone at
the top of the proverbial mountain, it was time to descend and plan my
move to the Valley of the Heathens—San Francisco! I would never be
the same. Not even close. I was leaving my dead reptilian snakeskin behind in the suburban castle.

San Francisco was the mysterious Emerald City where I hoped to find
the answers to many of life's questions and a lot of non-suburban fun. I
was excited about having all that great Chinese, Indian, and Italian food
so accessible and being in a city with action twenty-four/seven. But most
importantly, I would be around a high concentration of diverse people,
many of whom were also looking for something different.

Back in September of 2006, San Francisco was a much different place than it is today, with a lot more misfits and artists like me. There were, of course, a lot of LGBT folks. I had only met a very few of them in my life, and I had no LGBT friends. San Francisco had many clubs and bars that reflected various subcultures, and many of those clubs were just a five- or ten-minute cab ride from each other, as San Francisco is a very small city. You could discover multiple subcultures in one night of bar-hopping. And Tech was still isolated largely in Silicon Valley a comfortable thirty-plus miles away.

I'd been frustrated ever since I moved back to America when I was thirteen, and I was determined to take advantage of this opportunity to create a new life in the big small city. I needed a purpose, a quest. My soon-to-be ex-wife and I had cross-dressed for Halloween the year before. We had planned to do so again this year, but in San Francisco. Maybe I could do it by myself. Halloween was coming up in a few months. It sounded crazy, but why the fuck not? I just couldn't get it out of my head, and deep down I knew I was going to do it. But a little voice kept telling me it was ridiculous and embarrassing.

So, I figured the best way for one to stop a fantasy from constantly nagging you is to experience and conquer it. I was never one to turn down a challenge. I hadn't been so excited since Africa and Egypt. *Yes, let's do it!* I needed this, because my natural inclination was to have fun trying to date women. But getting divorced and moving to a new city was stressful enough. The last thing I wanted was to feel like a loser. I wasn't in the mood for the rejection, self-pity and being driven to the brink of insanity that came from my experiences with straight dating—and which led me to marrying the wrong person. I needed to get far, far away from that—and try something completely different.

I had my quest. Now I needed to find a beachhead to land on. But where to start? I only knew two people in the city, neither of whom I was close with—my cousin and a casual friend, both straight women my age. While I was still living with my soon-to-be-ex, but in the spare bedroom, I spent several weeks browsing around, sorting through loads of miscellaneous stories and information. I needed someplace to go where I could meet a bunch of people who knew about underground San Francisco. And then one day I found it.

I Love It Gurl was a club for cross-dressers located in Fremont, a suburb of Silicon Valley about fifty miles from San Francisco. It looked perfect. Strange it was in Fremont and not San Francisco. That made me uneasy. *What is this place? Well, it's not San Francisco, but they probably know what's going on there.* I nervously called and spoke to a super nice woman Joanne and made an appointment to go there. All of a sudden, this dark, mysterious thing I wanted to try was no longer shrouded in shame. I spoke with a real person, and she sounded pretty normal. This would be a recurring revelation—alternative people are just regular people vs. the toxic nonsense Hollywood had depicted.

I Love It Gurl cross-dressing club and my first night out as a woman

I Love It Gurl was located in an industrial park. As I pulled up, I wondered if I was in the right place. There were trucking companies, car repair shops, machine shops, and lots of big dudes walking about. *WTF is this?* I was nervous and would have just left if I had not spoken with Joanne on the phone. After driving around confused and frustrated for five minutes, I finally saw an entrance covered with flowery fabrics and feathers, and a little sign that said: *I Love It Gurl.* Very out of place . . . strange.

I immediately started second guessing myself, *what the fuck was I doing*? All that dude energy in the parking lot was making me nervous. But courage is not the absence of fear, it's action in spite of it. And it's easy to find the courage when sex is involved, especially something new. Onward.

I parked the car, and as I was walking toward the entrance, I couldn't help but wonder what all these dudes were thinking of me, as they probably saw all kinds of characters walk in here. But this would only be the first of many times I felt apprehensive. I just ignored it and went ahead. Of course, the dudes walking around the park probably didn't notice. They were busy doing their jobs. But when we're nervous, we often subconsciously think people are looking at us and judging us, when they really aren't. I call this the *Hidden Camera* implanted in our minds by my lifelong nemesis, the Monoculture Virus (The Virus), which has programmed us to always be worried about looking right and being trendy and normal. The sad thing is that today, we actually **are** being watched.

I rang the bell and Joanne appeared. A short woman in her mid-to-late fifties with long wavy hair, Joanne was bubbly and super friendly. "Hi," she said, "yes we spoke on the phone, come on in!" I entered a huge warehouse that was a cross-dresser's dream. It took me about thirty minutes to take in the whole place as Joanne gave me a tour while we were chatting. There was girl shit *everywhere*. It was shocking.

The entrance had little lockers where married men whose wives didn't know they were cross-dressers kept their stuff. Hundreds of wigs, boas, necklaces, and stockings hung all over the place, on top of cabinets, from the ceiling, and lying in piles. It looked like this stuff had been accumulating for decades. Then I saw the huge makeup room with five or six huge mirrors and powerful lights, and all kinds of makeup everywhere, plus loads of bras and more wigs. I was thinking, wow, how nutty sexy. What kind of transformations happen in here? I was both uncomfortable and titillated at the same time. *I could try out some sexy kinky stuff here and get out of my skin!* Even though I was excited and intrigued, I kept getting tugged by that damned Hidden Camera, telling me I shouldn't be doing this. And I kept ignoring it. This new excitement was no match for the Hidden Camera program. Pretty soon it had no effect on me.

We then went into the main room, which was the size of an airplane hangar for a small jet. There was a whole wall of just corsets, and another wall of frilly boas and foofy skirts. There was a kitchen and sitting area with several old couches plus tables and chairs in the middle of the hangar-sized room. The rest of the warehouse was full of clothes. There must have been a hundred thousand items—dresses, skirts, gowns, shirts, and belts of all different styles. My jaw dropped as we walked around racks and racks, plus there was a second floor of scaffolding with more stuff. It felt like the racks were imbued with unleashed feminine spirits of excited cross-dressers. I wondered what stories these items could tell!

And we talked and talked. This was the first person I ever spoke to about my straight romantic frustrations and the resulting cross-dressing fantasy I was curious about. Joanne was an incredible wealth of information. She was married with no kids and had been doing this for decades. She knew about the cross-dressing culture and the clothes. She knew about the scene in the Bay Area and the city, and the clubs and events to go to. And she even knew quite a bit about the psychology of cross dressing and being trans.

Joanne was my new best friend. I went to *I Love It Gurl* a few more times over the next several weeks as I planned my move to San Francisco. I met several other t-girls, some regular straight guys into dressing, as well as full-time trans women with breasts and soft skin. I was in heaven just talking with them about their lives, their attitudes, and, of course, sex and kink! Some of these guys were very straight sounding, others were a bit effeminate, and still others were clearly more women than men. But they all just loved all things feminine. I hadn't felt this excited to talk with people since those days so long ago living overseas. I was back in my element with people who were very different from me, all living interesting lives. This wasn't about sex or sexuality; it was about breaking out of the mold.

I rummaged through the warehouse and bought a wig and a cheesy, sparkly dark red party dress that a thirteen-year-old girl might like. I felt excited, but uncomfortable because without the makeup on, I felt like maybe I was turning gay. I had never been attracted to men, but at the time I didn't understanding the various LGBT nuances. I was seeking a total transformation to get me completely out of my skin. Experimenting with a new attitude and enjoying the dress would have to wait until the right time.

My first dress, which I bought at I Love It Gurl. This is several months later after I had moved to San Francisco.

I Love It Gurl had an outing in San Jose once a month, and they invited me to join them for the next one. I was planning to dress up and go out for Halloween in San Francisco, but on a regular day in the burbs? *No shit! Really?*

I had a week to get ready for the big night, so I went to *I Love It Gurl* few more times and sat in the makeup room playing around with makeup, clothes, and wigs. What a trip it was! I was nervous, but excited to do something completely different and learn a sex-related craft I never conceived I would. *Here's a really fun challenge, I can do this!* I tried a bunch of makeup, wiped off my mistakes, and tried again. I wanted to look like the sexy women I used to fantasize about. I wanted to look in the mirror and see somebody else. Seeing yourself in makeup for the first time is a transformative experience—the genie is released from the bottle. I knew I was getting ready for a long trip. I loved being excited and feeling like I was in trouble at the same time. I needed this.

Joanne helped me a little with foundation and eye shadow, but it was mostly trial and error. This was before the YouTube videos, so the only instruction I got was from the book *Making Faces* by Kevyn Aucoin. But his book was about making women naturally beautiful. I needed to figure out how to amp it up for my own trampy tastes. At first, I spent most of the time in the makeup room alone. I was too nervous to be around the other gurls when I was transforming. I was okay being around others *after* I was a girl, but The Dude didn't want to be around others during that intimate transformation. It was too "gay." I was either a gurl or a boy, nothing in between.

The night to go out as a gurl came. I rented a motel a few blocks away and stopped at the pharmacy to buy some black pantyhose. Sweet nylons! I was nervous about buying them, but I made up a story in my head that my girlfriend asked me to pick them up along with a few other items like toothpaste and Q-tips. I went to *I Love It Gurl* where I was joined by six other gurls, two of whom I had already met. They

Experimenting in the makeup room at I Love It Gurl in Fremont. First picture of me en femme.

had all been out before, and I was the newbie. They had plenty of wine for us to imbibe while we were getting ready. I started drinking . . . a lot. I guess I needed liquid courage.

I went into the makeup room, and now since I was tipsy, I started really enjoying the transformation. I covered my eyebrows with Kryolan eyebrow wax and used Kryolan professional grade concealer on my face. I powdered it all up and saw my face now as a blank canvas to create my dream. I took another swig of wine and looked for the most shiny, sparkly eye shadow I could find, probably blue, while chatting with the other girls . . . woo hoo! As I applied the eye shadow, a new person emerged. *Who is this girl?! I haven't had this much fun in twenty years.* I put on fake eyelashes, eyeliner, rouge, lip liner, lipstick, so much hot stuff available! As this woman emerged, I got more and more excited, and drank more and more wine.

Then came time to get dressed. I was well-oiled up with wine, but I needed to do this part alone, so I asked the other gurls for some privacy. I put on a black bra and some cheap breast forms and looked at myself in the multiple mirrors, where I could see from all angles. And then, the pantyhose. I loved slipping into those black nylons and seeing my white legs turned into shiny black sex objects. And the feeling of nylon on my legs and groin . . . ooh yea. I have big strong legs from lots of biking, so they looked fucking awesome. I refused to shave anything because I wasn't ready to make that commitment, and I'm really hairy, so I had to put on a pair of beige pantyhose under my black ones, and also cover my chest hair with a black mesh shirt. I bought some shoes from Joanne. Shoes are the hardest, I had a hard time finding something that fit, so they weren't ideal—better shoes would have to wait. I put on the sparkly red dress and enjoyed the new feeling of it on my body. *Wow, this is so fine. I can't believe girls have been feeling this soft and silky sexy wonderful feeling their whole lives. It's no fair they get to do this all the time!* I didn't realize until I put on girl clothes how important the *feel* was. I only knew about the look. This was a completely different way of being! I had *no idea* how much fun this was. I felt so good it was scary.

But it was too weird seeing my regular hair. So, the *big* moment came. I downed another half glass of wine, grabbed my dirty blond big hair wig, positioned myself in front of the big mirror, and got ready for that big moment. Several girls came back in to watch. I had wanted to be alone, but fuck it, I was tipsy enough. I donned the wig, and . . . *who is this sexy bitch? Yea!* What a difference now that I had the whole look going—I was a woman. I wanted to immediately grab my balls and start masturbating, but that would have to wait. Instead, I danced around a little to the music. I was holding back my excitement a bit, because I was still kind of nervous in front of these other people. But they knew. Joanne was clearly pleased. She had just unshackled another soul.

"What's your name?" she asked me.

"My name?"

"Yes, what's your girl name?"

Nobody had ever asked me *that* before. The other gurls had girl names, so I shouldn't have been surprised. But I wasn't one of them, was I? This was just a kink I was trying out getting ready for Halloween, right? I thought about it as I finished getting ready. I had always had a thing for Marie Osmond, fantasizing she was a lot darker in secret than we would ever think she could be, so I chose the name Maria. I didn't think much about it, not realizing this name would be with me forever. The other girls started calling me "Maria" and referred to me as "she" and "her." This made me really uncomfortable, but I didn't protest. It was weird for a *long* time until I got used to it.

It was time to head out to the bar. For years, I had a favorite fantasy about dressing up as a girl in a cross-dressing club in New Orleans— one I'd seen briefly with business associates while we were walking around Bourbon Street. In this fantasy, other t-girls invited me to walk the streets outside the club. I would imagine the moment my high-heeled foot touched the pavement outside, I would be stepping through a magic, one-way door into the life of a kinky cross-dresser. I had loved that fantasy to sooth my dating and marriage frustrations, and here I was really doing it! And it was a great antidote for my depression and anxiety over getting divorced. This was a helluva lot better than being some frustrated suburban loser feeling sorry for himself. *Will I be able to come back from this?*

But at this point, I was drunk and don't remember much. It was still light out, and I was thinking *what are these dudes in the industrial park going to think?* But I didn't have much time to worry about that. We piled into Joanne's van and were off to Tinker's Dam, a gay bar in the suburbs of San Jose. I had never been anywhere near a gay bar, but it didn't bother me at all. I basically had a protective shield on. I was a girl, and nobody knew who I was.

Tinker's Dam was fun, probably because it was mostly gay men. I chatted with a few folks, but I mostly continued to drink and look at myself in the mirror, amused at how totally insane this was. I don't remember much of the rest of the night, other than dancing in front of the mirror back in the hotel room and jerking off before going to sleep. I had asked the gurls where to go in San Francisco, and that's how I found out about the transsexual bar Divas. And that's where I would be heading next.

Transsexual Bar Divas

Should I just show up at Divas? Would I be dressed right for it? Was it safe to go alone? Joanne didn't have outings to San Francisco, so she told me about Jasmine, who ran a cross-dressing service there. I called Jasmine. She had an effeminate man's voice. That made me really nervous, as my prejudices about being judged bubbled up, but like Joanne, she was super friendly on the phone and that made it much easier for me. We met at her place in the lower Haight in San Francisco for a makeover. I was to learn makeup the same way I learned piano and guitar, mostly from *a lot* of trial and error, with occasional tips from others.

I was apprehensive about meeting a freak. I was expecting some weird, unemployed, drugged out, sex-crazed person, living in squalor amidst needles, dirty food, and hungover vagrants crashed out on a dirty, ripped-up thirty-year-old couch—the kind that has springs sticking out of it.

Hollywood is so misleading. Jasmine lived in a really cool and clean penthouse flat. She worked as a man as a news producer for one of the major networks by day but was a woman the rest of the time. Jasmine was the nicest, coolest, most open person I had met up to that point.

I could not believe how easy it was to yet again share all my frustrations and fantasies with another person. Everybody should have the opportunity to do it. We went through it all while she was putting makeup on me. She also told me about the various communities in the city—drag, trans, female-male transsexuals, gay, pansexual, and so many others.

Jasmine had quite a bit of business from both locals and those travelling to San Francisco from all over the world. They were from a very broad cross section—truck drivers, doctors, investment bankers, software engineers, chefs, and a lot of ex-military—who came to her just to cross-dress and fulfill their dreams of going out in public. And many of them were married or had girlfriends. Jasmine did makeovers, dress-up sessions plus pictures, shopping excursions, a night out on the town, and regular Friday night parties twice a month with other gurls. These parties included walking to Divas. Jasmine invited me to come to the next party in a week. Perfect!!!

Jasmine's soirees were held at an apartment where a t-girl named Jamie Faye lived. The apartment was five blocks from Divas. You could walk it in heels as long as they were four inches or less. I got a motel, stuffed Maria into a bag and went to the party, scared shitless of what I might find. I took a deep breath, paused for a moment and knocked on the door wondering who would appear. A nice, very feminine guy wearing a bit of makeup appeared. I immediately noticed much to my surprise that there was food spread out and people were drinking wine, just like any regular party. I guess I was still expecting a bunch of hypodermic needles, tweakers, and sex on the couch in front of other people. (I *would* see that soon enough). It took me a few more months to eliminate this preconception from my mind. Decades of programming take years of meeting all kinds of new people to undo.

I introduced myself as Maria, which was weird because I was still

dressed as a guy, but everybody else only used girl names and referred to each other as *she* regardless of whether they were presenting as a man or as a woman. This is all so normal to me now, but back then it was *really weird*. About a dozen people were at the party, and after having met the gurls at *I Love It Gurl*, I was pretty comfortable chatting with them.

After about an hour, a little mini orgy started up in the corner room. I walked in to use the mirror to put on my makeup, and several gurls and a guy were on the couch smoking weed and making out. I noticed a few bare cocks, too. I had never seen anything like this before. My first thought was maybe I shouldn't be hanging out with low-life scum like this, I mean I was a professional, what was I doing here??? What would my friends think? *There goes that damned Hidden Camera again. Stop it! Appreciate this new experience!* And again, I had to let those old prejudices die on the vine. The bunch on the sofa asked me to join, but I politely declined. Not ready to even think about that.

I finished my makeup and slipped on some fishnets with a crisscross pattern. *Oooh yea! There are them hot fucking legs again!* I put on that same dress, popped on the wig, and voila, there she was! I didn't drink nearly as much this time, but I was pleasantly stoned. Mixing weed and dressing as a girl—yes ma'am. Guaranteed fun and fulfillment. No frustrated man around here!

Then it was time for the big walk to Divas—my first time walking on the streets as Maria. We were near the very upscale Russian Hill neighborhood, so there were many straight people walking about on Friday night at ten thirty. Maria hadn't met any straight people yet. I expected them to sneer at me. But we were rolling, and there's safety in numbers. After partying for three hours at Jamie's and being chatty as we went down the elevator, I wasn't apprehensive when we took that big leap out the door into the street. I was actually excited. As soon as I saw my black nylon-laden, high-heeled foot touch the pavement, I thought about how many times I'd had that fantasy, even jerking off to it a few times, and here I was! Everybody fantasizes, but do you fulfill the deepest ones? Woo hoo, onward! And damned good weed!

Yet again I would discover fantasy to be a far cry from reality. Now that I felt confidence with my new friends, I couldn't wait to see the reaction from the straight people. For the first time, I wouldn't be just another guy being ignored, and I didn't care if the straight people sneered at me—at this point I was actually turned on by the idea. I wiggled around and swayed and was surprised how easy it was for me to simply let my feminine side out. I guess it was the performer in me who likes to role play, finding that relevant part of the character inside you.

We ran into many people on the street, and a lot of them looked at us—it's hard to miss a group of chatty t-girls clicking around in heels. But they weren't sneering, they were all smiling! Big smiles. And a few "Looking good, girl!" remarks. A myriad of thoughts went through my mind: *Are you talking to me? Does my makeup look good? Do they think I do this all the time? Do they think we're working girls?* I was elated, I felt special. I was no longer this run-of-the mill dude. Their smiles made all the difference.

It was hard stumbling those five blocks in heels, trying not to get them stuck in the various gratings and seams in the sidewalk. I had to learn to walk without twisting my ankle, especially downhill, all while enduring pain. But with all that excitement, the pain added to the pleasure. *Maybe this is how you're supposed to feel as a girl?*

San Francisco is so small; the scenery changes really fast. In just a few blocks, you could feel the vibe change as we walked toward the Tenderloin. We were coming up on Divas! This part of town was crawling with trans working girls—guys knew where to go to pick them up on the streets. About two blocks from Divas, I saw my first trans prostitute, walking toward us.

Wow, look at those insanely hot smoky eyes, big hips, large cheekbones and lips—and killer attitude. That's fucking crazy. I can't believe that's not a genetic woman. I couldn't help but look over my shoulder as I passed by her. I felt a bit embarrassed, but I had to. Then she looked right at me and said, "Great legs, girl!" OMG, we made eye contact. *A hot, real life t-girl is complimenting this average boring dude!* As we got closer to Divas, I saw more working girls, more exotic eye candy. It was art on the street, a part of life I had never seen. What a dreamworld. No Virus-infected person here. And then there it was . . . Divas lit up in purple neon. We had reached the nucleus.

Me in front of Divas with a gaggle of girls about six months later (I was usually a blond). I hooked up with the t-girl on the right several times—she was my first.

We gurls got in for free—the guys had to pay the ten-dollar cover charge. *I like this!* Divas had four floors. The first floor was a dive bar with a small stage for drag shows.

The first thing I noticed was tons of mirrors, a glittery décor, and a whole gaggle of unbelievably *gorgeous* woman—great legs, fabulous breasts and hips, heavy makeup. *They can't all be trans can they?* They were all smoking hot . . . Yup! OMG! *Wow, that would be so crazy if I had the surgery—the face, breasts, hips. I want all this attention and a ton of sex. I want to live—fuck being straight!*

Of course, I wasn't thinking about how I would feel after having sex, taking a shower, going to sleep, going to the store, getting a job, going to work, getting my car repaired. They all warn you. The best test to make sure you're really trans and not just a kinkster is to try to keep the clothes and breast forms on after you cum. And then live that way during the day. But it was great to fantasize.

The third floor was the dance floor, the fourth floor was a lounge, and each one had its own bar. The second floor was secret (wink). We quickly

1st floor bar
Credit: David Steinberg

ended up at the fourth-floor lounge, where we sat on the couches, drank and chatted, and played pool. We met several other groups of non-working gurls like us. The working gurls rarely came up to the fourth floor.

After a bit, we wandered down to the dance floor.

After more dancing and flirting in that first night than I had done in my entire life, we shut the place down at 2 a.m. and hung out in the front for about thirty more minutes. We watched people smoking and flirting and saw many guys jump into a waiting taxi with their t-girl for the night. Guys were also pulling up in cars, picking up t-girls. Wow, this part was like the movies.

On the fourth-floor lounge with friends

Divas Dance Floor—an orgy of mirrors
Gabrielle Lurie / © San Francisco Chronicle / Polaris

I didn't want this epic evening to end. We went back to Jamie's for an after party, and a few working genetic girls showed up. Around four, I thanked Jasmine and the gang for an insanely fantastic night. I didn't want to take my clothes and makeup off before going to the motel, because I wanted to be alone with Maria and a mirror for a bit before I went to sleep. I was feeling confident, so I just put on my sneakers, and walked about six blocks to the motel, fully confident and figuring it was so late at night, what were the odds of running into trouble? I got back to the motel, looked at myself in the mirror and smiled. *Oh gurl, you are in trouble.*

Divas would become my Cheers—where everybody knew my name—on steroids. We'll get back to Divas and the various subcultures. But next, I had to plan for the big move into the city and for Halloween. Oh, I almost forget, was I getting divorced?

CHAPTER 2

EVERY DAY IS HALLOWEEN IN SAN FRANCISCO

Yup, I got an apartment two blocks from Divas

I had an astounding view of the San Francisco skyline from my new apartment, but more importantly, I could see the roof of Divas summoning me. I now had my tower lair where I could get dressed while I stared at the city, reminding me that I was now part of the alternative weirdness. It was my *duty* to go out, which was easy. I could saunter over to Divas in less than five minutes, and then grab a cab from there to dozens of clubs.

The ground floor of my building had a market where I could pick up booze, sandwiches, fruit, and junk food till two a.m. without even crossing the street. This would come in handy for the many parties and fun that would soon come. The *Bread and Butter Market* was owned by three brothers from Jordan who loved all the weirdness—another reminder that we're all the same, and demographics don't mean jack shit.

View from my apartment

I was on the corner of Polk and O'Farrell Streets, right across the street from the famous strip club Mitchell Brother's O'Farrell Theater. Polk Street was the gay part of San Francisco before the Castro. There were still several gay and gay/trans-friendly bars, performance spaces for live shows, and many artistic and eclectic people walking around. Plus, many homeless living on the streets or in the shelter around the corner. Goodbye, quiet life!

I vividly remember the feeling of my first night in the apartment as I stared at the majesty of the skyline. I barely knew anybody in the city, and it was still a mystery to me. I was getting divorced, so there was a lot to be apprehensive about. But fuck the victim thing. I didn't have time to worry about that or whether I was crazy for doing this, because I was so excited about exploring the city and my new gurl power.

It was mid-September, giving me about six weeks before Halloween. I started going nuts doing as much girl shit as I possibly could because I wanted to be a super-hot, confident, kinky woman on Halloween. I also needed to find which places to go on the long Halloween weekend. My prep plan included going to Jasmine's parties every two weeks and to Divas as often as possible, plus discovering the drag scene in town. Each time I went out, I would try something new with makeup and clothes and get instant feedback from a wide cross-section of people. I got good at it very quickly. I spent a lot of time going to Walgreens, Kryolan professional makeup, Macy's, and stores in the Haight-Ashbury.

At first, I felt really nervous and weird about buying girl stuff, and again, I created a story in my head that I was buying these products for my girlfriend. But I wasn't going to run into somebody I knew from the 'burbs, and I was buying so much stuff that the girlfriend story just wasn't plausible anymore. And everybody was very trans/drag friendly, especially the Kryolan makeup store, which had many gay people working there. I dropped the story because I was quickly becoming part of this alt community, and the story was just too exhausting and unnecessary. I was so lucky to be in San Francisco, because a few bad experiences might have stopped me in my tracks. I don't remember a single bad experience during that time. Au contraire. Most people, even the taxi drivers when I would go around as Maria, were not only super nice, many were chatty and really interested in what I was doing. Many kept staring at me in the rearview mirror, and good number of them asked me out on dates. Literally unbelievable!

I was going out three or four times a week to shake off the remnants of loser-hood, become as fabulous as possible, and meet as many fabulous people as I could. I had several runs where I went out four nights in a row. I even managed to date two straight women I knew from the past. They both dumped me, but I didn't care because I had Maria. I was doing tech geek consulting working mostly from home, so I had the flexibility to manage Maria's hangovers. My body wasn't acclimated to all this drinking and weed. The Dude was not into partying, but Maria was a young teenage girl with money and no adult supervision. Danger! I was exhausted and confused living these multiple lives. But I was able to find the time for all of this by simply not watching any TV. I think I had cable, but I'm not sure. What was the point anyway? Real life was *much* more entertaining.

My first order of business was to get up the balls to go out as Maria by myself. I wasn't going to let a dependence on Jasmine's parties slow me down.

Maria's first time out by herself

For about a week I stared at the two-block walk between my apartment and Divas, wondering how dangerous it was going to be as a woman at night given the various shady characters and homeless people around. The Dude had walked those two blocks many times during the day and at night anticipating any problems and evaluating Maria's escape routes.

There was an empty lot with a broken fence around it on the first block[6] and anything could have been lurking in there. I also had a new problem I'd never had to deal with before. Where was I going to put my wallet and keys? My dresses and skirts didn't have pockets. *WTF is this?!* I'd never thought about such things. I had to buy a small purse I could strap over my shoulder and keep on while I danced my ass off. I went to (C) Ross Dress for Less and bought a purse and a little money belt I could Velcro to my thigh under my pantyhose. I was terrified somebody would snatch my purse and I would be left without money or keys. *What a pain it is to be a girl!*

I had a routine for getting ready. Pour a glass of red wine, smoke a little weed, put on some music and then start gluing up my eyebrows with Kryolan eyebrow wax. Covering my eyebrows was a royal pain. It took about thirty minutes because I had to apply three layers of the wax with a spatula, carefully smooth it out, wait for each layer to dry, and then put on a fixer, wait for that to dry and then apply the foundation and powder it up. I then care-fully drew on eyebrows with an eyebrow pencil, making sure to not screw up the wax or get the pencil caught up in the flattened hairs and end up drawing in a kinked line. And then at the end of the night, it took about twenty minutes to get the stuff off using various solvents.

Over time I improved this eyebrow process. For exam-ple, later that year I learned from the professional drag queens in the *La Cage au Faux* show in Vegas to simply use a purple Elmer's glue stick that costs only $2 and washes off with soap and water.

I love this hot picture of me in Vegas after a makeover from one of the La Cage queens

---

6. There is a retirement home there now

Getting ready took just over ninety minutes[7], but I allocated two hours—accounting for getting off admiring myself in the mirror and playing around with bras and pantyhose to disco music. My favorite parts were putting on the pantyhose, always black. And then that final moment of putting on the wig—who's that girl?

I had played around with makeup a lot the previous month, so I was looking quite fabulous. And then I always needed an extra ten minutes to strut around and admire myself in the mirror. This final step was important because although I thought my makeup was hot, I was worried queens and women would nit-pick my technique. When I looked in the mirror critically, I saw my strong male features, weird pointy chin and imperfections. But my attitude, personality, and constantly moving around compensated for that.

After admiring myself and dancing in front of the mirror as usual, it was time to leave the safe harbor of my apartment and enter the real transsexual world—but this time alone. I poured another small glass of wine, played the piano and sang a few tunes. This became a ritual, always playing the piano before going out. *Okay, no more procrastination.* I nervously grabbed my purse and headed for the elevator. It took me to a back door exit to Polk Street, which often had a homeless person wedged up against it on the outside. I stood by the door and took a deep breath, not knowing who was on the other side. *Here it goes!* With my heart pounding, I opened the door to a flash of wonderful, cool San Francisco air.

Good. Nobody is lying around by the door. The first few people walking by didn't appear to notice me. *Phew.* As I walked down the sidewalk, people started smiling at me. *Wow, really?* I still couldn't believe it. I walked past the dreaded empty lot, but it was no big deal because a lot of people were walking about, most of whom also smiled at me, especially the women. Women smiling at Maria touched my heart, it was the kind of deep smile from their soul that I never got as a man. *Wow, this is fucking phenomenal!*

As I approached the streetlight at Geary and Polk, the only light between me and Divas, I prayed it would stay green, because I didn't want

---

7. The makeup took around an hour (thirty minutes for eyebrows and foundation, thirty minutes for the rest of the makeup) plus thirty minutes for the clothes (twenty minutes to determine what to wear, ten minutes to put it on) and then another fifteen minutes to mess around with the wig/hair, earrings, necklace, and bracelets.

The ominous back door out to Polk Street

to stand on the street corner looking like a prostitute. I could see from the pedestrian light counting off that I would need to run to make it. But **not** in heels! I accepted my fate, figuring it was bound to happen sooner or later. As I slowed down and approached the yellow-then-red light, I started whistling to calm my nerves. Because there I was standing on the street corner looking like a prostitute. Yet other people standing at the light smiled at me. I giggled inside and smiled back. People driving by were slowing down to look at this gurl. I gave them a big smile, too. All this positive energy from other people made me positive. I had never experienced a cycle of positive energy like this before—without even saying a word! *Pinch me.*

The light turned green and I slowly crossed the street with renewed confidence, purposely smiling at the people in the waiting cars. I got smiles back, even a thumbs up. *Holy shit, are you talking to me? I'm adding to their fun on their San Francisco night. I'm part of the San Francisco experience. Imagine that!*

A lot of homeless people were on the next block just before Divas, along with an alleyway I was worried about. I was terrified of them. But as I approached, they started smiling at me, too. *Holy fucking shit, this night just keeps getting weirder and it's hasn't even been five minutes!* I got a few whistles and several compliments like, "You're looking fine, girl." How odd. I had been afraid of them and had considered them to be low

Video of a song I wrote about this walk.

lives living in a different world I wanted no part of, and here they were being really nice to me and treating me as one of them.

In my fourteen years of walking the streets as a gurl, not once did a homeless person harass me or be rude to me in any way. I actually felt protected. They would step aside and smile, saying things like, "Go girl!" I began to see the homeless as people, almost as if God was encouraging me to experience this and feel safe with them. That neighborhood had a lot of t-girls, and the homeless folk clearly respected us. We brightened up the neighborhood, and they considered us part of the family. The transformation of my view on things was just beginning.

On that last block, I also saw other t-girls, almost all working girls, and cars stopping to pick them up. Over the years, many guys stopped their cars and tried to pick me up! At first, I thought they were talking to somebody behind me. I was always very nice and learned to tell them I was meeting somebody. I had to learn

Credit: David Steinberg

all these new girl things . . . and little lies to survive. Now I turned the corner, and there was the neon sign—Divas. There was usually a gaggle of t-girls standing outside, smoking and flirting. I was usually greeted with a "Hey, gurl." I was one of them! I proudly walked into Divas, ready for guaranteed fun. That dude-loser was choking on his last breath.

I could not believe how easy it was to walk up to people and talk with them, and how many came up to me. And this was true at most other bars and clubs, even the straight ones—as long as the people were generally over thirty years old. Twenty-somethings were too busy trying to get laid. This would NEVER happen to The Dude. He hates walking into clubs. I don't remember exactly what happened on this night at Divas, as all the evenings all blend into one set of great memories.

I probably chatted up a lot of guys and the few genetic women who were often there, got free drinks, danced my ass off, and ran into people I knew from my previous visit.

While the rest of that night was a blur, I do know I ended up at a private party after Divas closed at 2 a.m. and was then back there at 6 a.m. getting a last drink after the club reopened. What a night! What a difference from just a few weeks earlier when I was miserable and hopeless.

Then next time I went out, I didn't bother with the money belt. There was a lot more love around San Francisco than I could have imagined.

Drag – Trannyshack[8] at The Stud

A t-girl is NOT a drag queen. Divas was a t-girl bar, and The Stud was a gay bar with a drag show. It took a while for me to understand the difference because this was rarely covered in the media at the time. Drag queens and t-girls are like bats vs. birds—at a distance we look the same but are completely different. Drag queens are typically gay men who dress up for the fashion/glamour and to get attention, usually to perform in a show. T-girls were born male, but want to look and feel like women, either full time or part time.

---

8. The term "Tranny" is no longer used, as it's considered derogatory by some. "Tranny" has been part of the San Francisco vernacular since way before it was considered derogatory at a national level. T-girls used to refer to themselves as Tranny in variety of contexts, some intentionally self-derogatory. The positive vs. negative sentiment of many terms depends on how people use them. However, given the controversy which started around 2011, most people in the community started to refrain from using it. Trannyshack was renamed "Mother."

To be more clear, when the show is over and it's time to fuck, the drag queens take all their girl stuff off and fuck as men, whereas the t-girls are girls all night long. T-girls typically don't have man-on-man sex—they're not gay[9]. Gay men didn't come to Divas to hook up—it wasn't a gay bar. Straight-identified men did. I'm a bat t-girl and the drag queens are the pretty birds.

Even in San Francisco I'm weird. The drag queens think I'm trans, and the trans people think I'm a drag queen. One easy way to tell I'm not really a drag queen is my name. I have a normal name. Drag queens typically have funny names like Hedda Lettuce, Penny Tentiary, and Scarlett Letters.

But I had a DNA test done:

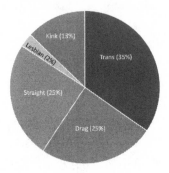

- **Trans:** I like expressing my fabulous female side and being trans has allowed me to resist being put in a box defined by advertisers and Hollywood.
- **Drag:** I like performing.
- **Straight:** I *love* straight sex, opposites banging. I just happen to change my sex whenever I feel like it and go where the opportunity to get laid is greatest—which basically means being a woman most of the time. When I'm a man I sleep with women. When I'm a woman, I sleep with men.
- **Lesbian:** ... well women too, because I sexually prefer women a great deal more than men, but sadly there are a lot fewer opportunities for that sort of thing. Plus, it's a whole lot more fun to just

---

9. I'm using the definition of "gay" in this context to mean a common lifestyle and culture of men who date other men, usually exclusively. There are many labels used in the context of LGBT, and they often mean different things to different people.

avoid all the complexity and drama in relationships with women. And me with another t-girl is fucking HOT! But t-girls are more complicated than genetic girls and thus have been a more rare, special treat.

- **Kink:** I find that certain clothes and equipment make me feel more like a woman. Or should I say, not a frustrated man. Very exciting.

That makes me 75% fabulous! My straight side pays the bills. It also prepares for the shows, but my fabulous side performs in the shows and gets all the glory.

Note that there is no gay in my DNA. When I would later play piano at the mostly gay piano bar, people would be confused when they would ask me to play Barbara Streisand, or showtunes from a musical like Rent and I wasn't familiar with the music. I would have to explain that I don't have the gay gene. I have the kink gene. I'm not a drag queen, I'm trans. I can play Sweet Transvestite, blues, rock, and jazz.

While most men who dress up like a woman are either trans or drag queens, I'm one of the few who is a cross between the two—a Trans Entertainer. And one who wants to fuck half the drag queens, but they want to do it as two boys . . . sigh.

So after exploring the t-girl scene at Divas, I wanted to check out the drag queen scene, which is very different in the same way that you generally don't see bats hanging out with birds. I wanted to meet a larger group of people, and the drag/gay community was a much larger and more active subculture. And since I used to play in bands, I had the performer bug, and drag queens are the performers. T-girls are into living the gurl life and generally like to stay a little more incognito. They say a t-girl can have fun just looking in the mirror, whereas a drag queen needs an audience. I get it, as I do both.

I found out pretty quickly that Trannyshack at The Stud Bar, run by the illustrious drag queen Heklina, had great shows and was a prime meeting place. This is where I really cut my teeth and met people. Walking into Trannyshack was like going to a spectacular Halloween party every Tuesday night that went till two a.m. Crazy outfits, wigs, glitter, lots of bling, leggings, you name it. Trannyshack had been around

The Stud Bar[10]. A most colorful and fun dive bar. The Stud went out of business during COVID-19.

since the mid-nineties, hosting many celebrities, such as Lady Gaga, Gwen Stefani, RuPaul, and Charo. When the use of the word "Tranny" became controversial, Heklina eventually renamed it Mother[11], which debuted in January of 2015 at her new, more modern club Oasis, which she opened with D'arcy Drollinger, a fellow queen who had been on Broadway.

Opening night of Mother:

Video: Drag queens Mama Dora and Tawdry Hepburnn are interviewing folks outside the club, and I'm interviewing people on the red carpet inside the club with drag queen Thee Pristine Condition.

A drag show is typically about an hour, with each queen performing for three to seven minutes lip-syncing to a song. Occasionally someone will sing live. Trannyshack had been among the best drag shows with

10. Credit: From Wikpedia, user Dreamyshade, License, modified: Face blurred
11. Heklina recently retired Mother

a high level of production—extensive props and artistic backgrounds along with background dancers. Many queens would slave away all week putting together their costumes, hair, props, and organizing other queens to back them—all for five minutes of glory. Very often, new queens would have their stage debut as a backup for one of these numbers.

The shows were really good, with tremendous variety and creativity. And one of the most magnificent aspects of the San Francisco underground is that it has an immense and rich history of community. When you went to an event like Trannyshack[12], you not only met people across multiple communities, you met people across the ages and would be exposed to incredible stories, attitudes, and lifestyles.

One of the first things I noticed when going to Trannyshack was who was open and friendly and who wasn't. Overall, it was *much more* open and friendly than any straight bar I had ever been to. Drag shows are way at the top of the list of fun things to do, and people at drag shows are really happy. I was surprised just how friendly most of the gay men were to me. There is no comparison with a straight bar where most people are aloof sticks in the mud. And I couldn't believe that they were complimenting me and calling me things like *fierce*. *I'm fierce? Really?*

But the drag queens were different. Drag queens were admired by the community and held a special status at the top of the food chain. Although most queens were really open and nice, I was initially rather dismayed when a good number of them were not. I was an outsider coming into this community, so it's no surprise some might treat me as such, but it was odd that pretty much everybody in this club was open to me except a good percentage of the queens. This was very reminiscent of high school cliques—a very unpleasant feeling. The **Diva Queen**—exemplified by *RuPaul's Drag Race*, aloof, competitive and catty[13]—was very strong in this community, and this *meme*[14] seemed to affect a lot of the queens.

One needs to understand the common history among many of the

---

12. The name "Trannyshack" was actually a misnomer, because it was a drag show with mostly gay men. There were rarely any trans people in the show, as most of us are not performers.
13. More details later
14. Ideas, feelings, cultural trends, that spread similar to a biological gene, but much faster. Love is a meme. Community engagement is a meme. Not to be confused with "Internet Meme" (a funny picture passed on the Internet).

queens to get a perspective on this. Many didn't feel safe or accepted in their communities of origin, and they found their true family in the San Francisco drag community. And getting into drag and working your way up to becoming one of the key performers acquaints you with the hierarchy you have to work through. Most queens first seek out a Drag Mother, somebody to help them learn the ins and outs of drag. Often the most experienced queens were inundated with people who wanted to connect with them—it was like being a movie star. And getting into drag is akin to putting on a mask and becoming somebody else. In many cases, the queens are shy as men and fabulous and outgoing as women, so this combined with the Diva Queen meme from *Drag Race*, appeared to cause many of them to be aloof, which came across as obnoxious arrogance, even though it was probably caused by a combination of shyness, insecurity, or just being really busy. The queens have a term for this, which is giving somebody "shade," something I've always despised, but at least now I understand its origins, and know the attitude has nothing to do with me.

It was odd the trans folks and the drag queens didn't mix—the drag queens usually hanging out by the stage, and the few trans folks in the corners talking amongst themselves. I was the oddball floating between the different groups, taking it all in. But we all were there because it was just such an awesome, diverse, dynamic, alternative world.

I was at Trannyshack every Tuesday for about five weeks before Halloween. It was surreal living part of my life as a technology guy and another part feeling like I was living on a different planet, meeting all these people, becoming part of their community, wondering if they had any idea who I was . . . complicated of course by my discovering who I was, too. I was part of the community, yet an outsider at the same time. I definitely did not relate to LGBT culture at the time. But at the same time, my ability to relate to my tech peers was waning. It was common for me to be in some tech meeting in Silicon Valley, run home, turn into a girl, go to Trannyshack, stay out late, and then end up at another tech meeting on Wednesday afternoon trying to remember where I was.

The contrast between these two worlds was so stark it was downright laughable. One Monday while having lunch with work colleagues, several guys were describing their weekends. One guy was jumping up and down with excitement. "We had the craziest weekend! We had incredible chicken wings at this Chinese restaurant in Mountain View. And then we drank all this great beer! You gotta check this place out!" I was waiting for the punchline. No drugs? No leather? No kinky sex? No prostitutes? No transsexuals? They asked me what I did over the weekend. What was I supposed to say? That I put on a garter belt and fishnets and ended up at a sex party with a bunch of transsexuals? I lied and I told them I ordered Indian food and watched TV. I must admit though, it made me feel special.

My first queer hookup

I also had my first queer hookup in that first month at Trannyshack. Melissa, a t-girl from NYC was visiting. We started flirting. She was cute and, hey, it was fun flirting as girls. *This is new.* I never had any interest in queer sex, but I wanted to cram in every bit of new post-divorce experience I could. So, I downed about three more vodkas, smoked some more weed, and off we went to my place.

I was really apprehensive about what I was going to do when the issue of the Dick came up, so I drowned that in more drink and smokes. It felt great to be touching somebody else's body after not having had sex for a long while, and the whole girl-on-girl thing suited me just fine. We did some making out and dry humping. I was intrigued, in my drunken state, by the feeling of that mound against me. It made me feel so gay I no longer cared about not being with a genetic girl. The Dude felt degraded and not worthy, and that made it so much easier to be kinky. I loved the way this headspace freed me.

But when Melissa's dick came out, I just couldn't go near it. That would take a lot more time. I avoided it, and we fell asleep. I woke up in the middle of the night still horny from all that weed, thinking I gotta try this, otherwise I'll keep thinking about it. But she was asleep, and it wouldn't be a good idea to jump the bones of somebody who was passed out next to me. So, I jerked off in the bathroom thinking about yet *another* crazy night, and I was then able to relax and fall back asleep.

And then the really awkward part. When we woke up in the morning, Melissa still looked great, but I was sober and halfway between being a nasty looking, melted woman and a pathetic guy. I needed to get her out of there, but I didn't want to be a jerk. Real life is such a pain compared with fantasy. I lied and told her I had to meet friends, but we planned to meet again in a few months to visit the Power Exchange sex club when she was in town again.

I was really excited that I'd had a trans/queer hookup. I didn't really feel queer, and I didn't feel apprehensive. I was simply having fun with these new experiences. I was concerned about going too fast into something that could drive me into drugs or dangerous sex, but I knew I could take it slow. There were clearly many more opportunities to have fun in this new life.

Other drag clubs and parties

Unlike the burbs, something was going on every night, and I hit it as hard as I could. I was learning about the various sub communities and clubs and was developing my female persona, which continued to come out naturally in this safe, fun, and inspiring environment. I probably met more people in six weeks than I did most of my previous life.

I went to Saturday night drag shows at Marlena's in Hayes Valley, a small neighborhood gay bar. It was one of those bars that displays so many pictures and knickknacks from its history, it looks like the home of an enormous extended family. When I first went there, I was nervous because it was a new place, and it was smack dab in the middle of the straight opera and symphony world. I sauntered on in all nervous, but that nervousness lasted about five seconds. Immediately I got

Many club bathrooms had memorabilia on the walls, like the bathroom at the Cinch, which had flyers from Charlie Horse

Michael Brown, taking care of people at the Cinch. You don't get more LGBT San Francisco than this. Michael WAS San Francisco. He had a purity and positive energy to his soul that I had rarely seen before. I loved this guy immediately. You should hear the dirty lyrics he has made up to popular songs.

comments like, "Hi lovely, you are fabulous!" And as I started chatting with folks, I was wondering when they would realize I was an imposter and not the fabulous queen they thought I was.

But that never happened. I guess I really *was* a fabulous queen. Marlena's attracted a lot of local straight couples, and I really enjoyed talking with them about what I was doing. They were insatiably curious, and I wanted to hear what they thought, because I had come from that world and still identified as straight. I was just on, uh, vacation. This was my entry into becoming a *Fembassador* between the different worlds.

Friday nights, I was at the Charlie Horse show hosted by the queen Anacoda, who always made sure I had free drinks. Charlie Horse was at the Cinch, now the last gay bar left on Polk Street. When I first went there, I felt like an outsider, but again within seconds, I kept getting comments like, "Wow, you are beautiful. Are you in the show?" This Maria get-up was becoming quite the superhero outfit. Very quickly, I was running into people I knew just about everywhere.

Thursday nights, I was at the Monster Show at The Edge in the Castro, hosted by the late drag queen Cookie Dough. Cookie was hugely influential to me. Despite being a veteran and one of the most popular queens in the city, she was the nicest, most supportive queen. Her attitude was most precious. It was so wonderful to see somebody in her position take time out for the new people in town. Cookie was just the kind of person I was looking to find in San Francisco. I was so fortunate.

Me interviewing Cookie Dough and clips from the Monster Drag Show:

Video   *Interview*

Video: This includes an interview with Cookie and is followed by clips from their Grease Tribute, a good example of the type of small-scale, underground neighborhood drag shows that occurs every week in San Francisco. In the video link, I jump to the segment which shows Cookie's positive attitude.

Cookie unfortunately passed away in early 2015 from a sudden case of meningitis in Mexico, which put her into a coma just two days after this later interview.

It was non-stop fun for the six weeks between moving to San Francisco and Halloween. It really helped me, because I pretty much forgot I was getting divorced. But what was so unexpected was this deep, supportive community I'd found. There was nothing like it in the suburbs. Most of the people I met as Maria were not married with kids, although I was surprised how many gay men were married to each other, legally or otherwise. This community therefore had more time and money available for a larger alternative family—fellow performers, supporting people in the community, including newcomers and those in need through a lot of volunteering and fund-raising events. I was inspired by the passions people develop when they had time to focus outside of themselves and their immediate families. They were propagating memes not genes. And good memes, too. Propagating memes is every bit as powerful as propagating genes, probably more so as memes are certainly the nature of our future.

I never expected how quickly I would be absorbed into this culture. So now what would this long-anticipated Halloween be like?

Halloween weekend

October 31, 2006, was a Tuesday, so I had parties to go to Friday, Saturday, and Tuesday. I had told my family and most of my close straight friends that I was going out in drag, as I didn't want even the slightest concern that I might get outed, so I came right out with it, sparing most of the details. I had to tell people about all this fun, and what better time to tell friends and family than on Halloween. I was doing this just for Halloween, right?

On Friday, I went to a straight party thrown by my cousin who lived nearby. I wanted to impress them with my new skills and state of being. *Hee, this is going to be fun! I'm going to blow them away, and this time I'm going to have a damn fucking good costume, probably the best one.* I wore blue eye shadow, long blond hair, a foofy vinyl skirt, a fishnet top and hose, and very tight boots.

Of course, I was the hit of the party. Despite the fact they knew I was coming in drag, they still didn't know who I was when I showed up. *Score!* I got as many questions from the straight guys as I did from the

At my cousin's Halloween party

girls. I liked all the attention. I deserved it after braving these totally insane last six weeks. But I was starting to get bored being the primary attraction at the straight party, and I left after about an hour. I ran down the street in my massively tight boots to grab a cab and was off to Castro for some club parties. My boots were so tight, I had numbness in my toes for several months afterward, but it was worth it. Kink will allow you to endure lots of pain because it feels like it's for a higher purpose.

The rest of the night is mostly a blur, although I found a few pictures. I hit various bars and shows in the Castro and, of course, Trannyshack on Halloween night, where I met Wilhelmina, a transsexual dominatrix with breast implants. She invited me to be her assistant for a session a few days later, whipping one of her clients at the Power Exchange, the big kink sex club in San Francisco. And this was supposed to be my last night going out as Maria. The best laid plans ruined by better opportunities.

CHAPTER 3

HOW CAN I GIVE THIS UP?

I came home that Halloween night, pondering what a journey the past six weeks had been and realized the journey into the San Francisco underground was the real adventure—not Halloween, which was basically amateur night. The original plan was to get off this train at the next stop. That seemed so depressing, but I had to, I couldn't keep doing this, right?

My new friend Wilhelmina told me I just "loved the jazz." I was afraid she was right, and it scared me. I thought about my favorite joke:

> *What's the difference between a transvestite and a transsexual?*
> *. . . 2 years*

I had to discover more of this new power. When Dude walked into a club, nothing happened other than a tiny breeze from the door. When Maria walked in, the Red Sea parted. Plus, hundreds of people already knew Maria in just a few weeks. *This is working, go with it! I need to stay on this path and rewire my brain in a positive way.* I had the opportunity to make up for lost time. For the past twenty years, I had rarely partied, and I never just had fun with sex. It was always about trying to find the right romance, which *never* worked out. I had fantasized about leaving all that behind and living in a big city, and here I was! There were more people to meet, more clubs to discover, more headspaces to experience, and I'd never have to be bored again. I was living in heaven on earth.

My relationship with women had also taken a 180-degree turn. As The Dude, I had never been able to talk to women with their shields down. But they were so nice to Maria, so happy to meet me. My first real shot of that happened at a late-night crêpe shop. Three young women were eating at a table, and when they looked up at us as my friends and I were walking in, one of the girls looked straight at me and gave me this deep smile filled with love and joy that floored me. I had been waiting my whole life for a girl to look at me like that. She opened her soul to me. We sat down next to them and spent the next thirty minutes giggling and flirting. That blast of feminine energy warmed my soul and softened my heart more than I could possibly describe. And I couldn't have cared less about the sex thing. This connection is what The Dude craved more than anything but could never get. And now I was a sister living in a world of female energy and love that I never knew existed. How could I ever walk away?

Left: *Flirting at the Lush Lounge, a straight bar across the street from Divas. It became a routine for me to leave Divas around 11:30 p.m. flirt with super sweet women at the various bars nearby, and then go back to Divas.*

Right: *People on the street, most often young women, were constantly stopping me and wanting to flirt, hug, and get pictures. This is crappy picture of me, but it brings back fond memories.*

Often, they would end up back on my place. I couldn't believe who was coming to my place for little soirées. The Dude is such a nobody compared to this.

I was loved for being fabulous. I was having the best time of my life. I was attracting all these lovely women like flypaper and was regularly having impromptu parties back at my place. I could not believe it. I always wanted to be Batman, but I found Batgirl instead!

Having a natural, person-to-person, shields-free relationship with women without all the BS trappings of straight dating was divine. And I never hit on women I had just met, because I didn't want to tarnish this precious relationship—unless they wanted to, which did happen occasionally. It was so hard sitting down at the piano or on the couch with these women, baring our souls, them telling me how much they admired me, wanting so badly to kiss her and not doing it. I found this connection I had craved so much for so many years, but not in the way I had expected. And I was perfectly content and happy, because connecting

Playing the piano came in handy for entertaining at home, and I developed my flair for playing songs I knew off the top of my head and channeling my emotions through them. Little did I know I would be soon doing this out in the clubs.

with a woman's soul and that female spirit was *so* important to me. I didn't want to screw it up by hitting on them. Since I was preparing for a divorce and had continued bad experiences dating as The Dude, I still wanted to stay away from dating women as much as possible. I was so much happier this way, and I was free to do anything I wanted and to express myself. Free as a girl!

I was worried about how dangerous all the partying, sex, drugs, and kink could be. How would I get work done, eat well, and not get hooked on drugs and alcohol? But I knew I'd just have to figure it out—I had decades of a bruised soul to heal, and I had found something *guaranteed* to provide me with fun and self-confidence every time I went out. I needed to stay here until I was ready . . . but for what I wasn't quite sure. I wasn't some oddball outcast anymore. I was loved for my uniqueness, just like everybody else in this subculture. And I felt part of a community, one with a deep, rich history. It was the antithesis of everything I had known in my suburban life. I was getting addicted to people liking my raw, fabulous energy. The more I pushed it out, the better it was received. This was in stark contrast to the suburbs, where being different and full of passion was not well received and was just considered weird. And to me, it wasn't at all about sex or labels. I couldn't believe how different these worlds were. And I wanted to stay on this train until I felt complete.

Why would I give this up? Why would I fret over what people thought and limit myself to the trappings of straight dating?

Maybe I could integrate this new power into my male side? It was too soon for that. I needed to stay on this train and see where it went. But The Dude would have none of it. Maybe he was clinging to his romantic dream? Well, Maria wasn't just dreaming.

Back to the present—late Halloween evening . . .

"No!" The Dude kept repeating as I finished dissolving the eyebrow wax. "You're done, Maria. We had a deal that you would do this until Halloween and stop. This was not meant to be a lifestyle thing."

I was starting to ignore him.

"I'm throwing this stuff out," he said.

Now I was paying attention. "Are you threatening me?!"

Well, it's easier to act than argue with somebody incessantly. Rather than wait for an answer from him, I took immediate action. At three in the morning on Halloween, I went online and bought a Wonder Woman outfit. *Ha! Now I have no choice but to keep going because there is no way The*

Dude is just going to throw the outfit out after spending money on it. I was getting to know how to werk men, including myself. We girls can be so sneaky if we understand where true power resides.

The train doors closed and I was on my way to the next station! And since it was early November, well, we both knew we would make it way past the holiday season. Choo choo . . . *whistle* . . . !

The Power Exchange sex club

The next stop on my train ride was two days later when I accompanied Wilhelmina to the Power Exchange, the preeminent sex club in San Francisco. I was to be her assistant for a client. Like most of her clients, he was a powerful, well-to-do man who wanted to switch roles and be dominated for an evening—more specifically, get the shit beaten out of him with a flogger.

Before going out, I went through a ritual, cementing the next phase of my new life. I shaved all my body hair, including my legs. That was a big symbolic deal for me. Now putting on a bra with no body hair was extra sexy. *I'm feeling even more like a woman!* I suddenly wanted to buy a bunch more bras, which I started to see as art. Without the hair on my legs, I only needed a single pair of pantyhose, and it felt *so* good putting them on. I smoked some extra weed to get all excited for the club, took one more good look at myself and ran downstairs where Wilhelmina picked me up, and we were off to the Power Exchange on Otis Street[15].

When you walked into the club, you had to sign a disclaimer. There were signs notifying us safe sex was required, with jars of condoms and little lube packets all over the place. And best yet, all types of girls got in for free. We could wear any clothes we wanted—typically fishnets, garter belts, leather, and the like. Guys had to pay, and they also had to strip and wear just a towel[16]. Girl privileges kept stacking up.

The lounge was quite nice and clean, but a bit cheesy with red walls, memorabilia, and a cheeseball Elvis statue. This wasn't what I expected from a sex club, but it worked because it made you feel comfortable. The lounge also had a little shop with snacks, lube, condoms, small whips, and other useful knickknacks. The woman behind the counter was

---

15. It has since moved to a much smaller location in the Tenderloin a few blocks from Union Square.
16. If they wanted to wear their clothes they had to pay more, but few did.

super cool. Again, I expected some drug-crazed person, but she was an awesomely nice, chatty goth girl.

We were to meet Wilhelmina's client in the **King Arthur Room**. It had a throne, a St. Andrews cross, and a horse similar to a pommel

The lounge, lockers, and gift shop area had lots of memorabilia. Strange seeing this décor in a big sex club.

The King Arthur room

horse[17], but with metal rings you could tie people to. I started getting weak in the knees as I thought about all the things I knew I would be doing in that room someday. I still felt a little residual embarrassment about my own kinky feelings, but I would find that most of the people at the Power Exchange were pretty experienced and cool about the whole thing.

Wilhelmina started setting up while I went on a little tour.

The next room had a cage with chains attached to a leather sex swing. My jaw dropped as I thought about the number of people who got fucked on that swing, and I just knew I was going to get fucked on that swing. That was as certain as the sun rising. It would be on my mind until I did it, so I needed to get it over with soon, and I would.

The first floor had various other cages and benches as well as a dance floor with mirrors and a few poles. A lot of men of all ages and races were walking around in towels. The girls were in the minority, and were almost all t-girls, mostly Asian.

The cage and sex swing with my name on it

Guys immediately started hitting on me, but I had a job to do, so I declined. I had learned how to say no gracefully.

I saw a dark staircase going to the basement. Down I went and entered a huge room with a playpen and a bunch of guys tied up and getting whipped by huge muscle men. *That looks like a lot of fun.* I'd seen this sort of thing in the movies, but this was real. There were lots of little rooms connected by dark passageways, black lights, strobe lights, creepy music, and benches and leather beds everywhere, with people fucking all over the place. I wandered around and felt so sleazy, because I wasn't used to

17. The familiar kind one would find in a school gym class

The Power Exchange also had many little rooms with various types of beds like this fucking podium.

being so fucking turned on by this nasty shit in a public place. I felt weak in my stomach and I couldn't help myself. I tried not to touch too much because I could smell the sweat and body fluids. There were also second and third floors, but I didn't have a chance to get up there until I visited again a month or so later to get my brains fucked out in that swing.

I went back up to the King Arthur room to assume my role as Wilhelmina's assistant. The guy she was to beat seemed like a regular early-forty-something professional guy. My job was like an operating room nurse—to hand Wilhelmina the whips, lube, collar, harness, and restraints as she needed, and also help her tie the ropes and leather straps around her subject. This was all happening while people came in and sat on the many benches in the room and watched while they jerked off or got a blow job. Another checkmark off my list. I couldn't wait to tell this story to my select friends. I knew I would be back soon, next time with more details about what *I* did.

CHAPTER 4

SHOPPING FOR THE NEW WOMAN

I was off to the races, and now it was time to really go shopping. I was never good at picking out clothes when I was a guy. But I discovered I had a pretty good knack for putting sexy women's outfits together— well, mostly trashy outfits. I understood the saying, "It costs a fortune to look this cheap!" In fourteen years living in San Francisco, I must have spent fifteen grand on girl clothes and only about two thousand on men's clothes, mostly underwear and boring shirts and pants. I'm not good at picking out men's clothes because I have zero interest in them. Men obsessing over their clothes just seems narcissistic to me, probably due to the trauma of my parents having *obsessively* bitched at me about clothes *all the time* to the *exclusion* of all else.

But when I'm a girl, it's different. I'm interested in women's clothes because I'm interested in women. Why would I be interested in men's clothes when I'm not interested in men? When I'm a guy, I just want to be myself without all the pretense. When I'm a girl, it's a dress-up thing, so being preoccupied with the clothes makes sense. The whole world seemed upside down to me. But that's just me, I'm weird. I'm still a misfit, but I'm fabulously misfitted, like a good mutation.

At first, I would only go going shopping as The Dude. One of my favorite places to shop was Macy's in Union Square. It's a great place to go for cool blouses and nice dresses, and it ended becoming my best place for women's underwear. Victoria's Secret and Fredricks tended to be for smaller women—I needed lingerie for a queen or a goddess. Macy's is very trans friendly, but The Dude never asked for any help because he felt nervous shopping for me and still pretended I was his girlfriend. He never tried anything on. I just took the risk that it might not fit. If it didn't, I gave the item to one of my drag queen friends. I considered that a convenience tax.

However, during the holidays, I said *fuck it, I'm going shopping as a girl.* And as an extra incentive, I decided to trip on mushrooms while looking at bras at Macy's. And it *was* a trip! As soon as I started tripping, I left my apartment, freaking out because the elevator walls were shrinking, and so were the doors to the cab. It was so bad I almost jumped out even though the ride to Macy's was only six blocks. Thank God I lived in the city. By the time I got to the lingerie department, I was tripping balls and feeling really giggly happy. What an incredible joy it was to feel like a girl going bra shopping. I was taking my time and picking up the bras and feeling them. I actually thought I was a girl, and I couldn't stop gig-

Bra racks at Macy's. They had a wide variety and lots of sizes at great prices.

gling, because it was so much fucking fun. I didn't think about the past, the future, all that guy planning I was always doing. I was spiritually present in this girl thing.

I had just gotten huge DDD professionally realistic silicon breast forms[18]. My previous size was just a D I created with men's white socks. What a fucking trip it was trying on these huge bras with these huge breasts. I was entering the big leagues, baby! I even got up the balls to ask one of the Macy's women for help. When she saw how huge I was, she explained to me exactly what a minimizer bra was. I'm pretty sure she thought I was had just gotten implants and needed guidance on controlling these huge girls. I had so much fun talking with her while I was tripping.

There was a three-panel mirror in the dressing room so I could see my front, back, and side of these sexy bras while tripping balls. This started my love affair with the combination of dressing up as a girl, extreme intoxication, and three-panel mirrors. Talk about releasing your inner joy.

The trip lasted about three hours, and I somehow ended up with multiple colors of polish on my fingernails. I think I put them on at Sephora. I ended that day at Divas tying on a few drinks while chatting with the bartender, Cassandra Cass, a well-known post-op[19] transsexual Hollywood starlet who worked part time at the bar while building her career. We started talking about breast implants and sex change operations. Crazy, I was talking with a real transsexual about sex change! Cassandra told me about the psychology of it and what you needed to do

Cassandra Cass, a transgendered actress, later appeared on Under the Golden Gate

---

18. For $450 back then from a specialty online store, where today you can get them from Amazon for only about $90

19. "Post-op" transsexual refers to a man who has transformed into a woman and has had his penis converted into a vagina with surgery.

to prepare, and she encouraged me, telling me, we girls have no choice. I didn't really think this was for me, but then again, maybe it was for the rejected Dude. I mean, if I had a ton of money or if it opened up doors . . .

A few days later I was walking down Castro Street with my new, huge DDD breasts and sexy lacy bra from Macy's, and let me tell you how totally rad it was—walking down the street with proper huge breasts bouncing around. I learned how to walk, matching the natural vibration of my breasts. I also started to wiggle my hips like a woman as I walked, doing it so much that my hips actually started hurting and I had to tone it down. I also noticed more people were looking at me with my huge, new breasts. Guys were buying me more drinks. I broke even on my four-hundred-and-fifty-dollar investment pretty quickly. It made me more self-conscious because I wondered even more *what are they seeing and thinking? Am I just a woman with big tits or more than that? How do you get used to this?* But once I went DDD, I never went back. It just felt too good! It reminded me constantly that I was a woman.

Another notable shopping experience was when The Dude was working on Wall Street on a consulting project for Merrill Lynch. During my lunch break, I went to a boutique which catered to drag queens, crossdressers, and transsexuals. It was located in the Greenwich Village Meatpacking District, a dirty and sleazy place at the time. The boutique had an unmarked door. I hit the buzzer and nervously went upstairs and voila, what a place! It was huge and had transsexual mannequins, racks of kinky bras, boas, clothes, and a whole backroom with serious European trans magazines. The other customers walking around were all regular looking Wall Street dudes with really nice suits.

I bought my first real corset there. The t-girl helping me insisted that I try one on. It was pretty, but I didn't see the point of spending a hundred and fifty dollars on it. She insisted again, and while she was lacing it up, I looked in the mirror and told her I didn't think it was worth it. She said, "Gurl, wait until I tighten it." I replied, "Huh, what do you mean?" She finished the lacing and then tightened it, and *wham!* I got it. Holy shit, I felt like somebody grabbed me and was making love to me. I'd just found a new religion. It's hard to explain how it feels to be grabbed by something sexy and shaped with curves. *I'll take it, ring me up!* She put my new garments into a brown paper bag, which I put in my backpack and brought back to the office. I had trouble concentrating at work the rest of the day as I stared at that brown paper bag through the partially

Piedmont in the Haight: *Famous for the fishnet legs above the door plus great flashy outfits to wear when you want to party or just try to be somebody different. One of my favorite places, so friendly. And what HOT pictures in the dressing room!*

Piedmont is owned by a couple, the wife is Israeli, and the husband, from Germany is posing in the picture.

opened zipper of the backpack, chuckling how a transsexual's corset was in the office and nobody knew. Hee hee. I couldn't wait to fly back to San Francisco to wear it during my next outing! I wondered what they'd think when I put my luggage into the X-ray machine at the airport.

When it came to makeup, I learned to find the products I needed at a wide variety of stores. I didn't trust any brand based on reputation or buzz. I needed to try it for myself, and I was very picky about quality and functionality. This is where The Dude's view of the world was helpful. He was immune to the psychological manipulation of advertising. I also rapidly discovered that so many of the really cool colors weren't strong enough for t-girls and queens, so I learned to mix cremes, lose powders, and shadows. Much of it was trial and error, plus getting tips from queens. I especially liked sharing tips with other girls in the dressing rooms at shows. This is where the magic of kink and professionally creative artistry mix.

CHAPTER 5

TRANS ENTERTAINER

Piano gurl

I started going to the piano bar, Martuni's[20], which has open mic singing 9 p.m. to 1 a.m. every night accompanied by the regular piano players. There's a bar in the front and a piano room in the back with a classic piano bar feel. Martuni's was a lot classier than Divas or the dive bars and underground clubs and parties I was hanging out in. It's a mixed[21] bar and was great place for straight guys and curious visitors to meet classy t-girls like me, and you would regularly run into many local characters, performers, queens, politicians, and activists.

Martuni's is located halfway between Gay San Francisco (The Castro) and Straight San Francisco (City Hall). It's an epicenter where straight and gay people mix—ideal for my tastes. It was about seventy-five percent gay, with a lot of theater lovers singing showtunes, but very

---

20. It's still on the corner of Market and Valencia.
21. Queer and straight

Singing with Katy

chill straight people and couples also came to hear the music, sing, mingle, and run across the various queens and performers who often stopped in after a big event. It was a great place for straight people, especially men, to feel at ease singing or connecting with their feelings and feminine side. You could shed a tear at Martuni's without the fear of being thought of as a sissy by a bunch of meathead douchebags. And people didn't care if you weren't any good, as long as you were having a good time.

Performing as a woman had never crossed my mind. But one night, my t-girl buddy, Miranda, and one of the regular piano players, Katy Stephan, dragged me up to the piano. It didn't take much dragging. Now I really was out there, a fabulous t-girl who could really ham it up. I discovered how much easier it was performing as a trans women vs. when The Dude would occasionally play somewhere over the years. The audience *wanted* to like me. I found myself at Martuni's twice a week usually performing a few songs. Sometimes I was fucking awesome, and sometimes I sucked. I quickly learned some simple rules of performing. Eighty percent is choosing the right song for you and then choosing the right key. It really helps if the audience knows the song and it's upbeat. And the more fun you have and the drunker they are, the better!

One of the legendary pianists, Trauma Flintstone (aka Joe Wicht), took notice and asked me to be in his show. I thought he was just being nice. The whole idea seemed ridiculous. *I'm not good enough, plus singing isn't my forte.* But he kept badgering me and invited me to perform in his variety show called *Bijou*. I reluctantly agreed, and chose a few songs I knew really well, hoping people wouldn't notice I was a fraud and not a real musician.

When we were organizing the show, Joe asked me, "What's your last name?" Huh? Nobody had ever asked me that before. Most drag queens had funny names like Tragic Fantastic-Titt'es, Scarlett Letters, or Peaches Christ, and I wasn't a drag queen. I thought about it for a few days and just chose the last name Konner after Sarah Conner from *The Terminator*, but I changed "C" to "K," as it was more unique and sounded German. So my name was Maria Konner. I didn't think much of it. Yet again, little did I know it would be with me for the rest of my life.

The show came and they loved my bits. I thought at first they were just being nice, but I kept getting asked to be in more variety shows and to play piano for other people. After a while I thought, *Okay, I guess maybe I'm pretty good.* I mean, I was just playing how I feel and having fun—I think that was the secret. People like Joe Wicht, who have been in the scene for decades and reach out to help and encourage new people in the community, are the soul of San Francisco.

Video interview with Joe Wicht in front of Martunis:

Note: Bad audio quality (before I started using a handheld microphone).

At Martuni's, I met Dennis Sanchez, a singer with a voice of velvet. I remember looking at him while we were sitting by the piano, thinking, *wow, here is a guy from this other gay world that I know so little about. What is his life like, his attitudes?* The gay men I knew up to that point all hung out in the trashy party bars. One night, Dennis came walking into Divas with a friend and saw me. "Hi, Maria from Martuni's?" Within fifteen minutes, we were back at my place with him singing and me on the piano. In a short time, we were doing our own shows at Martuni's and various other clubs. I thought I wasn't good enough at first. I didn't know all those show tunes, and I was terrible at reading music. But I knew how to play from the gut and could easily read chord charts with just the lyrics to guide me. I knew jazz/blues and rock/pop and knew how to jam on a good riff. And so, I just did what I knew, and we killed it.

Video playlist of Dennis with me on piano:

We played two consecutive nights at one club. The first night I went as The Dude. The second night, I was Maria, and the crowd went crazy. The owner grabbed me and said, "Wow you're incredible, who are you?" He didn't know I was The Dude from the previous night! They all liked Maria a whole lot better. I never performed as The Dude again—what was the point?

I started singing a few songs of my own in the show I did with Dennis, and this allowed me to build up my own presence as a performer. That's the way a lot of these things develop. I had vague dreams of performing as a musician over the years, but reality happens when you just put yourself out there and meet people like Joe and Dennis.

My own show: gateway drug into sex parties

The owner of Martuni's noticed me and asked me to do a monthly show. It was a great opportunity to have a platform to work with musicians that I met and try new songs, many of which were originals or spoofs on popular songs. My show gave me access to some fun action. I hooked up with two lesbians. They started chatting with me after the show, and we just naturally ended up in a threesome. This is the way life is supposed to be—doing something fun that leads to a connection and sex. One of them was *butch*, short hair and tough looking, and the other was *lipstick*, long hair and pretty. I was more interested in the lipstick girl, but it was the butch girl who was most interested in me. Oh well . . . I'll take it. This same situation happened several times. In a *billion* years, The Dude would never have an opportunity to hook up with two women.

I had heard a rumor about a trans woman who lived upstairs and had crazy sex parties and a bed with mirrors all around it with a view of Market

Street. I didn't think it was real, or perhaps this was a tale from a decade ago. Then one night after performing, as usual, I ended up at a table having drinks with people who'd seen the show. One was a trans woman, and another was a guy wearing a shirt that said, "Trannychaser." The trans woman said she was having a party upstairs and invited me to join them. *Holy shit, this is real, and I'm invited!* We sauntered on upstairs and lo and behold, there were about a dozen people making out and doing various light drugs like alcohol, weed, cocaine, and whip-its.

It seemed too dirty at first, so I just smoked some weed and chatted with those who weren't having sex or doing heavier drugs. Then I wandered into the bedroom, and there it was—the bed with tons of mirrors overlooking Market Street. *I really have arrived!* The guy with the chaser shirt followed me in. He was a nice guy, and I had fun flirting with him a bit while we got more stoned off our asses. I jumped up on the bed and saw my gurl self in the mirrors from every angle. I felt sexy, and I started role playing as a sexy bitch. And then he jumped up on the bed behind me, grabbed me, and started dry humping me, thrusting his dick up against my ass. This was the second time a guy grabbed me, but this was much more intense, and it was on a bed. When you're stoned, getting touched by anybody on a bed feels really good. Well, that's my excuse.

Our bodies were locked together with me as the submissive. *Whoa, I really like this.* I looked at the five different angles of myself in the mirrors and rejoiced at watching this fucking slut while he was thrusting into me! I felt weak and excited, but I couldn't stop The Dude from thinking,

The night I ended up at the sex party, I had my rare, short dark hair dyke look going.

you shouldn't be doing this, and if you try it even once, you'll never have the op-
tion of being with a woman again.

The problem was that I knew I wanted to see where this easy and
kinky sex led. I knew I would be back for more. It made me feel so much
like a girl, so different from being a man. He wanted to fuck my brains
out, and this dry humping was getting me so fucking hot and bothered.
I wanted it so bad, but I was too afraid of feeling labeled "gay" and thinking I might get hooked on queer sex. I chickened out. Later I couldn't stop
thinking about how much I wanted to try that again, and I frequently
jerked off thinking about my own sexcapade. Next time I was determined to go through with it. I was not going to give up the opportunity
to see what it felt like to be a sex queen.

Rocker chick

Andy Woodhouse could play ANYTHING on bass and kill it

Over time, I started adding more singers and musicians to the Martuni's
monthly show. Then I started bringing my acoustic guitar, then my electric guitar, then a bass player, then a drummer, then a harmonica player.
We started calling it a rock-and-roll cabaret, but we needed to move to a
different venue because we were getting too loud.

So, I formed a band called *Sex Industry* with Flynn Witmeyer on vocals, Davey J on bass, and Syndi Heart, who had previously played in an
all-trans band Lipstick Conspiracy, on drums. We played drag shows,
then larger clubs, then underground parties, then street fairs including
Gay Pride, Castro Street Fair and then Folsom Street Fair—the world's
largest BDSM leather street fair. People loved the trans/drag thing, but
when you add rocker chick to the mix, it became thermonuclear!

Left: Flynn Witmeyer (center) and Shakey Gibson (right) on vocals, Davey J on bass.
Right: I love when Marilyn Mitchell backs me with her searing blues guitar riffs.

Credit, right photo: https://photosbygooch.com

Folsom Street Fair with the band. I wanted to look at queer as I could, so I added butterfly decals on my legs.

Left: Gay Pride at the Fairy Village Stage
Right: Playing at a street fair in the Mission

Playing in the basement of a funky mission antique shop. I used to wear wide foam hips created by drag queen Ginger Snap, but I had to wear opaque tights under my hose to cover the foam which went down almost to my knees to create that fuller female shape. However, the two pairs of leggings made my legs too hot and crushed my toes, causing constant pain after about an hour of wearing them, so I eventually stopped using the hips.

Video of us playing Glory Box (including my short, searing guitar solo) at the club in the picture.

Playing at a Rave in an industrial warehouse

Castro Street Fair

Playing underground parties was a lot of fun. We got to meet a whole gaggle of weird underground SF folks, while also learning a lot about the history of San Francisco culture. The above party was at the Purple House in Oakland, a community house where several old school San Francisco queens, The Cockettes, lived. I loved the mixing of the ages, cultures, attitudes, and art.

We recorded a CD of original music in my home studio—something all three of us always wanted to do. Recording music was very different from playing live, as it took a lot of painstaking work and experimenting to get the right sounds. Fortunately, our bass player Davey Jay was a producer and audio engineer.

We made several music videos. Flynn was in film school, and Davey was also a video producer. Collaborating with my bandmates and bringing multiple complementary talents together on a project was a dream come true.

Playlist – *Music videos plus live performances*

Purchase CD: *from Apple*

Purchase CD: *from Amazon*

Davey became instrumental in our *Under the Golden Gate* show, where I learned about professional lighting and using multiple high-quality video cameras.

I was starting to create, perform, and disseminate real art. I never would have met any of these extraordinary people if I hadn't moved to the city and become Maria. I was also learning how to be an entertainer. One of the most important tasks in performing is to screw up as fast as you can and get used to it. This way you're not uptight on stage. If you're having a good time, the audience will have a good time—it's all about energy. I loved the advice I got from a San Francisco professional pianist and performer:

"If you try too hard, you're gonna suck. Just have fun."
—*Erik Walker*

My biggest train wreck gigs were the most appreciated. I've lost count of the number of times where things kept going from wrong to worse, and I was so embarrassed I was counting the minutes until I could make a mad dash for the door. But I kept playing my best until the end, and I couldn't get to the door because people would keep stopping me and buying me drinks, telling me much how much fun they were having. God bless!

Music is very precious and personal to me. I've always seen it as the ultimate authentic connection to the universe and to the energy that envelops us. When you combine the mood of a great piece of music with a powerful story and lyrics that match, you have divinity. Having the opportunity to be intimate in front of an audience and spread energy that inspires is a genuine privilege I cherish more than anything.

I increasingly found myself being asked to perform both as a solo artist or sit in with a band in some pretty big venues, like the Independent

Bottom Right: *Playing Purple Rain, in the rain (hence the sneakers). Golden Gate Park for Easter.*

in San Francisco and the Fox Theater in Oakland. At the Fox Theater gig, we had incredible dressing rooms, hospitality suites, a dinner spread, roadies, my own monitor with a great mixing guy, and a fun party afterward with the headliners, Franz Ferdinand and Sparks. Sometimes I would get paid five hundred bucks to dress up as a fabulous woman, play music, and party. Good deal!

Narcissistic Cabaret

Video Playlist highlights (other artists as well as myself): I created my own cabaret and started learning how to film a live show. I was into recording live music with high-quality audio on individual channels to get a great mix with multi-dimensional sound. So listen with headphones or good speakers!

My own band "Not from Jersey!"

Playing on the Main Stage at Folsom Street Leather Fair:

Bottom left: Getting whipped by Sebastian Keys, a porn star and producer from Kink.com, while playing Black Sabbath's "Fairies Wear Boots." Sweet Jayne on drums, Andrea Hensler on bass.

Several years later, I formed my own band, *Not From Jersey!* I started playing mostly naughty original songs on the guitar because I initially focused on underground clubs and par-

Playlist – *"Not From Jersey!" on the main stage at Folsom Street Fair*

Still drinking and partying, with Kelli Perry, after a long day at Folsom

ties. I learned pretty quickly that to keep the audience's attention, you either have to play dance songs, songs they know and can sing along to, or funny or naughty songs. I was asked to play the main stage at Folsom Street Fair and was paid for it! Maria was a pro now! The naughty songs were perfect for the biggest BDSM kink fair in the world!

CHAPTER 6

BECOMING BATGIRL

Jamie's legendary kinky parties

Every two weeks, there was another gathering of new and veteran t-girls at Jamie Faye's place for Jasmine's outings. Jamie also had sex parties after Trannyshack on Tuesday nights. At one of these parties I walked in and a guy greeted me and said, "Wow, you are gorgeous. What awesome lips. I want to stick my dick in your mouth!" I had learned how to layer my lipstick to create great DSL—Dick Sucking Lips. A little premature, as I wasn't into sucking Dick just yet, so I probably said something like, "I need a drink." But it was really confidence building. Then, seconds later, I saw a guy sitting on the couch with his hard dick standing at attention and another guy jumped right on top of him and they started fucking in front of everybody while the guy on top was screaming really loud. It was as if he was so proud of being out, he was enjoying shouting his joy. *Where's that drink?*

I wandered into the master bedroom to find two people fucking on the sex swing hanging from the ceiling. I felt like a square. I couldn't tell

Walking into Jamie's Party

if this scene was basically a bunch of perverted sex addicts acting like children without adult supervision, or if this is what healthy adults liked to do when they are free. I saw the baboons doing it in front of us in Africa, so maybe this was natural? This was no regular wine and cheese party. Well, they did have wine and cheese, but it wasn't *about* the wine and cheese.

But there were plenty of people who didn't fuck at the party, and they seemed to be as amused by the whole thing as I was. I especially loved that in this trans/kink environment, I hadn't found any judgement or too-cool-to-talk-with-you people. Everybody was accepting of whomever you were, drugs or no drugs, sex or no sex, professional sex worker or civilian, beauty or no beauty. However, I did draw healthy boundaries. When somebody lit up a glass meth pipe, and I could see the white cloud of meth moving toward me, I decided it was time to immediately head out to Divas. I also made a mental note to not have sex with that person in the future.

I had met fellow t-girl Miranda at one of these parties. She became my best buddy and wing-gurl. At first, I wanted to fuck her as I was anxious to try trans-on-trans sex. I was excited about the idea of easy, kinky sex, but when it came to looking at somebody in the eyes, and touching and smelling them, and actually fucking, it wasn't nearly as easy as the fantasy. It would be a little more time before I slipped into being a slut.

So, Miranda and I just became good friends, and once I saw her as a dude, there was no way I was going to fuck her. She was new in town, but not new to dressing. She was a skateboarder and surfer dude who skated with many of the big names in the competitive skateboarding scene. None of the dudes in that scene knew about Miranda. It was difficult for her to dress because her surfer dude roommate didn't know she had girl clothes stashed in her trunk. She had to dress in secret when he wasn't home, which created all kinds of funny logistical problems. Miranda had a really smart daughter who eventually learned about Miranda's dressing and was totally cool with it. She was pretty evolved, probably because she had

Jamie at her place with porn star Kelley Michaels, and also dressed for fun

With Miranda in front of Marlena's, an old school drag bar which has since been sold

cool parents—plus the newer generations generally don't have the same hang-ups as my generation. Thankfully, they'll be taking over our world.

A lot of gurls lived two lives. One worked at a very exclusive conservative club as a dude and knew many big politicians and Hollywood actors. She eventually transitioned and came out, and the guests and management at the club were totally on board with it. I also frequently ran into a group of t-girls who were guards at a state penitentiary, and one of them was the assistant warden. She always had a few hot genetic girls at her side when we went out to the clubs.

I met trans porn star Carmen Cruz at one of Jamie's Trannyshack after-parties. At first, I didn't recognize her. I was chatting with this hot t-girl, only to find out she was Carmen Cruz! Carmen had just released a new series on shemaleyum.com where she was fucking a few guys at once. The postings were so new, she hadn't even seen them yet, but I had! I logged into my account and sat down next to Carmen at the computer and showed her own videos. She was all turned on and stroking herself while sitting next to me watching herself getting nailed by all these hot guys. She kept exclaiming "That is so hot!" Now that's a party!

Then they started having the parties at my place. I had resisted having monthly parties at my place because I was afraid it was going to impact my ability to maintain some semblance of normality.

With trans porn star Carmen Cruz. I looked like hell after a night of hard partying at Trannyshack.

But normal conversations didn't work for me anymore. When I went to visit people outside San Francisco, the conversations about kids' soccer, kitchen tile, TV shows, and patio furniture bored me so much, I had to start bringing joints. But I needed to ensure I kept at least one foot in the real world, after all I did have nieces, nephews, and a mother. The parties were so much fun, I wondered which of my two worlds was the real one. Only one way to find out—keep going down the unexplored path!

Club gurl

Kinky Salon

Kinky Salon was a frequent private sex party. On my first visit, I finally had a chance to use my Wonder Woman outfit. Kinky Salon was held at Mission Control, a large commune on the second floor of what looked like a run-of-the-mill, three-story older apartment building in The Mission. When I first arrived, I thought I was in the wrong location, as it was so dark and quiet outside. But then I saw a person standing in the vestibule by a gate. I had the secret code word, which unlocked the hidden treasures inside.

The front room had a dance floor with mirrors and a stripper's pole along with a little bar and several bedrooms off it. It reminded me of Jeannie's bottle in *I Dream of Jeannie*—they were full of plush couches, hanging beads, and dreamy fabrics. Each room held multiple people who were making out and smoking weed. In an outdoor smoking area, I managed to convince a few visiting straight people to explore an alternative lifestyle, and one of them decided to move here from the Midwest. In the two official orgy rooms, I saw nothing but mounds of bodies wriggling around. I think there was a bed under them. I was getting used to people having sex in front of everybody at a party, but this was something else. I felt privileged to be there, but also like a bit of a dork because I wasn't jumping on the pile. But then I remembered, all types are welcome[22] in San Francisco with no shame, even those who aren't in the mood for filthy group sex.

I start chatting with a really hot, flirty genetic girl, but something was wrong with the conversation. I couldn't put my finger on it. I got these weird sexual vibes from her like it was too easy for me to just grab her. I wanted to chat more first. I was still wired to be a conservative straight guy who likes to have a little connection with someone before rubbing up against her. I told her I was going to grab a drink, and when I came back, she was getting banged from behind against the wall by some dude. In front of everybody. That was quick. I was actually shocked. And then I fantasized both what it would be like to fuck her and what it would be like to be her, getting fucked by some random dude. I was both excited and scared to be in this scene. I

---

22. As long as you're not an *asshole* (an annoying or detestable person—as defined by Webster).

figured I had to check these scenes out before I decided what I wanted to do with this. I had all the time in the world to explore, and I wasn't sure if fucking anything that moved was the best way to go.

I met another genetic girl at the party, and she loved Wonder Woman. I had a date to meet her the next week. Score! The problem was that she simply knew me as Maria, the Wonder Woman. I tried converting her to The Dude. Fatal mistake. I told her I would be The Dude when we met again, but when she saw him, I could hear the hissing of the balloon of our new relationship deflate as I saw the disappointment and horror on her face. We walked around the city, but you could hear the sad trombone playing the entire time. *But I'm the same person!* Or was I?

I eventually learned that this *never* works. There I was, this fabulous person when I was a woman, yet people seemed to think The Dude was horrible. I feel nauseous even thinking about it. At first, I thought people would have a hard time first meeting The Dude and then meeting Maria. That wasn't hard at all, people loved it. But meeting Maria and then The Dude? Ew. I felt like the man in the movie who pulled off his mask to reveal a monster underneath.

The Fembassador Oracle

I got tired of The Dude ruining conversations and relationships. I thus established my cardinal rule: Do NOT try to convert people to The Dude if you meet them as a girl first. As a result, I had *a lot* more fun. I had to basically gag The Dude and make him irrelevant. That's when I started really bonding with women. I was turning even more into one of them and letting myself get really girly. And when they asked me what kind of guy I was into, instead of telling them I was into girls, I lied and told them I liked big muscle guys with no body hair and a big shaved cock, who could really fuck my brains out. Wow, that opened the doors even further! I would find later this actually became true. I guess I was asking for it.

Even my most homophobic straight friends couldn't deny the allure of this life. Maria walked into a bar with one of The Dude's straight friends. As we entered, I flashed my arms around in a "here I am" gesture and got a bundle of smiles and hellos. He said, "Okay, go up to that group of hot girls and get them to talk to us." I walked up to them and said, "I'm conducting a little survey. Do most girls swallow after they give a blow job?" And I got a slew of detailed responses. Several said they don't really like blow jobs. They do it because their boyfriends love it, but they don't like to swallow. Some think it's too gross and try to avoid it. A few said they *love* all of it and swallow every drop.

Then with a huge smile and sparkle in her eye, one of them asked me, "What about you Maria? I bet you swallow." I wasn't expecting that! I had never experienced that kind of bond with a woman before. The look of pure girl sexual excitement in her eyes was *intoxicating*. Somebody sprinkled stars on me. I was talking to her about sex as a fellow person.

I didn't know what to say because I hadn't done so yet, so I just said, "Oh yeah!" and smiled. And the girls' response was so sexy and seductive, "Yeah girl, we knew it! Fucking hot." The look on women's faces whenever we talked about the Dick told me I had been admitted to the inner sanctum of female bonding. I liked this. A lot. But the problem was I didn't get it. I thought maybe I should try sucking Dick to find out what all the fuss was about. I wasn't into the Dick, but that would change soon enough, as there was plenty more humiliation of The Dude to drive me to it.

On another occasion a group of girls in their early twenties flagged me down with an urgent request. One of them had never given a blow job and she needed some tips for a hot date coming up. The excitement and nervousness on her face was precious. And she was smoking hot. Her friends asked me to help out.

"You look like you have a lot of experience," they said. At the time, I had no fucking idea how to give a blow job, but I wasn't going to give up this opportunity. The Dude was helpful here—he knew what craziness happened when you gave a man something he wasn't used to. "Girl, you are going to have a lot of fun. Remember, we have the power, and you need to use it. Just give it a little lick, then pull back, and make him wait and beg for more. Give him a little more, taunt him a little, then wait and then take your time to get into a good position."

Her jaw dropped as her friends said, "You tell her, Maria, that's how to do it!" I couldn't believe I pulled this off. This bonding with women wasn't just hot, it was spiritual. I couldn't believe women were doing this shit. What power. What excitement. It would take me years to fully grok this female lifestyle and process everything I had learned.

Women I met started asking me for relationship and sex advice. I must have had dozens and dozens of "sessions" with girls, sometimes right there on the street. The advice would include statements like:

"Fuck him, you're the one with the power."

"Tell him what *you* want and see how he reacts."

"Tell him the truth and let the cards fall where they may."

"Okay, so he's a Republican. Find out what you have in common. Make him talk more."

"Make him wait a week."

How the fuck did this loser Dude become an oracle, a fembassador between the sexes? I guess I was now both sexes. How odd.

Bottom Left: I loved my red leather skirt custom made by Piedmont in the Haight. It got ruined when a heel poked through it. Not sure how that happened.
Bottom Right: Sometimes I looked awful as I experimented a lot—I was still basically a teenager. But it didn't appear to matter.

The bathrooms!

It was inevitable that I would have to start using the women's bathroom. In San Francisco, you're legally allowed to go into any bathroom you want. Many places had individual stalls in unisex bathrooms, where a lot of sex and drugs would also take place. But most had traditional men and women's bathrooms, and I wasn't going to use the men's bathroom dressed as a gurl[23]. Using the women's bathroom was *really* uncomfortable. First, I was simply not going to pee sitting down. Girls, I know I should, but no negotiation on this one. Pull down the pantyhose and sit on the dirty toilet? Not going to happen in this universe. So, I would pee on the side of the bowl and cough when I started if there wasn't any noise like a hand dryer running. If a woman was in the stall next to me, there was no good way to hide it, but I tried to not think about it when that happened. I also slouched because I didn't want my hair sticking up out of the stall advertising my predicament. But I believe in karma. I always wiped and put down the seat.

The weirdest part was washing my hands and putting on lipstick and fixing my hair in front of one of those huge single mirrors when other girls were standing next to me doing the same. Most of the time they didn't look at me, but I couldn't help but wonder . . . they *did* notice, right? What were they thinking?! Maybe there was a code to not look at each other in the mirror in a women's bathroom? I had no idea because most straight dudes don't look at themselves in a public men's bathroom for more than a second, tops. None of the women was ever mean to me or looked at me askance. On many occasions, I got compliments and a smile. "I love your outfit." "Great lips." I'd passed through yet another level.

At the Stud gay bar, I wondered why the one private bathroom was always so hard to get into. And then I was chatting with a guy and he followed me into that bathroom and told me he wanted me to suck his dick. At first, I was thinking, okay, I'm drunk enough. This will be a fun experience. But I was hesitant. Who was he? Was I going to get a disease? The floor was a fucking cesspool, so that put the kibosh on that idea. Then I realized why so many gay clubs had both private bathrooms and ones with multiple stalls or a trough—people were busy.

The purse challenges

I also had to learn simple things like make your lipstick easily accessible by putting it in one of the pockets of the purse so you don't have to fish

---

23. Unless the women's line was too long. WTF is this? If the men's room was a trough, I would have to be really drunk and desperate to use it.

around for it at an awkward moment like being dressed as a woman in the women's bathroom. Also, I kept forgetting to wipe down the lip gloss so that shit don't get everywhere.

And I kept forgetting to empty the change I would normally empty from The Dude's pockets every night. My purse got at least two pounds heavier over a five-year period when I finally realized how much change I was hauling around.

And where do I put my extra pair of comfortable shoes? I was getting tired of going home early or getting stuck in a chair at the bar because my feet were wasted. What the heck do you do with a big purse to hold your shoes when you want to get drunk, dance your ass off, and flirt? If I was playing piano, it was easy. I would arrive in crazy sexy heels, and immediately take them off while sitting down at the piano. But most of the time, I was sucking up the pain till two or three in the morning. At any given time, my one pair of comfortable shoes looked like they were put through the dryer with thumbtacks too many times.

All this little stuff was a really big part of being a girl. But I did draw the line at not bringing my wallet. I put my man's wallet in my purse to this day, despite gurls bitching at me about it. Fuck it, I ain't dealing with transferring all that to a purse. I had done that until one day I went to the airport without my driver's license and had to go all the way back home and grab it out of my purse, narrowly making my flight. Fuck that. Dude has his limits.

The lesbian bars

I also checked out the lesbian scene. The Lexington was a dyke[24] bar in the Mission. I really got to like dykes. They were dude cool, but they were girls. Lesbians have always been open and nice to me when I'm a girl. It feels really good to chat with them. We can talk about anything, without all the programmed pretense of the straight bullshit memes. I see them as the flip side of my personality. They're women, but often with a hard and sensible edge I really admire—and wish I could see in more straight girls, sigh. I didn't care that there was no sex possibility. I was just so glad to check this all out and become part of their community as a sister and a friend.

---

24. Lesbians who are more on the butch side.

And there was Mecca for lipstick[25] lesbians, which was a completely different scene. The first time I went there, seeing all the beautiful women making out and hitting on each other was shocking. Check. And many of these women were tech professionals who made a lot of money. Smart women are such a turn-on. It broke my heart that I was a platonic sister, but being a sister was definitely the way to go here. I went there once as The Dude with a male and a female friend who looked like a lesbian, but it was not a pleasant experience. The reason for the disconnect between fabulous Maria and The Dude's experiences is crystal clear when you look at it objectively, but my internal experience was depressing and felt really absurd at the time.

Fetish / S&M Clubs

I went to several parties that were mostly straight people who were into various crazy outfits made out of rubber, PVC, or leather. It was basically a costume party. We used to refer to these S&M parties as *Stand & Model* because many of the people were so caught up in the clothes and presentation, they just stood around and didn't say much. Strange. The vibe was almost the same as going to an average boring bar in Silicon Valley.

The clubs that were more queer-oriented were a lot more fun, probably because queer people in general are definitely more sexually charged, open, and free. The Cat Club is a goth, queer/alt dance club where I liked to dance like a slut to 80s and disco music in front of the many big screens and mirrors. This was a great way to work through my childhood dancing traumas.

Bondage-A-Go-Go[26] at the Glas Kat was a huge venue with a mezzanine, stage, multiple bars and dance floors, and little rooms off to the side where people were getting it on, often with whips and a piece of equipment.

The Eagle, leather bar

One of my favorites was the Eagle, an old school San Francisco hardcore leather bar. When I first went there, I felt out of place and intimidated. I was overwhelmed by so much concentrated gay man energy. I couldn't believe how intense these guys were with the sexual vibe and

---

25. Lesbians who are more on the feminine / pretty side. Mecca was on Market across from the Castro Safeway, but only on Thursday nights.
26. Bondage-A-Go-Go has since moved to the Cat Club.

how totally comfortable they were with themselves. All these buff, good-looking guys were making out and hooking up. It was shocking. Check.

But just as before, I quickly found them to be a lot of fun, really open, and a sheer delight. What straight person woulda thunk they were like regular people? I guess I thought they were going to be tough, mean, and so oversexed they wouldn't even talk to you. Reality was in stark contrast to what Hollywood makes you think.

The Eagle also had a great stage and sound system. I ended up playing there with my band many times. We also did a monthly piano show tunes night. There's nothing like seeing hardcore leather daddies get excited about getting up there and singing show tunes with all their heart!

Playing at the Eagle

Paul Nathan and his theaters

A magician named Paul Nathan ran various theaters[27] which typically had sexy, dark shows. He threw dark parties that were always full of dark passageways and sexy, strange, colorful characters. These parties *were* right out of the movies.

---

27. Climate Theater, Konservatory, refurbished Great Star Theater

Paul (on the far right) at his Dark Kabaret at the Great Star Theater

The Radical Faeries

The Radical Faeries is a worldwide community of gay men who put on shows, dress up outrageously, have sex parties, live in collectives, promote art and discussions of culture, and put on community events and fundraisers. They were probably the gayest group I had ever met.

I ended up at many Faerie parties. At the first one, I was enjoying chatting with the faeries and discovering this incredible subculture. After a while, men started slowly lying on the floor, at first just hanging out, and then lightly touching each other, and then more men joined, and then dicks started coming out, and then a few started blowing each other, and then it turned into a full-on orgy. When this started, I was trying to continue chatting like I didn't notice, but I was making less and less sense as I saw this unfold. The Dude would never have survived there. I was so glad to be able to see this from my super girl window. They asked me to join, but I politely declined because that wasn't my scene. But I did appreciate the privilege of having seen it. I went into the other room and talked to folks as if it was a normal party—while the others were screwing in the living room. And I would end up at many such orgies. San Francisco!

Gurlfriends

I was also going to many trans and LGBT events. *Trans Gender San Francisco* (TGSF) had an annual formal event where trans women and their partners would get dressed up for a formal party. My friends and

Left: I always wanted to wear one of those sexy bridesmaid dresses
Right: With Kim

I saw a smokin' hot, tall blond woman from a distance and remarked how we wished she was trans, but she couldn't possibly be. We saw her again at a club that night. It was only when I was a few feet away from her that I realized, yes, she was trans! Woo hoo! I reported back to my gurl friends, and soon we started hanging out with her.

Kim and I became good friends as both girls and Dudes. Kim was married, was an equally good-looking guy. I found the relationship I had with mostly straight[28] t-girls is the most intimate straight man/man relationship I've ever had, other than my brother and a few very close lifetime friends. We talk about guy stuff, our deep feelings, women

With Lola early in our gurl careers. Lola got pulled over by the cops her first night out as a girl!

---

28. T-girls who almost exclusively date women when they are a man. And usually also when they are a woman.

Saying hello to the illustrious LGBT organizer and host Donna Sachez at one of the formal events.

challenges, and of course all kinds of kinky girl stuff that only a guy would talk about.

Relationships with women

I was still only interested sexually in woman at this point, but I was determined to pick up a guy because I wanted to experience easy raunchy sex. I would get stoned off my ass so I could go through with it, only to find myself often catching a whiff of a woman's smell and gravitating to her.

One night at Martuni's, I saw a woman staring at me from across the room. And being a girl, I could easily act on it, so I went up to her, and we started flirting. I still couldn't believe it—The Dude could never do this. She was totally into me, and she was a lesbian cop. A lesbian with a gun who was into me—it doesn't get any better than that! And she was duly impressed when I escorted her to the secret performer's bathroom in the back when the main bathroom had a line. She gave me her number. I was nervous wondering what she would do when she met The Dude, but I figured I would hang out with her as a girl first for a while.

Me with my new cop friend. I look like a mess after all that making out.

Dawn and me in Vegas. I had the dress custom made by my friend Susan Harris—we designed the dress together. I even had acrylic nails done. Sexy as shit! I always wanted to try that.

I had learned my lesson. But it wasn't to be. When I called, her girlfriend intercepted the phone and started screaming at me about stealing her girl, and they had been fighting over this whole thing. Oh, fuck lesbian fights. On to the next thing. I don't need this. Damn, that had *so* much potential.

But I found a new forever friend. Dawn is a lesbian I met at Aunt Charlie's, a dive bar with a really old school drag show. She was the first person I shared my deepest kinky drag and trans thoughts with, and her response was, "Wow, that's hot." I responded, "Really, I'm not totally the most twisted person in the world?" Dawn chuckled, "No, not even close!" Dawn told me stories about her drag and queer friends back in New Hope, Pennsylvania, and we talked about the frustrations of straight rituals and culture. Wow, I wasn't alone. *Where were you when I needed you in high school? Cool, I can have a great relationship with a woman.* I didn't care at all about the lack of sex and romance.

We did fuck several times, first with me as The Dude, and then she fucked Maria in the ass with a strap-on. That was painful, but fucking hot. We did it a bunch of times, and I got used to combining the pain with the pleasure by jerking off while she fucked me. The human mind can do amazing things. Pavlov's sex—associating pain with pleasure. Very advanced human constructs. And then one time while she was fucking me, I suddenly had enough of the pain. The novelty had worn off. I told her to stop right in the middle as I realized I preferred traditional sex without the pain. That, of course, was a fantasy, because traditional sex was only rarely available to me. But that didn't affect my friendship with Dawn. We were evolved adults who could explore and then move on.

Who the hell are you?

I now had a lot of platonic women friends in my Maria life. And it was such a bummer going back to being a guy. On one occasion, I was having a soirée of about five people at my place. It was three in the morning, and my eyes were itching. I got up and went into the bathroom to change back into The Dude without saying anything. I came back out as The Dude and continued partying. About fifteen minutes later, one of my friends asked me who I was. I was like, "Huh?" She responded, "Who

I was trying to look more girly over time instead of being a tramp. Typical pattern for a cross-dresser.

are you? I didn't see you come in." "Oh . . . I'm Maria." "Whaaaat!" She had never met The Dude and how no idea who he was.

The Dude just keeps failing

The separation of my two lives was starting to get pretty extreme, so I started to get interested in having a relationship with a woman as a man again. I had tried socializing as a guy, attending lectures at the Commonwealth Club and private parties hoping to find eligible women. But it was really hard getting people's attention. I was so used to dazzling with Maria, I wasn't used to how difficult it was being The Dude. I gave online straight dating yet another shot, going on about eight dates in a six-month period. None of them knew anything about Maria. But the dates all sucked wind yet again. I got tired of all the online fishing around only to occasionally end up on a lousy date, compared with the many hundreds of people Maria was meeting each month.

THE DIFFERENCE IN POWER BETWEEN MY REAL MARIA LIFE VS. MY ONLINE BULLSHIT STRAIGHT DATING LIFE WAS
MASSIVE

With the awesome Batgirl lifestyle I was living, did I need Dude's aggravation that made me feel like a nobody loser *every single day of my life*? My work life was full of enough stress and rejection[29], the last thing I wanted was to go home and also get rejected by women. I needed at least one thing in my life that worked well consistently, and Maria was it. Just like in sales, I needed to choose actions that generated *results*. I needed to be the star salesperson for myself.

I was Maria Konner, fabulous San Francisco queen. Fuck this straight dating. I was now ready to focus on a Maria sex life instead of just flirting. Everybody else was having sex, now it was my turn. I had to be sexually fulfilled in order to go to the next level of being fabulous. I had been increasingly fantasizing about kinky sex and acting like I didn't need real people for sex, and that was not healthy. I couldn't get to true fabulosity without a whole lot of fun, positive sex. Them's the rules, so follow

---

29. I had shifted my tech work from engineering to marketing, business development, and sales.

the good love wherever it may come from. And the difference between The Dude and this girl is that she can actually make sex happen. *And have the whole process be fun, not the misery and fantasy The Dude experienced when he longed for women.*

My divorce was now complete, so it was time to shift to the next gear. I needed to turn off this desire to date women completely and stay away from the toxicity of straight dating so I could be free to have fun Maria sex. I no longer cared if I had to switch teams. I was changing my whole approach to life. *I'm going where I like the people and they like me for exactly who I am—and I'm talking about being fabulous, not about being a woman.*

I knew exactly where to start spending more time—back where I started all of this. At Divas. All aboard for the sex train!

PART 2

DIVAS BAT TRAMP

CHAPTER 7

EASY SEX HOOKUP

At this point, I'd only had that one hookup with the t-girl from NYC, and that hadn't been much of a hookup. The problem was I wasn't attracted to guys, and to me the Dick was gross and scared me. I was *really* disappointed that I wasn't into guys. It was really frustrating, because they were such easy pickings. But I was *determined* to experience easy and fun sex as a girl. There was a simple answer. More drugs.

A lot of the t-girls were using drugs, and I felt compelled to experience the trifecta of cross-dressing, drugs, and queer sex. I had been strait-laced most of my life. I was tired of it and needed to experience the other side. I figured it would make me a better person. I was afraid of really fucking myself up with hard drugs, so it was time to ramp up the cannabis and alcohol. I got the strongest medicinal grade weed I could find—edibles and vapes—and made sure I was always stocked up with enough hard liquor, forget the beer. Now, getting super stoned while putting on my makeup, bra, and pantyhose was even hotter and more exciting

After closing, the crowd outside Divas would still see lots of action
Gabrielle Lurie / © San Francisco Chronicle / Polaris

because I was looking at myself as a slut, knowing this could really be the night! And Maria always delivered.

It's amazing what you can do when you just put your mind to it. After about two weeks of spending more time at Divas, I saw a hot t-girl at the bar with fucking incredible legs. I didn't get a chance to speak with her because she was flirting, and it was really crowded. Closing time came, and the usual gaggle of gurls and t-girl chasers were hanging around out front hoping to catch a last-minute hookup. And standing outside was that hot t-girl. I have never had such an easy hookup in my entire life. This is how it went down:

> I walked up to her, smiled, and said, "I live two blocks from here."
> She said, "Let's go."

Wow, was that easy!
Leanne was wearing a hot little black dress, stockings, and very high-heeled lacy shoes. As we walked back to my place, we locked arms and started talking mostly nonsense with a quiver in our voices because we were both so excited and nervous. It felt so good to be walking down the street as two hot bitches getting ready to fuck. I couldn't stop thinking,

"I'm going to get laid, I'm going to get laid. I like how easy this is. I don't need girls, na na!" I had absolutely no idea how this was going to work, but I didn't care. I wanted to have some fun NSA sex.

Up in my apartment, we smoked a bowl and mellowed standing by the window. Leanne took in the great view and we got to know each other just a little. She was married to a woman who didn't know about this part of her life. She did a lot of rollerblading and biking, hence those fucking awesome legs enrobed in black shiny nylons, just screaming sex.

We sat on the couch and rubbed our black nylon legs against each other. *I fucking love this shit!* We put our hands together and played with each other's clothes. She had on a really tight shiny blue corset laced in the back. I wanted to fuck her corset and lacy shoes. I was turned on by kinky women's clothes, but being this close to an actual real t-girl who was wearing said clothes was really weird to me. The Dude resisted, but damn, I was going to go through with this.

SORDID DETAILS

Leanne pulled off my short skirt and panties and started sucking my cock. I had trouble enjoying it because it was just too weird. But she was having a lot of fun. T-girls love sucking dick because it makes us feel like women.

Then she pulled out her dick. I looked at it with fear, never having sucked a dick before. But it was a clean, good-looking dick—as far as dicks go—and pretty damned big and super hard. I was worried about getting a disease, so I insisted she put on a condom. She wasn't really happy about that because I hadn't. While she was putting it on, I took a big hit of weed from my bong.

Okay, here it goes.

I put her dick in my mouth. Well, it tasted like latex covered with some kind of oil, so I really didn't get much of a sense of a dick being in my mouth. But I was a trooper, and I went through the motions, periodically pausing to lubricate my mouth with vodka. It was actually boring because there was no sensation, but I was turned on by the idea of doing something kinky and rebelling against the Culture Virus telling me I shouldn't do this.

Finally, she pulled off the condom and started jerking herself off. This was so bizarre to me, *but hey, this is part of the experience.* She had her eyes closed and was probably fantasizing about the same kind of kinky shit I would. I was afraid of what would happen when she came. I didn't want it on my face. I actually *did* want to see what it was like to have her cum on my face, but I was so concerned with getting a disease, I just let her come all over her nylons. Then, after she came, she *immediately* and aggressively started sucking my dick, probably to make it part of the orgasmic experience. Leanne clearly really loved the Dick, which I found strange, because I knew she was married. I couldn't yet relate to being obsessed with the Dick like that.

The whole thing freaked me out, and I couldn't cum. She was disappointed because she didn't get her dessert. But she didn't say anything about it, and here's the best part—she quickly left. She wasn't rude or anything. We chatted for a bit while she collected her stuff. It felt super sleazy for somebody to leave right after cumming, but it's actually what I wanted. I found that to be the norm and cool with everybody. It worked well because after she left, I harnessed that fresh kink energy, looked myself in the mirror and jerked off while contemplating what I had just done. It wasn't a fantasy anymore. Celebrate!

I felt so empowered. *Now I can have fun sex almost anytime I want instead of being a desperate loser guy.* I had absolutely no feelings of shame. I felt like an explorer who'd been crowded out of his home territory and was in search of new lands. I thought a little bit about what my friends would think if they knew I tried this, but it had no effect on my self-esteem. It was more of a practical issue. They simply didn't need to know. Why complicate those relationships with something they couldn't or wouldn't want to understand? They weren't going to listen to *why* I did it, only *that* I did it.

I ran into Leanne again a few weeks later at Divas. She came up to me and said, "I like you." And again, we immediately headed back to my place, this time holding hands on the street, which I wanted to try. As we walked, I smiled at the homeless folks who enjoyed seeing two hot t-girls doing the about-to-fuck walk. I had a fuck buddy! The second time was similar to the first, and again I insisted she wear a condom, a rule that disappointed her, and one I would later ditch.

After the second time we fucked, I did something else that girls do that The Dude hates. I started ignoring Leanne as if I didn't know her. I saw her several more times at Divas, but I got cold feet. I was afraid of getting too far into this. I was worried her insisting we don't use a condom would result in me getting a disease. I didn't see this relationship going any further. Ignoring her was a jerk thing to do, but I would unfortunately do it a few more times to people I fucked. Okay, The Dude now gets why girls sometimes do this. I needed some more time to discover this Diva's lifestyle without the pressure of having even a fuck buddy relationship. I guess I was still a teenager.

CHAPTER 8

THE FULL-TIME T-GIRLS

Divas had many subcultures within this milieu. These various subcultures are referred to by many different terms and labels—discussing which is the correct term and how one could categorize t-girls could generate hours of discussion[30]. And many would fit into multiple categories—I myself would be considered a t-girl, transvestite, cross dresser, and sometimes a drag queen. So, when I describe these various subcultures, this is just my way of providing a broad overview of the way I see the various groups of people within a culture that has as many subcultures as there are people.

The working t-girls

Most of the t-girls at Divas were working girls who had extensive surgery. Many had voluptuous hips and huge breasts which often hung out of awe-inspiring lacy bras. Most had beautiful faces and oversized,

---

30. e.g. transsexual, cross-dresser, transgender, shemale

inviting lips, and they were surrounded by guys at the bar flirting and seducing them. But most of the t-girls at Divas had not had the bottom surgery. They still had their male parts, because that's what the guys want. Once a t-girl gets bottom surgery, many of the guys weren't interested anymore because they figured they might as well go for the real thing. The t-girls who did have their bottom surgery were usually not living such a promiscuous lifestyle or were over at Asia SF, a t-girl club that provided a nice dinner, put on shows for mostly tourists, and wasn't a hookup scene.

It took me a while to realize something very simple—the t-girls were girls. You could tell by their demeanor. I had that "aha" moment when I was standing next to two of them in the women's bathroom at Divas futzing with my hair. The way they looked at themselves, messed around with their makeup, and talked with each other, there was no question. They were pure woman.

Although many of the working t-girls were friendly, most of them were very aloof. It took me a while to realize it was because they were working girls. At first it annoyed me because I was there to have fun and meet people. But when I realized it was a job to most of them, I respected their attitude and that they didn't like us taking attention away from their customers, the guys. But this generally wasn't a problem because they were way hotter than me.

I became casual friends with several of them and learned quite a bit. Not only about the various types of surgeries and the best doctors, but, more interestingly, about their lives. Many lived nearby in SROs (Single Room Occupancy hotels that charged by the week) and travelled to different cities, working off of sites like eros.com. Others had regular rent-controlled apartments in the city or in Oakland. Some even commuted to the city from the suburbs around San Francisco. Many transitioned to being a woman at a young age and had to work as a prostitute to earn money because they couldn't get a job as a trans woman. And a lot of them didn't have strong support from their families because they were ostracized or came from overseas, typically Mexico, Thailand, and the Philippines. Almost all of them dated only men—they were women through and through. I had envisioned they would be having smoking hot sex all the time with hot guys, but much of the time they were having sex with really gross guys—anybody who would pay them. I was shocked to learn several hired male prostitutes, usually hot muscle guys, when they wanted to have some good fun sex. However, some had older sugar daddies they slept with for the financial and emotional support.

I really appreciated seeing the working girls as people who didn't have the same incredible advantages I had in life. I couldn't judge their lives, because there was no way to know what I would've been like had I had been born in their situation. Many of my straight friends wondered why I hung out with prostitutes, but I learned to ignore the judgement of people who were living in a monoculture. I always remembered a key lesson I learned in Jerusalem: There are good and bad people in every demographic, every locale, every profession. You take from it what you choose to see.

The hottest ones walked the street in a very specific area about a block around Divas[31]. Their heavy makeup and enormous breasts were breathtaking. On my way home, I would often take a one-block detour down the seedier Larkin Street just to see them. Most of them recognized me and said hello, so I always felt safe and part of the family, but I wondered who they thought I was.

I loved walking past the Thai restaurant with the huge window, where I could see my reflection as I smiled at the patrons, wondering if they thought I was a working girl. Hee hee. On two occasions, some nice young straight girls offered me food on the street like I was homeless. That was nice and cool. I politely declined. These were moments when I really felt the absurdity of how you can't really know about a person by the way they look, and how I felt like I was two different people.

And when I entered the lobby of my building, I wondered if the security guards thought I was a working girl. Whenever I walked in as The Dude, I wondered if they made the connection with the gurl by my mannerisms, the way I pressed the elevator button, or my strange chin. I didn't really care, but I loved thinking about it.

The non-working t-girls

A fair number of t-girls had regular jobs or were retired. Many had surgery, often bottom surgery[32], but they didn't have the cosmetic surgery on their breasts, face, and hips at the level of the working girls. They

---

31. Mostly on the Larkin and Post street intersection and one block north, south, and west toward Divas.
32. Their penis turned into a vagina

were from all walks of life. Some were older, retired men who had children, careers, and a home in the suburbs, but got to a certain age and said to themselves, *fuck it, I want to be a woman now.* Some had been high-powered executives, or engineers, or firemen, and an unusually large number were from the military. One was a Special Forces/Green Beret type, another was a salvage diver with the Navy. Some still had a relationship with their wives, some were divorced by choice, and some were divorced because their wives didn't want anything to do with them. Some dated women, some had moved on to men, many dated both.

I found most of these women to be very mellow, very friendly, and very unassuming. They were super interesting to speak with. They tended to have a very deep, emotional perspective on life. They had great stories to tell, and they were also a wealth of knowledge about the transition process. They didn't screw around and party a lot. They were happy to just be women and hang around this scene of diverse, open people.

The younger ones were a mix. Some were quiet like the older t-girls while others were having a great time partying. One of the more striking t-girls, Nicole, transitioned really fast, over a period of about three years. She was a death metal dude guitarist and singer in a band who originally looked like one of the ZZ Top guitarists with the long hair and beard. When she started coming to Divas, I would sometimes chat with her. One night she showed up with a really refined, pretty face and huge breasts, wearing a kinky leather collar with a hook on it for kink play. I looked at her with my mouth agape. *Oh shit, now I know somebody personally who had her breasts done, this could be trouble, I could be next.*

I could not stop thinking about her. I remember looking at her black bra slipping out from under her clothes, wondering what it was like to have to wear a bra all the time. And she was having fun. I often saw her making out with guys, girls, and t-girls—in the elevator, in the stairwell, on the dance floor. I was jealous. Of course, I didn't really think about the cost, the surgery, the pain, and dealing with being a girl *all the time.* I just loved the fantasy of doing it.

About a year later, I saw Nicole with shiny, tight black spandex pants. It was clear she now had a pussy. *Oh shit*, I got weak in the knees, as I convinced myself *this is what I want.* For some t-girls, getting your pussy done is the Holy Grail of sex change. You're never coming back from that. I related to this very differently from most gurls. For them, it's their true self. They want to truly be women. For me, I was running away from the trappings, expectations, and *constant* rejections of straight dating. It was my fantasy of diving into perverted hedonism to escape the ravages of the Monoculture Virus. But I know that kind of surgery has all kinds of complexities, and it's not an easy life. There are also many unknowns. For example, Nicole told me she wasn't as effective on thrash metal guitar because she just didn't have the same level of aggression "without her balls." But her band totally embraced her transition.

Nicole got into the latex and vinyl fashion scene and had some pretty fucking hot outfits showing off her new body. What a woman, what power! I felt strange talking with her because I so admired what she did. She was like a goddess to me. She eventually settled down and got married to a really cool guy, and they only occasionally came to Divas to hang out with old friends. And during this whole time, she had a professional job.

Divas embraced all different types, all of whom shared a love of expressing the feminine.

CHAPTER 9

PART TIME T-GIRLS & MORE SEX

Most of the part-time gurls were like me—they hadn't had any surgery. Some liked to party like me, and others liked to be lower key. And some were on hormones and intended to transition to full-time. Part-time gurls were the most in between the sexes and had the widest variety of sexual inclinations. There is not a strong correlation between **sexual expression**, how you present, and **sexual orientation**, who you sleep with[33]. We pretty much covered the whole seven-point Kinsey scale, just as you would find in the general male population—some exclusively date women, some are curious to hook up with guys occasionally, some are 50/50, some prefer men, and some hook up with men only. However, we tended to be more into women than men. And some, like me, had different preferences based on whether it was sex or romance.

---

33. According to many studies, and also my own experience

I'm only interested in women for romance. I can't conceive of falling in love with a man, and I feel really uncomfortable when a guy likes me that way. I'm a lot more flexible with casual sex, depending on how much weed or alcohol I've consumed. But even then, I prefer to have some kind of connection with somebody. I can't relate to fucking somebody without talking with them for at least thirty minutes or so. It's also safer because you can better tell if they are a decent person and if they are the kind that fucks the first warm body they find.

Labels are extremely misleading. Many new gurls would ask me nervously whether they were a cross-dresser, transvestite, transsexual, or gay. For example:

> **They would ask**: "I like to occasionally suck a dick when I'm dressed as a girl, but I really like women and could only fall in love with a woman. What does that make me? Am I gay?"

> **I would reply**: "You're somebody who likes to occasionally suck a dick when you're dressed as a girl, but you really like women and could only fall in love with a woman."

I would explain that labels are just an *attempt* to try to broadly categorize behaviors, and that each person is unique, and people often exhibit behaviors from multiple categories. They would usually be so relieved. They were so worried about being given a label that would degrade their position in life, they often forgot to just *enjoy* and *be*. I was glad I could help nudge them towards seeing this curiosity as a gift of fluidity, wisdom, and joy—not a curse.

I would confuse people when I told them I identify as straight. They would look at me confused and say something like: "Girl, you're about a straight as a bolt of lightning!" They couldn't conceive that I like having sex with women as a man, but I was willing to have sex with men as a woman because it was simply easier and a lot more fun. I don't identify as gay or bisexual, because I would never have sex with a man as a man. Not because I'm afraid or I disapprove, it's just not my bag. I have a simple rule when it comes to the sex I'm involved in—there has to be a girl in there somewhere, even if I'm the girl. The Dude and a girl works. Maria and a guy works. Maria and ten guys works. Maria or The Dude and ten girls works, although my doctor recommends against doing cocaine and Viagra at the same time. I'm flexible, and without the availability of women who like The Dude, nature finds a way to have sex.

And when it came to finding that alternative way, it was very natural for me to first start fucking a bunch of t-girls. Call us trans lesbians. We love the fun and the kink, but we understand and relate to each other. Most of us are tired of the trappings of the straight dating world where people didn't understand us as dudes and were constantly judging us. Most of us no longer cared to try to figure out why our straight life sucked. It was time to put on our sunglasses and say *WTF* and move on to something easier.

How much easier? I actually calculated it, using my own empirical data:

IT'S 250 TIMES EASIER TO GET LAID AS A GIRL.

To get your head around these numbers consider this. As a girl, I could have sex once a week, but as a guy, I could have sex once every five years. Imagine The Dude could only get laid about another six times for the rest of his life. That's a *colossal* difference. My straight friends would say to me, "Hey, it's twice as easy to get laid if you go both ways." No, it's 251 times easier.

So, I was experiencing something else that was completely new to me—learning how to say "no" to sex! Over and over. It was getting to be ridiculous. Guys wouldn't leave me alone. My whole world was now upside down, but in a good way. Now *I* had the power and had to learn how to use it. I had to learn to ask for what I wanted, to put the brakes on when necessary, to ensure the person was safe. And I had to learn how to say no without being an asshole or putting myself in danger. Girls, I can't believe you have deal with this shit! How do you do it?!

Maria was becoming more and more fabulous and killing it on the stage, and even The Dude was killing it at work. It would be intolerable being on the top of my game in life, yet go back to subjecting myself to straight, online dating. Maria was just no match for The Dude, especially in the realm of fun. I had to *be totally* fabulous, and there was only one way. So there you have it, this straight guy just justified why I went for the Dick. Pop out that cork!

Getting fucked in the ass by Jennifer

I couldn't get that night above Martuni's out of my mind, when the guy was dry humping me doggy style. I *had* to try getting fucked in the ass. I figured we've all been figuratively fucked in the ass many times in our lives, why not try it on my own terms and see how it makes me feel? Otherwise, there was no way I was going to get it out of my head.

I met Jennifer at Divas one night when her gaggle of three t-girls was making so much noise, I could hear it across the loud bar. This gurl had to see what fun was going on, and that's how I met Richie Leeds and Jennifer. I couldn't figure out if they were transvestites, circus performers, or just came from an S&M session. Maybe all three. They were part-time sex partners, and like many other poly folks, their full-time sex partners didn't care who they fucked. I was to find that many poly couples even enjoyed hearing about their partner's sexcapades. It all depended on the agreed upon rules of the relationship—for example, no falling in love with somebody else. Richie, a self-declared polyamorous bisexual fetishistic transvestite, was a longtime SF Bay Area resident who took part in much of the San Francisco underground alternative life in its heyday.

Video Interview with Richie Leeds (several years later): We talk with Richie about polyamorism and about partying in the old days. He sings a few of his songs about the fun life. While he's playing his song "Princess," (at 16:40) I realize he's singing about Jennifer, who I had fucked several years earlier!

This interview was one of our longest, but he was such an interesting, really cool, awesome guy, and his songs were so fun, I didn't know where to cut. I loved all the weird people I was meeting, and I wanted to ask them questions and document as much as I could. Richie unfortunately passed away unexpectedly in early January 2019. He was loved by so many people and left so many good memories. Deep love to Richie. He is part of the heart of San Francisco.

Back to the present—the night at Divas . . .

I figured I didn't need Richie's permission, so I told Jennifer I wanted her to fuck me in the ass, and that I had never tried it. She was glad to oblige, and we set up a date for the next weekend. She recommended I buy a dildo to practice.

SORDID DETAILS

Dildo practice

Jennifer recommended I start with a small finger and lube to get used to something going through the anal sphincter, and then work my way up to a bigger finger, then the dildo. It's not like I hadn't stuck my finger partway up my ass before, but I had never tried to get it all the way past the sphincter before, and it was *not* easy. My sphincter was very stubborn, but I managed to relax, and I reminded myself I couldn't be the only formally straight person whose sphincter would refuse to oblige. *Just keep going and enjoy. Okay, keep pushing, ooooh, ah, okay, yea . . . got through! Oh, not bad at all.* Pretty weird, but I kind of liked it. I wiggled it around a bit, damn it felt good!

Okay, I got the smaller index finger in. Check. I smoked some more weed and started again, practicing going back in with the longer middle finger. *Oh yea, oh yea, fuck yea. I get it. Not sure if want another guy and a smelly dick attached to this, but this actually feels kind of cool.* Check. On to the last step.

I grabbed the dildo and thought, oh god, this is ridiculously large. But I was determined. I put a generous amount of lube on it and spent about two minutes trying to figure out from what position I would put it into my ass. I couldn't visualize which body position matched the dildo position or what the best angle should be. Eventually I gave up trying to analyze the solution and just started trying every which way. Finally, with lube leaking out all over my hands and ass, I finally found it.

Okay, just a little nudge as I recognized the now familiar sphincter barrier. But ouch, *this is huge . . . fuck this.* Pause. *Okay, relax. You can do this. Failure is not an option. Lesser men have done this. Okay, push . . . ouch.*

Okay, now in and out. I had fantasized about this for years, and now that I was actually doing it, it hurt like fucking hell. I mean I knew it was supposed to hurt, I saw that in the movies, but *damn*, not like this.

Okay, back and forth, relax, back and forth relax, okay . . . hmmm, it's starting to feel more like the finger, I guess I'm stretching. Okay, I know I'm getting close to full penetration of the sphincter because the tightness is getting nonlinear. Oh yea . . . oh fuck, this is hot, fuck yea . . . oh . . . shit that hurts . . . no it's not that bad . . . . Courage . . . courage is not the absence of fear, it's action. Just fucking do it. Push, ow, okay, wait okay, yea, that's good, yea, just like that. Oh keep going, yea, that's it, one more push, make it good . . . oh, aaaaaaaaah, it's in!

It didn't hurt as much when it was in. I felt like I was stuffed, but it was kind of hot if I just wiggled it around a little. It was kind of like snorkeling through the rough surf and suddenly finding serenity and astonishing beauty from a whole different world on the other side. *Is that's what it feels like to get a dick in my ass? Wow, that's actually pretty fucking hot! This is so different. Okay, with enough weed and vodka, I can take a dick.* I was so excited to have a whole set of new options! Freeeeeeedom!

Okay, I took it. Now I had to fuck myself. I pushed back and forth repeatedly without pulling it out. *Okay, oooh, that is weird. It sort of hurts, but not really. Yea, that's weird. Yea that's hot. But oh, damn I feel like I need to take a wicked shit!* I popped it out, and oooh, it felt like I just took a great dump. I mean it feels great to take a good clean shit. *Is that what getting fucked in the ass feels like?*

That was fun, but it hurt. I didn't know if I wanted to do this regularly. But I needed to keep trying. I decided to jerk off while I did this. After all, that's what they do in porn when they're getting fucked in the ass. *But how the fuck am I going to do that with only two hands when I have to also shove the dildo up my ass and balance myself?* I was going to take another hit of weed, but I was too hot and ready, and my hands were loaded with lube—too messy, fuck the weed. I made a mental reminder to use edibles next time, so I wouldn't have to keep loading up on weed to make this work. *Fuck it, let's roll.*

I had a brilliant idea. I was going to ride the dildo dick pole by pressing it against the bed and holding it straight with my left hand and jerk off with my right hand. *Here it goes.* Oooooh, I got it in in pretty quick because I knew what to expect, but it still hurt, and I needed to call upon my new faith that I would get back to that beautiful serenity on the other side of the sphincter. *Aaaah, there she is, yea . . . swimming in the warm surf.*

I started imaging a body touching me . . . anybody . . . I don't give a shit what sex. Yea nature does find a way . . . find a way with me, baby. Enlighten me. Take me into your warm arms, remind me what love is. After about a minute of sheer kink ecstasy, it was starting to take a lot of effort to relax my ass. *Oh, shit it's hurting more and I'm getting tired. Oh damn, I'd better cum soon. But it hurts.* I started jerking off really hard . . . oh, weird pain and pleasure combined . . . *Oh yea, I get it, I'm getting it. I get the whole fucking thing! It's all so very clear to me now. The human mind can bridge pain and pleasure . . . how amazing, how beautiful. Fuck that hurts, oh shit, that's wild, oh that hurts, oh that's wild, hurt, wild, wild, hurt, hurt, hurt, oooh, wild, oh fucking cum now. Yaaaaaaa!* . . . .

Aaaaaaaah . . . . . .

. . . *breathe in. Oh, yea, I did it!* I popped that big dildo dick out of my ass like a wine cork—POP! Oh, wow. That was the best part, and I felt so much better, so relaxed. That was hot. But ouch, my ass hurt. I couldn't imagine putting that thing back in. Not ever. I mean it was hot, and I felt like a fucking kinky superhero who was even more invulnerable to the scourge of modern straight dating, but my ass hurt. *Hmmm, do I really want this? Am I okay?* I ran straight for the bathroom, throwing the messy lube covered dildo dick into the sink, and while the shower was warming up, I wiggled my finger around back there to make sure there weren't any strange holes or bulges, and nothing red. *Oh, good.* I got in the shower to wash that itchy lube off.

Once it was washed off, I enjoyed the warmth and serenity of being on the other side . . . a nice post-cum long shower. I had reached spiritual nirvana. I was ready to dry off and go to bed dreaming about the tough mission I was able to complete. *Oh, shit, there is a huge wet spot of lube on my damn sheets! Fuck it,* I grabbed one of pillows and put it on top of the lube, smiled, and fell right asleep with my body on top of the pillow.

Never again shall anything go up my ass? Well, we'll see. I was ready for Jennifer.

Time for our date

A "date" in San Francisco really just means you go out and do something, anything, before fucking. The simplest is to meet at a bar, have a drink or two, and if the person seems nice, safe, and clean, down another quick drink, go home, and fuck. We went to a drag show, which was a good way to ease into the idea that I wanted Jennifer to fuck me in the ass. While at the show, I avoided thinking about the fucking. I just wanted to see if I got along with her—a strategy I highly recommend to reduce the stress. But the inevitable came. It was time to get on with it.

I was excited about the idea, but every time she started touching me, I had to deal with the fact that I wasn't attracted to her. I was not physically wired to have sex with anybody but a genetic woman. I was kind of hoping she would get a text with an emergency and have to dash. But I had learned how to deal with this problem by eating cannabis edibles. Just smoking weed required me to puff every twenty minutes or so, and that was really inconvenient during sex. Edibles lasted a good three hours or more and often you would periodically get some great head-rushes which if you were lucky happened right when you were getting into something hot. And the more I had queer sex and watched kinky porn with cannabis, the more I could train my brain to like it.

SORDID DETAILS

Getting fucked in the ass

We got back to my place, and Jennifer immediately jumped into my bed and pulled out her dick. It was shocking to see her with a grin on her face and see that pink torpedo of flesh standing up, both waiting for me. I was not turned at all, but I was determined to complete this night according to the plan. I lit a candle, turned off the lights and put on some music. I've found candles and a good long playlist of bubble gum disco or ambient electronic jazz to be essential. I still wasn't yet sucking Dick without a condom, but I let Jennifer suck my dick without one. I had to give her some good foreplay to work with. After the foreplay, I got into the doggy position while Jennifer put on a condom and came up behind me. Feeling a dick behind you is really hot. I loved feeling like I was being forced to have this kind of sex because I was a reject. I imagined that several of the women that had rejected The Dude were seeing me do this.

Jennifer was really good in working that dick past my sphincter. Without practice, I would have recoiled in pain and horror, ran to the bathroom, thrown her out, took a shower and grabbed a Ben and Jerry's Phish Food ice cream and watched TV. But I wasn't going to couch potato fantasyland again. I was ready to suck it all up. She thrust deeper and deeper. *Fuuuuuck, almost there, yea keep going, yea, deep and deeper, yea, yea, almost* . . . and the final thrust hurt like hell for a second, but then a moment of pleasure and serenity as we got through the surf. *We're there. I have a dick in my ass . . . awesome!*

Once she was in, I was in a different world. Jennifer started thrusting slowly, then faster and faster, and I felt her balls against my ass. That was more intimacy then I had expected, but it made me feel like a girl. I felt like I was a fucking animal and I liked it. Talk about living in the moment! I started playing with myself with one hand while she grabbed my other arm and pulled me toward her, locking our bodies together. I really liked it. It scared me, but it was just what I needed. The combination of pain, feeling like I had to take a shit, being locked with her, and playing with myself was a novel combination that just fucking worked and got this San Francisco slut so excited and hard.

We took a brief pause and enjoyed wiggling around to find the right position for the big final pounding. I knew I could only hold that dick in my ass for maybe five more minutes, so I screamed my kink and porn fantasies. *Fuck me. Fuck me hard and cum in my ass. Make me feel like a woman. I'm doing things that girls do! I'm a girl, fuck me!* Jennifer was pounding so fucking hard now. I didn't expect just how violent it was going to be and how the raw animal took over—thrusting, bodies in unison, no thoughts, just pleasure. *I don't need genetic girls. I don't have to act like a certain type of guy. I'm having hotter sex than you are! This is the way sex is supposed to be!* Holy shit, pain, pleasure, screaming. I told Jennifer to tell me when she was cumming. All I could think about was how much I wished the women that rejected me could watch me now, having hotter, kinkier, better, and more sex then them. God, she's going to come in my ass . . . pump, pound, she screamed, "Oh god, I'm coming," and then our bodies, locked together . . . oh fuck, I never felt so much pure sex before! Thrust one, ah, thrust two as those balls bang up against me. *Wow, this is fucking rad, look at me girls!* And then Jennifer grabbed for my cock during her final thrust! Deep breath and hold . . . slow exhale . . .

And then a moment of quiet as I felt the pressure of her body behind me. *I did it. I don't need girls, I can have this kind of sex anytime I want with no bullshit!* I enjoyed a few aftershocks as our embraced bodies quivered, making me feel like a relaxed sissy. Nice . . . .

Okay, I need this out of my ass right now. POP! Ah, one of the best feelings in the world. And then, like a good t-girl, she didn't want to hang around much after that. I grabbed a shower, and my little pint of ice cream....

I felt alive! I wanted to get better at it. Doing it one time is just trying it, whereas the second time is experimenting with getting into it, and it spirals downward from there! Jennifer wanted to meet again the next weekend. But Dude was fighting me. He started coming up with all kinds of excuses about maybe getting a disease, getting hooked on drugs, girls finding out I was doing this, permanently losing interest in women. Fuck him. I knew I would be doing this again. I made the date with Jennifer.

But a friend of The Dude set up a double straight date that next week with a girl I had already met and seemed to like me. My brain had not been fully reprogrammed to be a girl, so I postponed the date with Jennifer because I really wanted to go on a date with that girl. I told Jennifer the truth. The Dude's date was mild good relaxing fun, but as usual my date had zero interest in me romantically. *Sigh . . . here we go again. Fuck this shit!!!! I could have gotten fucked in the ass again. Why did I waste my time? Dammit, when am I going to learn!* Now Jennifer was annoyed with my postponing her over a genetic girl, and our relationship fizzled. Fuck, now no opportunities. For a moment, I was frustrated with the whole situation, but the beauty about being trans fabulous in San Francisco is that frustration doesn't last long at all.

Getting fucked in a cage at the Power Exchange

Melissa, the t-girl I'd spent a night with a few months before, sent me a note. She was visiting in two weeks. There was no doubt in my mind. We were going to the Power Exchange. And she was going to fuck me in the ass in that swing in the cage. Unlike the straight world, fantasies actually came true on a regular basis in my new world.

Melissa was just as excited as I was to go to the Power Exchange. The Power Exchange is the kind of place where it was best to bring your own fuck buddy instead of finding one there. I was hoping she would be willing to fuck me in the ass, and fortunately she was. The great thing about dating other t-girls is that we have a lot in common—the same kinks, no explanation needed, no embarrassment, and no need to feel like a complete degenerate.

We warmed up on the horse in the King Arthur room. Whenever ner-

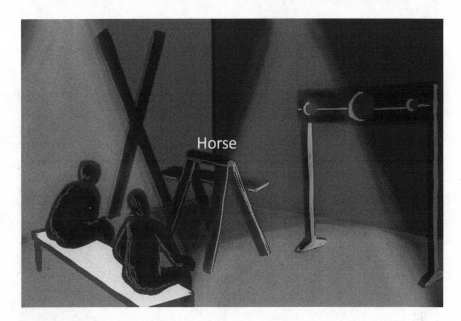

Horse

vous about doing something new in the kink realm, always fall back on something simple to warm up and get to the know person better. No need to feel more sleezy or uncomfortable than you have to. Kink is first and foremost about trust and feeling comfortable with the person. Don't pay attention to the Hollywood Disneyfied version of subjects like kink, often written by people who have never lived the lifestyle and are sensationalizing everything for entertainment purposes. Make your fantasy real, but don't let the fantasy control or frighten you too much. Your interest is there for a reason, and your destiny is to proudly discover why on your own terms and enjoy the ride.

I mounted the horse doggy style and Melissa tied me up on it and tickled me with a flogger. Then she spanked me with her hands, and then whipped me with the flogger. Every lash must have released a blast of endorphins into my system, because each one felt so damned good. I was wearing a leather miniskirt, which worked out really well because the spanking and whipping against the leather protected my skin while giving me the pleasure of Melissa strong arming me. I was wiggling around, screaming for her to spank me harder, and as I rotated my head, I noticed about a dozen people sitting on the benches watching us and jerking off! I couldn't see their faces, but I didn't want to. I felt like I was in the movie *Eyes Wide Shut*.

Then Melissa said she wanted to switch position to sub while I

A flogger similar to the one Melissa used on me.

dommed[34]. I had no interest in being a dom, but I told her I would love to. I didn't want to be selfish. Shuffling around switching roles was awkward with the crowd still jerking off in the silence. All while, I was wondering how exactly I was going to beat her, something I had never done and was never interested in. I was uncomfortable, but figured I might as well put my all into it. Besides, I *am* an entertainer and I *do* want to please the crowd. *Think gladiator.*

I tied her to the horse and started with a spank on her ass. Then I paused to get everybody juiced up, and tickled her, screaming things like, "Okay, you fucking bitch! You've been naughty, I'm here to do justice!" It wasn't difficult for me to find a fun cadence and schtick and get into it. Then

I started flogging her, periodically building up the tension and then releasing it with a spank or a hard whip. I found I had a real knack for being a dom. And the spectators clearly loved it. In the corner of my eyes I could see the speed of the jerking off increasingly rapidly. I added being a dom to my bucket list and immediately checked it off.

After the horse session, we took a break and wandered up to the second floor, an enormous room with a stage where a woman was blowing twenty or more guys. It's hard to describe what it was like seeing a woman surrounded by so many guys that those on the outer ring had to stand on their tiptoes

Once again, the blessed sex swing in the cage

34. Submissive, Dominant

to see what she was doing, all while vigorously jerking off, waiting for their turn. Their faces were contorted with raw, male pig energy—an image impossible to unsee. It was shocking, seeing a woman voraciously sucking these dicks as if she was licking an ice cream cone but at ten times the speed. I looked around at the little groups of fuck clusters and wondered *who are these people and how often did they come here? Is this a regular hobby? Do they have relationships? Do their partners know?* What a trip it was to be there, essentially incognito. The Dude never would have felt so at ease walking around.

It was time for the fucking cage. Melissa and I smoked a few magic puffs in the bathroom to get all horned up.

SORDID DETAILS

Getting fucked in the swing

When we got to the fucking cage, I jumped right into the swing. It felt *so good* to feel the leather forming to the shape of my body and sway-ing around as I wiggled. *Wheee, this is definitely a playful way to get ready for some sex.* I grabbed the chains and pulled back and forth, finding the natural rhythm of the swing. Then I put my legs up on the chains and wrapped my ankles and fuck-me shoes in the chains, waiting for it. It felt so natural, and Melissa knew exactly what I wanted. She grabbed my arms and wrapped them in the chains while she shoved her cock up against my ass. I had to shift backward and raise my legs more to get into the right position.

And there it was again, those balls against me, making me feel all kinky and bad and wrong. "Fuck me, baby," I screamed, "fuck that ass." I'll spare the intimate details about getting that thing rammed into me, but it was easier this time. I squirmed back and forth in scream-ing pleasure as I was grabbing the chains getting us both into the sway of the swing—total fucking animals locked in visceral sync. The bigger thrusts were so shockingly painful, I had to raise my ass a little bit off the leather seat in order to take them. But it was hot dropping back down on the seat and while rubbing against her balls.

And then, as I turned my head to enjoy the next thrust, I was shocked again. There must have been over two dozen people right there on the other side of the cage watching and jerking off. Hot! I was a *fucking* rock star! Talk about confidence building. I screamed in pleasure to make sure the audience got their money's worth! Melissa screamed too as she rammed into me and came. I jerked off and came with Melissa's cock still in my ass, and then she pulled out, leaned over and slurped up my cum. She told me how much she loved the taste. Weird and hot!

It was so much fun, but it still scared the shit out of me. Was this going to be my life? Sorry to say, but I did the thing I hated again. When I saw Melissa at Divas a month later, I ignored her. I was worried she would want to do a lot more fucking, then want me to not use a condom, and I would be hooked on Dick. Or maybe since I already had her and I was still new to this, I just wanted variety? Regardless, I was still not versed in the ways of being a woman, like how to politely say no. Eventually I built my confidence up enough and stopped being such an arse.

Challenges hooking up with t-girls

I hooked up with several other t-girls during this period. Some were highly experienced, and we played around and shared our hot stories. Others were less experienced and often didn't want to fuck, but it was fun chatting. Most were visitors from out of town, had only gone out a little and were thrilled to meet a real-life San Francisco t-girl.

One of them was a high-powered lawyer, had a girlfriend, and had hardly gone out at all. What a treat it was to meet somebody so powerful in her male life, but who was timid, scared, and excited in this new female life. She was so happy to finally talk to somebody who shared her secret. I thought of her as a girl, and she was so cute talking on my couch about how much she loved being a girl, especially her new fucking hot shoes. I couldn't help it. I went to jump on her. "No, I don't want this," she said as she held her hands up. I apologized and said, "I'm really sorry. It's the complexities of being trans. So many combinations." She smiled and said she understood, and we kept chatting as if nothing happened. Aren't t-girls awesome? The Dude would have been so flustered, I have no idea how he would have handled that kind of rejection. It also helped that I was getting laid regularly, which helped me feel absolutely fine with her turning me down. I was more concerned about not ruining this great night for her. I could afford to be emotionally generous, whereas the Dude couldn't.

I started meeting t-girls online to extend my reach. We would meet at Divas, then I'd often go to their hotel room where invariably the place looked like a t-girl exploded in it. Nylons, garters, shoes, magazines, bras, and all kinds of shit everywhere. I expected to see a cash register and price tags on everything. We usually first drank and smoked, played around with clothes, and shared our best porn videos. When it came time for sex, it was often clumsy. We were usually two bottoms trying to fuck with dicks that just weren't programmed to anchor the tower of power. So, we'd ended up just dry humping with the challenge of finding just the right position so we could hump each other while looking in the mirror and jerking off to *those* two t-girls in the mirror fucking. After we were done with the fun, we would often have a nice discussion about gender, marriage, life, liberty, and the pursuit of happiness. Several of the girls gave me a little present, a cincher, a garter belt. I think back and it was really special connecting with others like that.

I met several t-girls who were online famous. I'd had dreams of them telling *me* all their kinky stories. But as I hung out with them, I began to understand most of these girls lived in the burbs, were often married and in the closet, and *I* was the one with all the experience and great stories. I just didn't spend a lot of time online because I was trans fabulous in San Francisco, and lucky to be living here.

I frequently ran into a group of Carla's girls. Carla's was a cross-dressing club in San Jose similar to *I Love It Gurl* but they had frequent outings to Divas. For many of Carla's girls, coming into the city from the suburbs or from out of town was a big event. For some, it was their first time. I was typically on my own, and it wasn't long before *I* was the cool San Francisco veteran showing them around and sharing seedy stories. In a few months, I had done what some girls took ten years or more to do— because I was so fortunate to have the opportunity to explore this subculture and become a true part of it by living right in the middle of it. I never expected to discover a large community, this sisterhood of men and trans women who had an admiration for the feminine.

The ability to get laid often now presented me with a new set of problems. I had so many epic nights, *how do I keep this up?!* Even though it was easier by far to hook up as Maria, I discovered it was not always *that* easy to hook up with t-girls. There are several challenges with t-girl-on-t-girl sex that often makes our trysts dysfunctional:

1. We are almost all bottoms.
2. We watch way too much overcharged kinky porn and have trouble getting it up enough to top.
3. Many of us are hot messes.
4. We have a tendency to be selfish in bed.
5. The drugs don't help you perform, which is a catch-22 for girls like me who aren't wired for this. Hard to have sex as a top with the drugs, but can't have sex without them.

The drag queens are very different

So, I started hitting on the drag queens. They are the best illusionists of female glamour, and there were many more of them in San Francisco. A lot of queens wore padding, which gave them a fabulous, sexy female body, so many of them got hit on by straight guys. Every queen I went after without exception only wanted to fuck after stripping and becoming men. I was like, no fucking way. Why? You're so hot! When I first started, I had this vision of super kinky sex in the drag world where drag queens would be having easy sex with each other. Unfortunately, drag queens are only very rarely into sex in drag. It's almost considered taboo. They have a word for it—Kai Kai.

Video interview with prominent veteran queen Ginger Snap: We talk about the difference between drag queens and t-girls, how drag is about glamour not sex, how it's changed over the years, the drag life, community support, how to get into drag, and how Ginger moved from bartending at gay bars to working with dudes at a machine shop. And we have a straight man's perspective from my co-host Andrew Roberts.

Video of Ginger in drag at Union Square during Christmas when we took a "Drag Bus" out on the town.

The drag queens were their own separate group at Divas. They were there mostly for the Friday and Saturday night drag shows and had little to no interest in flirting with t-girls or straight men. Many of them performed throughout town, and Divas was just another drag venue.

Alexis Miranda, the "mother" drag queen at Divas

Alexis Miranda was the "mother" queen and basically ran the bar and the drag shows. She is a drag queen, but she also knew the working t-girls very well, so she was an ambassador between the two groups. She had been at Divas for many years and was a great source of information and support for new girls. I learned a lot from Alexis and the queens by just chatting with them about hair, makeup, clothes, shopping, and hearing fascinating stories about girls transitioning. I also had somebody to talk with and great stories to share when I went there alone on a quiet night.

At this point, I needed to accelerate my getting laid hit ratio to keep up with my insatiable desire to keep taking this alternative sex thing to its logical conclusion. *Okay, so drag queens are off limits. I'll have to give the guys a try.* This was going to require a pretty charming guy and moving up to neat whiskey.

And who *were* these guys?

CHAPTER 10

THE GUYS WHO LOVE US

The t-girl lovers

Before I moved to San Francisco, I spent hours surfing the Internet for pictures of skanky trans clubs hoping to get a feel for what it was like. Not until you actually go there do you realize that people are just people. My first experience with the guys at Divas was that most were nice, clean, and curious. I was fascinated by how open they were about their fantasies, frustrations, and their deepest feelings. This was incredible compared with the "regular" world where many things just weren't talked about. They also were tired of the trappings of straight dating and not being allowed to be themselves in so many ways. They admired t-girls for their strength, how they worked so hard to be beautiful women, and how much they enjoyed and appreciated being women.

Many complained their girlfriends or wives didn't like giving blow jobs, or the sex was getting boring. I loved titillating them by saying, "Do you know why t-girls give such great blow jobs?" They would look at me with intense eyes and a little smile, eagerly waiting for the response.

At the Divas fourth floor lounge on St. Patty's Day

"Because sucking Dick makes us feel like women, and we love doing it. To be really good at something, you gotta love it." They found that really hot. And it's so very true.

After chatting, these guys would invariably hit on me, often by putting their arm around me, sometimes by asking me where I lived. I was wondering . . . do these guys have any idea who I really am? Did they know about all the padding under here? Most guys thought I was a full-time girl and had breast implants. And I felt like I was deceiving them because I wasn't really into guys . . . well, until I had a few more drinks.

I was sexy, but nothing compared to professional t-girls, with their tens of thousands of dollars of surgery on their faces and bodies. Why would guys choose me over these girls? I didn't understand why anybody would want to fuck me. It's hard for any guy dressing as a girl to look in the mirror and not see the man behind the mask—all the male features he doesn't like about himself poking through. But when I moved around, that's when I would see the magnetic field come up. It was about the attitude and the overall look, and that's how the fabulousness made me burst.

Many of the guys told me they prefer non-working girls, because we were nicer, more honest, and more real. This made sense, because it's hard to really be interested in somebody when having sex with men is your job, and it shows. A lot of men complained the working girls haggled over money, didn't seem at all interested in them, and tried to get it over with quickly. And they also figured we were cleaner.

The younger guys were much more likely to go straight for the working girls, as they were enticed by the large breasts, big hips, and gorgeous faces and had not yet appreciated the importance of the true feminine, which was the loving attitude.

Tim, always with a smile, surrounded by t-girls

I was initially just flirting, as I wasn't sure what I really wanted. I developed a lovely relationship with several of the regular guys. One was Tim Carmody, a straight Vietnam vet and a mercenary who managed to escape from a Brazilian prison after being involved in a plan to overthrow the government of Ghana[35].

Tim was retired from military operations, and at the time managed a bar called The Encore a few blocks away. But he was a big lover of trans women, always with a t-girl by his side. And instead of being at Encore, he was always down at Divas because it was a lot more colorful.

Another was David Steinberg, a professional writer and photographer who focused on human sexuality. He published a book of stunning photographs of the trans women at Divas.

Bottom Left: *David Steinberg*
Middle: *Kevin*
Right: *Steve Berkey – Divas owner*
Credit: David Steinberg

Divas of San Francisco: Portraits of Transsexual Women

---

35. It's quite a tale: http://l.mariakonner.com/timc

The dance floor had the pole surrounded by mirrors

Gabrielle Lurie / © San Francisco Chronicle / Polaris

The shows at Divas were similar to what you would see at a straight strip club, but the guys liked something more interesting.

Credit: David Steinberg

And there was their friend Kevin, a hardcore ex-marine and biker. What muscles.

It was a pleasure to be able to see totally cool, awesome straight dudes like this when I walked into Divas. But I couldn't fuck some of these guys. They were too nice, and I respected them too much. I hate when girls do that!

It's hard to believe, but the guys that hung out at Divas were straight. Gay guys rarely went to Divas, and if they did, it was generally to see the show and meet friends—and they were always so friendly and easy to talk with, especially the older couples. Only straight guys are into t-girls . . . because we're girls. It took me a while to figure that out. Gay guys aren't into girls, thus they aren't into t-girls. The love of t-girls has nothing to do with the Dick. And the straighter they are, the more they want to fuck you. We need this as part of sex education so guys can better enjoy the unusual things that turn them on or spark their curiosity. T-girls work hard to be girls, and we do great makeup, wear fun clothes, and have great legs. And we know what guys want, and we want to get to it quickly.

Finding a guy to fuck

There comes a point when you can't go any farther learning how to feel like a woman, and it's time for getting the Dick from a regular guy. The Dude *hated* casual, silly flirting. But Maria was young and had budding power. She *loved* the casual, silly flirting. She knew how to werk it, and this teenage girl was just getting started. I was going to find a man and discover what it was like to be a woman. The next time I met genetic girls at a club, I wanted to be an authentic sister.

One big problem was that many guys wanted *me* to fuck them in the ass, or they wanted to suck *my* dick. No! After a while I learned to just ask them early in the conversation what they wanted to do with me, in order to optimize.

I found that:

- Some wanted to suck dick but would never do guy-on-guy.
- A rare few wanted me to fuck them in the ass.
- Some liked just talking and found the whole t-girl thing to be "oddly very interesting."
- Many liked that t-girls were usually nice and appreciative of men.

Unlike genetic women, we haven't had men hitting on us our whole lives. Many of us were incredibly frustrated as guys and were so happy to now be loved—in my case by almost anybody.

- **MY TARGET:** The guys who wanted to top a t-girl like they would top a girl—fucking them and getting a blow job.

In the past, I had been interested in chatting with all guys because I just loved this whole scene. But now I was switching to sex cruising mode. I had to find a guy who wanted me to blow him, and he had to be the right guy. So, I had to turn down a lot of guys quicker than I usually did. Given the power bestowed upon me, I felt a responsibility to be nice about it to ensure that I didn't dissuade anybody from pursuing their fantasies and desires. Yes, I was indeed becoming a woman.

And then one night I found the perfect guy for my hookup.

He was a nerdy guy, really nice, and clearly in love with t-girls. I figured he was safe and clean. However, the problem was even though I was starting to really enjoy flirting and wanted to try the sex, I was really uncomfortable with the chemistry of being with a dude. But we found something in common. We both loved the old *Transformation* magazines, and he wanted to show me the stack he had in his hotel room. *Okay, this will work—let's look at those hot magazines.*

Transformation Magazine was high quality, powerful stuff

But, oh shit, now I had to think about safety, ugh. What if he's another Ted Bundy? At this point, I had to start figuring out how to manage my risk. I introduced him to a friend. In other cases, I made sure they knew the bartender saw us or found a way to get them to send me a text, or had a picture taken by a friend. It was also probably safer if I went to their place or hotel. Guys don't have to worry about this stuff. *Damn, girls. What a pain! Any tips?*

We walked to his hotel, where he made two screwdrivers. Best to start with a drink and flirting. We talked about how hot t-girls are and enjoyed going through his *Transformation* magazines. These magazines, for The Dude, was confusingly hot. For me, now as Maria, I wanted to *be* these girls. It was expanding, sitting there with him, thinking about how hot this was from *both* the male and female perspective. And it was fun sharing this kink with somebody. This was something I couldn't do as The Dude. It would be too uncomfortable.

As turned on as I was, I really didn't want to suck his dick, but I had to complete my assignment.

SORDID DETAILS

I figured he was probably clean being a nerd and all, so why not suck his dick without a condom, slipping down that slope. I asked him if he minded if I took a few hits of weed. Fortunately, they never protest. So here it goes, he pulled that dick out. Dammit, not shaved, *oh gross, ew!* I looked at it, contemplating another few hits of weed, but I figured that would rude. *Fuck it. I must really want to be a girl.* I started licking the head of his dick. Getting started, it was really not much different than licking salty skin, other than it smelled and tasted like sweat that has been fermenting for too long. But things started changing quickly. I started feeling the stickiness of his sweaty public hair on my nose while his dick started getting hard. But my new friend wasn't snapping to full attention—probably because he'd already jerked off a bunch of times that day. I know kinky guys can't focus and relax without cumming a few times a day. So, it wasn't as crazy hot as I expected. That would come later. As usual, I fantasized that girls who had rejected me were watching, but that fantasy was getting old. Since he wasn't getting very hard, and his pubic sweat wasn't exactly turning me on, I didn't need to stay on this train.

I had done enough to declare victory for the night, so I stopped to get a drink of water and used a little trick I'd learned. I grabbed the magazine, showing him a picture and screamed, "This is so fucking hot!" and that fortunately triggered him to jerk off. Thank god. He was a nice guy and wanted to see me again. We met a few months later and went through pretty much the same thing. Well, it was great seeing those magazines, and for once not being the one responsible for ensuring the Dick got hard.

✻ ✻ ✻

Shortly afterwards, I had sex with a guy I met online. We first met in person at Divas. You always meet them at a bar first so you can run for the hills if necessary. Fortunately, I rarely had to do so.

SORDID DETAILS

He wasn't getting that hard, either. He probably surfed too much porn or jerked off right before the date or neglected to take Viagra. Sigh. My turn to complain—guys, have some patience! So he jerked himself off while looking at me. At this point, I wasn't going near cum. I really enjoyed making somebody that excited and happy as they fulfilled a dream. I was happy for him and felt genuinely sexy. Actually, a pretty good experience.

But then this guy wanted to cuddle in bed with me and stay over. I had to throw him out. Right after having sex with him. How crass. I was really learning how to be a woman. I was getting more effective at throwing guys out, "Sorry, I need to get up early." Well that's easier then saying, "Get the fuck out of here, I'm not your girlfriend!" So, getting it wasn't *quite* as easy as I expected, but I was still getting laid about once a month even with being selective. Still hundreds of times more effective than being a loser straight guy. I could have gotten *a lot* more if I was willing to fuck the t-girl chasers.

The t-girl chasers

A t-girl chaser[36] is a guy who loves t-girls so much, the obsession drives him into unhealthy and obnoxious behavior. Most of the time, I would get hit on by t-girl chasers who were just gross. They would come up to me and immediately put their hand on my hip without saying anything. Or their opening line would be, "Hey, you live

TO OUR PATRONS:

THIS RESTROOM IS FOR PISSING AND POOPING

NOT SUCKING OR FUCKING

IF YOU FEEL A NEED FOR THE LATTER, PLEASE GET A ROOM OR GO TO THE POWER EXCHANGE

Credit: David Steinberg

nearby, want to go somewhere?" What losers. You can't get a girl like that! They treated me like an object. Dude, get out of your head and say something charming. Do a little dance, sing a little song, do something to make you stand out relative to the other johns around. Then I realized they probably thought I was a prostitute. I couldn't imagine anybody would take me for a prostitute, but apparently many did.

There were several guys who had *actually* been chasing me. They had been coming to Divas regularly for months specifically looking for me. I was shocked, because I didn't remember talking with any of them except maybe one. They were nice enough guys, but I didn't see anything compelling about them at first glance. I felt terrible, because now I was the one who only cared about what they looked like. I was grokking the Dude's humiliation. I knew what it was like for a guy to think about a girl for months only to find your fantasy collapse into nothingness. And now I also knew what the girl was thinking about the guy's dream—basically "ew." Ugh! What the heck was I supposed to say to them? Because they were chasing me, I didn't feel safe. I didn't even think of being sensitive. I simply went with the tried and true tactic. I lied. "Oh wow, that's cool, but I'm into girls. I'm really sorry." I hope my lying eyes weren't obvious. But I never showed any interest in these guys. Or maybe they thought I did because I smiled? Ugh.

---

36. Were really called "Trannychasers." We don't actually use the term T-Girl chasers because it sounds awkward, so a lot of people end up saying "Trannychaser" in private, as it's so embedded in the vernacular. Some girls use the term to mean any man who loves t-girls, but in my experience, it is a largely derogatory or sarcastic term.

Other times guys would *not stop following me*, when it was clear I wasn't interested. They followed me out of Divas and onto the street. What the fuck do they think they're going to accomplish?! I couldn't go home because I didn't want them knowing where I lived. So, I would stop and talk to other t-girls and ignore them until they went away. In some cases, I had to take a taxi two blocks to go home to get away from them. I certainly didn't want them knowing where I lived and then loitering around for me. I also had to leave parties and clubs way too early in order to get away from guys following me. I guess my being treated as a sex object was payback for my being a guy. It certainly made me appreciate what women go through, because not only was I clued into something I heretofore didn't know jack shit about, but I also could now *empathize* with them.

I never found out the deep feelings and motivations of the t-girl chasers. They were such horn dogs, I had little opportunity to see what was behind the curtain. Were they just kinky sex addicts, or did they also really appreciate us like t-girl lovers did?

The curious dude vs. the scared bro

A lot of the guys were just curious. Many were visiting and had heard about the world-famous Divas. I was excited to give them a good experience, just chatting about the whole scene. I especially loved people visiting from overseas. It was wonderful being their information guide and ambassador to this underworld. Many had no interest in sex, as they were happily married with kids, and just really wanted to see what it was all about. I was spreading love and color to thousands of people. But the t-girl world is hard for most guys to process. The really confident ones seemed to be the coolest. For example, the two Steve's.

The two Steve's

I don't know what it is with the name "Steve," but they seem to love the t-girls. I suppose it's just a non-nonsense, tough male name.

Steve #1 (The Curious Confident Dude)

When Maria was born, I told my friends and family right out of the box. I didn't want to be encumbered by a nagging feeling somebody would out me. Just about all of them were really cool with it, but I was hesitant to tell Steve #1. He was a hardcore dude, a man's man, a Vice President of Sales executive type. But I decided, fuck it, I'll tell him. I prefer experience over too much safety. When I told him, I fully expected him to say something like, "Dude, don't fucking talk to me, you faggot." Much to my surprise, his reaction was, "That's fucking awesome! That's fucking hot. You're a deity, man! Let's go out. I want you to dress me up and let's do the town!" He then called me the next day and told me he already had a girl name, "Stephanie." This is the reaction of a confident straight man.

Steve #2 (The Obnoxious Scared Bro)

When I went out for Halloween, my friend Dianna was dating Steve #2, a real macho dumb fuck type. Out of all my friends, he was the *only* one who had a negative reaction to Maria. "Fucking faggot" was Steve's reaction. I've only busted one guy at Divas, and guess who that was. Steve #2! Hypocrite! I was standing outside Divas one night, and guess who didn't recognize me and came sauntering in? I couldn't resist. I sat down right next to him. First thing I noticed was that he knew the t-girls' names! He was a regular t-girl chaser. I chatted with him a bit, and then I said, "Well, it was great chatting with you, Steve." He said, "Wait, how did you know my name?" I said, "Oh, sorry I gotta go, but don't worry, I won't tell Dianna." He exclaimed, "Huh, huh, wait a second, stop, who are you?" As I left, I waved. "Goodbye, Steve." He deserved it. That's the reaction of somebody who's in the closet. This is an extremely common behavior. He doth protest too much, me thinks!

I suppose we should have compassion for certain behaviors. Maybe one way to help is to liberate people by letting them know:

THE STRAIGHTER YOU ARE, THE MORE YOU ARE INCLINED TO LIKE T-GIRLS.

The liberated guys look so peaceful after realizing nothing is wrong with their interest in trans. Recently, I met a man who had previously admitted to his wife that he wanted to play guitar performing as a woman.

After one of my shows, she approached me and grabbed her husband. They were both so relieved after chatting with me. I loved being of service to untold number of people.

It's rather ironic how some of us t-girls may live in the gutter, but we get the best intel on what's really going on at so many levels.

Steve #3 (The Straight Owner of Divas)

The owner of Divas was another straight guy named Steve. Steve Berkey was a quiet gentlemanly guy who liked to sing Elvis songs during Sunday night karaoke. Before owning Divas, Steve was a nuclear engineer who also owned a construction business. Walking past *The Motherlode* transsexual bar, he had met a t-girl, and they eventually fell in love. He wanted to get her off the street, so he decided to buy the bar even though he had no experience running a club.

The owner of *The Motherlode* was hesitant to sell because he wanted to ensure it remained in the hands of somebody who would keep the club running as a transsexual (TS) bar. It wasn't just about the money—he was a t-girl lover like Steve, and he wanted to ensure the community remained intact. Steve's new t-girl friend, who eventually became his wife convinced the owner to sell to Steve. At this point, the club had moved across the street to a building the owner purchased, and he renamed

Credit: David Steinberg

it Divas. Steve purchased Divas and the building along with it. He was later shocked to see many of his macho construction workers at the club!

Steve was dedicated to creating this environment where the TS community and their admirers could meet, adding a huge amount of color to the city for thousands of people to enjoy—and to learn they weren't alone in their love of the mixing of the masculine and the feminine. He struggled to keep it going in the later years as SF nightlife went into rapid decline because of online alternative dating (boo), when he could have simply retired and sold the club and the building, but he waited for a buyer who would maintain the community. Sadly, that was not to be.

It was always pleasant running into Steve at Divas. You could sense his dedication to and protection of all the girls, including myself. I viewed him as the king of the trans underworld and somebody who would always protect all of us weirdos. Steve sadly passed away in January 2020 at the age of seventy-two, not quite a year after retiring.

CHAPTER 11

DIVAS TOWN SQUARE

Although Divas was the perfect place for me try out my new sexual power, I also cherished it as a Trans Town Square. It drew the various trans subcultures and their lovers and chasers together, creating a colorfully vivid milieu of real people. When somebody came to visit San Francisco, they could meet a community of t-girls by going straight to the Trans Town Square. And since the city is so small, they could pop over to the lesbian or kink town squares, too. That was San Francisco.

A night at Divas often included a few straight couples and groups of girls who were on a bachelorette night. They were there to see something different, and I enjoyed telling 'em all about it. I was proud of my community, and I wanted to help make sure they had a memorable night. I especially enjoyed chatting with straight couples. Although I had to distance myself from straight relationships, I still loved and missed straight romance. Seeing straight couples adding to the canvas of their life by discovering this subculture made me happy. They were always absolutely fascinated, and both the guys and the girls would grab me sepa-

Credit: David Steinberg

rately and ask me a *whole lot* of questions. I would wonder, what do they think of me? Do they see the natural elegance and beauty of the juxtaposition of spirit, femininity, fabulousness and kink? Do they see a woman? Do they just see kink? They were so inundated with this new experience, I'm confident they weren't quite sure what they saw.

And this town square even had a church.

God is everywhere

One of the weirdest and most wonderful things I saw in San Francisco was a man of the cloth sitting at the bar at Divas.

What the heck was he doing here amongst all these TS working girls? I had to know. I sat down next to him and started chatting. Reverend Lyle Beckman was the head pastor of the Night Ministry, an organization that provides social services to those in need after hours, the most likely time for people to be in crisis. The Night Ministry raises money to provide support mostly for the LGBT nightlife community. Lyle and his group literally bar hop, meeting and

Lyle Beckman (now retired) Pastor of the Night Ministry.

helping people. That is awe-inspiring. I was in a vibrant community. And what a great job.

Lyle is one of loveliest and most supportive people I've ever met. Just like I had learned in Jerusalem, there is wonder and greatness everywhere you go, even from members of groups that you wouldn't expect. Religion, like all things, has both greatness and scum. Organized religion gets a bad rap, but without it, many important institutions over the history of humankind would not exist. I would see Lyle periodically out and about, and he truly lit up the evening.

Video interview with Lyle:

It was rather ironic that we interviewed Lyle at the Kink.com Armory during one of our shows there.

San Francisco had a lot of these wonderful support systems. Others included the LGBT Center, transgendered support groups, and health care groups that would come to the bars to encourage HIV testing and the use of PrEP to prevent HIV infection. The people working for these groups devoted their lives to supporting the community, even though they were paid a meager salary that barely allowed them to live there. This is what it's like to live in a major, progressive city—a wonderful feeling of community and family. San Francisco has been a major destination for people who have been rejected by their families for being different and I deeply respected and related to that. I didn't *feel* like I was LGBT, and I wasn't rejected for any sexual reasons. Instead, I was rejected from my culture of origin for not being a consumer that *worshipped* money, prestige, and power over all else. And to me, these had similarities, as they were about being ostracized, humiliated, and emotionally abused by our community or family for not conforming to whatever their misplaced standards are.

Most heroes are the untold number of people who provide service to their community instead of focusing all their energy on the rat race of a consumer culture. Another is David Robinson, who was with Keshet, a nonprofit organization working for the full equality and inclusion of LGBTQ Jews in Jewish life.

Video interview with David Robinson: As most people, I have a love / hate relationship with my community of origin—Judaism in my case. It was touching and interesting to see the LGBTQ challenges in the Jewish community. While the Jewish community on average is pretty good about LGBT issues, its biggest issue is schools and children's organizations not knowing how to best accommodate children who have a different kind of sexuality.

We're just getting started here

Years earlier, when I lived in my suburban house, I had fantasized in the online virtual world of "Second Life" that I was a transvestite living two blocks from a transsexual bar[37]. And here I was. And with no end in sight! They say we are in trouble when our fantasy becomes our reality. What kind of trouble? This gradual descent (or ascent) into becoming a girl was a continuous journey, the immediate problem being that the ordinary now bored me.

And I found those fantasies, in reality, to be so entirely different and so much more than I expected. When I started, I wanted to get off on being a reject. This was my way of working through my traumas. But I didn't even have the chance, because my experience was so unexpectedly positive. I was so exuberant and happy that I was routinely lighting up people's day and giving them a night to remember. I was intoxicated with life. No matter what crap I had to deal with during the day in my tech job, or family crisis, I couldn't wait to slip down the Batgirl pole, to

---

37. A lot of guys have this same fantasy

emerge as a superhero and go out and be fabulous, and see people's re-action and go out and spread love and joy by simply being me.

And the fun just followed like never before.

A lesbian and rubber gloves

On an ordinary Wednesday night, Dude was working with my business partner preparing for an important tech geek meeting the next day. When we were done around seven, we lit up a really good joint, chatted about the world, and he went home to his wife and kids. I needed to do something with the great high and surfing porn or watching TV wasn't going to do it. *I'll go down the Batpole and go to Divas!* Not a good idea when I needed to get up early the next day, but the rebel girl inside of me won. *Fuck the rules!*

I walked over to Divas around nine thirty, and it was dead. I hate get-ting all dressed up and finding I'm the only interesting person there. As I was walking out the door, a hot genetic woman around thirty years old walked in, smiled at me and went to the bar. I did the proverbial turn around with my jaw dropped and looked into the "camera." My first thought was, *I'm already walking out with my jacket. I can't go back in there.* Well, that's The Dude talking. I took off my jacket, walked back in, sat down next to the woman, ordered a drink, and said, "What are you doing at a place like this?"

"Hoping to find somebody to fist me," she said. Shocked, I smile and held out my hand without saying anything. "Nice hand. That will do. Where do you live?" I actually picked up a (genetic) girl in a bar for once in my fucking life! I wasn't excited about the prospect of shoving my hand up her ass, but I wasn't going to turn this down. I'd figure out what to do. Laura was a nursing student and worked at the Mitchell Brothers O'Farrell Theater as a stripper to make extra money. She was a lesbian, like many of the girls at the theater[38], but she liked having men fist her

---

38. The word is that many claim to be lesbians so the guys hopefully will annoy them less

because they're stronger. Sounds good, let's go! The Dude never had somebody so hot, and a young stripper! Yippie! And a woman!

The moment we walked into my apartment, she went straight for the bedroom and pulled out green latex gloves. I was in shock and didn't know what to do, so I said to her, "Can we sit on the couch for a few minutes and just talk and get to know each other?" She said okay. I was turning in a girl! She was so cool, and it felt so good to be cuddling and chatting with a lovely girl. I was in absolute heaven. And for a change, I didn't need any more drugs. I didn't even think about it. After about ten minutes, she abruptly said, "Are you ready to fuck?"

I was scared about fisting her ass, but she clarified—she wanted me to fist her *pussy*. Thank god. That's cool, that's weird, but okay!

SORDID DETAILS

I immediately tongue kissed her and took off her clothes. *So* nice to be kissing a woman. Her entire back was covered in tattoos. Nice ones. It had a rough texture in stark contrast to her soft front. Out came the green latex gloves on my hands. I pushed her down on the bed, lubed up, and started with two fingers in her pussy. It was hard finding her clit through the latex, but she wanted me deeper. I wondered how I was going to fit my whole fist in there. I got four fingers in, but couldn't manage my thumb, so I proceeded with the four fingers.

It felt like I was looking for something at the bottom of a soft flesh purse that moaned as I wiggled around. I started going back and forth, hard and harder while she moaned louder and louder. I pounded her with the full force of my arm. I wanted to make sure she got what she came for. Bam, moan, bam bam, scream, yea, fuck yea. And I had the strangest experience. I was *really* enjoying pleasuring her. Since I had been pleasured *as* a woman numerous times in the past year, I knew how awesome it was. And I *liked* her. She wasn't an uptight, upwardly mobile corporate type.

I pumped her harder and harder, until my arm was so tired, I just couldn't do it anymore. She rolled over and exclaimed, "Wow, oh yea, that was awesome." And then something took over. I stripped off the gloves and the girl clothes and jumped on top of her, locked our mouths together, and fucked her brains out. I loved hearing her scream as our cheeks were pressed together—so wonderful, I could really get used to this. I then played with her clit until she got off. Smokin' hot! I guess The Dude showed up.

Never in a million years could I have hooked up with this killer girl as The Dude. As we laid there catching our breath cuddling, I started lightly stroking her body with my fingertips, admiring her curves and just started speaking my mind. "Amazing art. Billions of years of evolution did much better than Michelangelo could ever do." She said, "I've never had anybody say anything so sexy to me!" I was in pure heaven. I suppose this is what it's like being a lesbian.

For me, being with a girl was *so* much better than being with a guy. After cumming with a guy, I wanted to just wash up and throw him out. But with Laura, I loved cuddling afterwards.

She hung out for a bit and said she wanted to see me again. *Yes!* She gave me her number, and I contacted her a few days later but never got a response. What the fuck? Maybe I should have waited a week. The Dude probably screwed things up by being too anxious. Or maybe she was too busy with nursing school. Maybe this, maybe that, blah blah. But I put a quick stop to obsessing over what happened. My level of caring about what other people did had been dramatically reduced because I could easily go out and flirt around as a sex kitten and get me some Dick. It's great being a woman and having options.

The next morning just before our meeting, I told my business partner I got laid after he left. "What!" he responded. "How the fuck did that happen?!" I told him it wasn't exactly me.

It was Batgirl.

PART 3

WE ARE SAN FRANCISCO

CHAPTER 12

I AM SAN FRANCISCO

Warning: There is no sex in this chapter. It's mostly about me and love. Skip ahead to keep going for the naughty stuff.

Gay Pride

When I was a straight dude, I loved coming to Gay Pride in San Francisco to see all the colors. I never thought I would end up being part of it. I got invited to march with the TGSF (Trans Gender San Francisco) float at the parade. I walked in front of the float and started working the crowd like I was a gladiator, raising my hands and getting a whole part of the crowd to cheer. *Are they really cheering with me?* I raised my hand again and yes, they cheered on cue. Just to be sure, I walked up to the barricade and dozens of hands came out to touch me. It's amazing how fast love and fabulousness spread! You couldn't help but feel like god was watching and blessing us all and smiling. I wish everybody could know what this felt like.

I was astounded by the diversity and the looks on the faces of the people on the streets watching the parade. Looking in the eyes of thousands of people cheering, smiling, and effusing love and pride at you is indescribable. Every race, age, sex, and demographic you could think of were cheering. It was so touching. There were older Asian men, older Asian women, older Hispanic women, older Hispanic men, young Hispanics, young straight white girls, young black men and women, old black men and women, kids, regular folks, old Indian men, young Indian women, queer and alternative folks, regular looking folks, folks all dressed up, just to name a few. They had the biggest smiles *I had ever seen* and were cheering, throwing kisses, and holding up their children to see us. It felt like we were all part of the same super being.

I wondered what were they most excited about? Was it the love of those who are willing to be themselves? The colors and diversity? Did they have a desire to do it themselves at some level? Did they have a family member or friend who was queer? Did they love those who bucked the system? All of the above? To me personally, Pride isn't about being queer. It's about breaking the mold that forces are trying to program us into, and embracing the love of life, diversity, and joy on our own terms instead. I had loads of people asking to take their pictures with *me*! I always wondered what photo albums I ended up in.

I brought in my own stereo guitar processor and sound system. What a great feeling to hit and bend the guitar strings back and forth, hear a clear righteous sound blasted to the audience, and bend it just a little more while the crowd went wild. While we were playing, I saw people outside the fence of the enclave, climbing up light poles and the façade of the buildings to get a look. What a long strange trip it's been!

After marching, I usually went to the celebration at the Civic Center which was jam packed with hundreds of thousands of people[39]. There were performances on multiple stages, booths, food, and gaggles and gaggles of people dressed up every which way. I always ended up at the Faerie Freedom Village, put on by the Radical Faeries. It was an oasis of underground San Francisco in the middle of the mainstream Pride. My band, Sex Industry, played at the Village one year.

Video: Pride a few years later in 2016 on the ABFAB (Absolutely Fabulous, the Movie) bus:

I was asked to shoot a promotional video of their float and march with them. We talked a bit about the movie and, of course, being fabulous! Also, you get a feel for what it's like to be behind the scenes waiting to march, and the march itself.

One of my trans-sisters was harassed by the staff of a restaurant in Half Moon Bay, a sleepy oceanside town about thirty miles from San Francisco. They fucked with the wrong girl. A Vietnam vet, she raised such a stink with Town Hall, the restaurant was required to host a Half Moon Bay Pride event—and it continued for years after.

Half Moon Bay Pride was mostly straight people who were excited to have some color in their town. Families with kids of all ages came. I met several single women my age there, and they were infatuated with me. The Dude wanted to figure out a way to get one of them on a date, but I refused to let him try because it would stink the whole thing up.

---

39. About a million people total come to all the weekend events.

At Half Moon Bay Pride

At the Cinch after a long day of Pride where hundreds of people from all over the world would pile in. I'm jealous that girls get to show their underwear through their clothes.

Dyke March at Gay Pride

Video: The main Gay Pride celebration in San Francisco is on a Sunday, but many events take place over the weekend. Friday is the trans march, and Saturday is the dyke march, which starts off with Dykes on Bikes—hard core biker women who ride their Harleys. They are followed by marching lesbians who range from tough to pretty.

Every year we go to the House of Fish, a house on 18th street in the Mission, along the path of the dyke march. This house has been occupied by drag queens for thirty years. Originally, the producers of the cult film *Vegas in Space* lived there. The House of Fish throws a party attended by gays, lesbians, straight people, trans people, and drag queens. Now, that's a party.

We catch the march, then interview folks at the party to talk about what Pride means to them. I'm in there responding as well. I love being around a lot of diversity and getting away from people who define themselves based on their possessions.

Spreading piano love in Golden Gate Park

"Flower Piano" is an annual twelve-day event in the middle of July when a dozen pianos are put in the Botanical Gardens at Golden Gate Park for anybody to play. I went there first as The Dude to play the pianos. I had a good response, but I later went as Maria. What a difference! I wasn't there for five minutes, and I found myself entertaining about a hundred people. I was like a tornado, pulling in crowds at each piano I sat down at. At one of the pianos, I was singing a beautiful jazz song by Basia, and a group of Indian women came up to me with such love in their eyes, I was shocked. I still hadn't gotten used to people looking at me like that. They said they we're from Pondicherry India, and I said,

San Francisco Botanical Garden[40]

40. Credit Wikipedia / Stan Shebs, link to license: http://l.mariakonner.com/ggparklic

Playing at the Moon Viewing Garden

"Oh the home of Sri Aurobindo." They screamed, "We're from the Sri Aurobindo Institute!" They couldn't fathom that a queen like me had read his work, *The Life Divine*, a massive volume on the nature of consciousness vs. matter.

On another day in the Moon Viewing Garden, I played "The Rain Song" by Led Zeppelin, an exquisitely beautiful, quiet song I adapted for jazz piano. A young couple started dancing intimately. Then he got down on his knees and pulled out the ring. "Oh shit," I thought, "I better not screw up"[41]. When I was done playing, I didn't know if I should say anything, so I paused and the woman finally said, "We just got engaged," everybody clapped, and I became the MC! The man said, "I was waiting for the perfect San Francisco moment, and I found it!" He asked, "That was such a beautiful song, what was that?" I told him Led Zeppelin. "Oh wow," he said. He didn't expect to get engaged to Led Zeppelin music. I then played and sang Cole Porter's "Night and Day" for them as they danced. They got my contact info to invite me to the wedding.

Even after performing in front of so many people over the years, I'm still not used to the smiles on so many people's faces. It's indescribable—so strange and wonderful. I have a hard time reconciling how

---

41. And I didn't screw up. But it's hard sometimes for entertainers to enjoy the moment because we're such sensitive perfectionists. No matter how many times you play, it's hard to shake that fear and accept that live music is meant to be imperfect and visceral.

Playing at the Redwood Grove

they treat The Dude, ignoring him or assuming he's just an asshole bro, with how the feathers of love fluff up when they see Maria. It's like an opaque scratchy window has been removed, allowing us to see each other's soul and humanity. I still don't know if they see mostly the outside of me, or does the outside compliment the essence of my inside? Maybe it's just the raw unadulterated energy and love that comes from enjoying being such a fabulous super girl.

One of my favorite schticks was singing my song, "Living as a Girl," where I tell the guys to give it a try, you might enjoy it and learn something. I could see the reaction from the male/female couples, with the guys mesmerized, and the girls elbowing their guys to pay attention.

Video: A brief clip of the end of my song, "Living as a Girl":

When I was around eleven years old, I saw a transvestite in London for about thirty seconds. I was confused and shocked, but I loved her

CULTURE IS ALIVE!

Me with friend Gypsy, who found this Twitter post later that day

attitude. She had a big impact on me, and she didn't even know I existed. And now I think about how many hundreds or thousands of people saw me at Golden Gate Park, and I can't even imagine what they thought of me. Everybody had a big smile, but I wondered the most about the many children who could not stop staring at me with faces of bewilderment, curiosity, and joy. I wonder what imprint and sparks I might have left, but I'll never know. We all create a huge impact that we can't measure. Of course, when you're changing your sex and entertaining folks, your presence tends to hit a little harder!

Kinky tour guide

I loved bringing in visitors who had never seen this wonderful circus before and experiencing it again for the first time through their eyes. I had spent a lot of time in Ukraine for work, and one of the senior managers where I had previously worked moved to the US from Ukraine. He was a hard-core Ukrainian dude. He said to me, "I want to see something crazy! Show me crazy America!" The Dude took him to Divas. He didn't know about Maria and her world, and he didn't know this was a transsexual bar.

When he saw all the smoking hot t-girls, he loved it. Then I dropped the bomb. "These are all men who have become women." "Huh?" "Nobody here was born a girl. They all became girls." He looked back at the crowd and said, "No . . . no," and walked out. A few minutes later as I was just about to go find him, he came walking back in with a huge smile on his face screaming, "This is crazy! I love America!" and he stormed into the main bar to meet the t-girls. He not only loved it, he started bringing his Ukrainian colleagues into Divas and blowing them away. It was beautiful to see the cultures mix at this level, something so unexpected.

My Ukrainian friend and his wife started coming to our shows and bringing their friends. When we brough his wife to a gay bar in the Castro, she was on the phone with her friends back in Ukraine exclaiming, "I'm going into a gay bar. Yes, a gay bar, isn't that exciting?!" My Ukrainian friend later sent me a very touching handwritten letter about how much he cherished being exposed to the world of San Francisco and how different it was from the coldness of the Ukrainian and Russian cultures.

I considered this world to be my family. I felt like a proud sister or cousin who wanted to get their loved ones on video. And I did.

CHAPTER 13

UNDER THE GOLDEN GATE

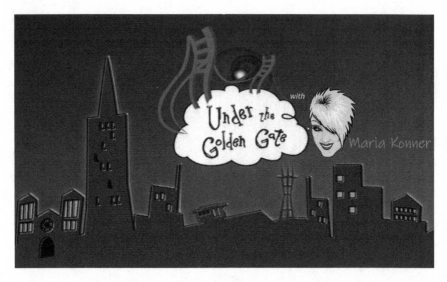

You've seen several videos from *Under the Golden Gate* (*http://underthe goldengate.com*). What's that all about?

Living in San Francisco and seeing all the passion, talent, community service, and excitement of the fantastically diverse underground world had changed me. For the first time in my life, I was not only accepted, but loved and encouraged for being a misfit. I no longer had to feel ashamed and in the closet for passionately wanting to express myself, for seeking out people who were different, or for expressing my joy of life and new experiences.

I no longer wanted to devote my precious and divine passion into to the black hole of a passionless, pointless business and political community focused on money, power, and drama. Instead, I felt compelled to share the wonderful spirit that encourages us San Franciscans to

168

be ourselves, harness our intuition and passion, and fight the forces of American culture that try to control us and tell us who we are.

WE ARE ALL SAN FRANCISCO

I was a performer, public speaker, engineer, marketing professional, manager, and lobbyist, and I knew I could adapt some of those skills to produce my first show—about underground San Francisco. The concept was to highlight the people, events, and places of one of the most fascinating, diverse, liberal, kinky, and colorful cities in the world. I was particularly interested in capturing great and interesting performances, interviewing people about their alternative lifestyles, and talking to members of the community who contribute to the working of this dynamic city—politicians, newspaper folks, activists, and community support people among them.

We did the show for about four and a half years and had about one million downloads. Some of the videos shot on porn sets, our most popular videos, got pulled from *YouTube*. I'm very proud of that.

San Francisco personalities

Many of our early interviews were done in my apartment. We would transform the place into a studio, complete with a backdrop and a tarp to block out the sunlight[42]. We called this our "Wayne's World" venue. They were very informal, and we always had a small, friendly audience,

---

42. At first, we thought it would be cool to show my great view of the SF skyline, but that was not to happen given the reality of cameras and lighting—oh well.

which made the interviews high energy, fun, and informative. I could spend twenty or thirty minutes exploring and finding the best material with our guests and then edit it down to around five minutes. I wasn't just interested in the "what" about a person's experience, I wanted to know the "why" and "who" they really were. I didn't want bland euphemisms and tabloid references to pop culture, I wanted to be moved and hear real, unique stories and deep experiences and feelings.

Michael Soldier, gay porn star

Video: I had never met a porn star. I guess I expected an oversexed, raunchy person. However, Michael was one of the nicest, most fun guys I had ever met. He was also quite sharp and talented. Michael is a very well-known San Francisco actor, performer, and drag queen[43]. Yet he didn't carry a chip on his shoulder and act like a diva. I keep repeating this because it's so important to be reminded that the most successful and powerful of us don't need to be aloof assholes. I subsequently found porn stars to be the most confident and fun/cool people I would ever meet.

Michael talks about how he got into porn, the kinkiest/hottest thing he's ever done, and life after porn.

Sitting next to me in the video was DJ Dank, my critical partner in *Under the Golden Gate*. Choosing a partner is one of the most critical

---

43. Precious Moments was his drag name. He won the Miss Trannyshack pageant one year, which is a big deal. He was also in a prominent drag queen band Pepperspray.

things one can do in any under-
taking. The beautiful thing about
our partnership is that Dank is
so different from me. He's somebody I would not normally have
socialized with in my life. He's a
gay man, very tied up with gay
culture and gay history, and he
went to school for film, writing,
and the performing arts. Dank
worked for Oliver Stone on several of his movies and on the TV
series *Dallas*. Dank is from Texas
and brought a big Texas bravado

DJ Dank (aka Dan Karkoska)

with him. But we complemented each other. He brought much to the
table that I didn't have—professional knowledge of how to tell stories
on film, producing shows, knowledge about LGBT San Francisco, and a
lot of contacts in the community. But most importantly, we shared values that made this partnership very fruitful and fulfilling. Dank has a
strong passion for culture and a focused determination for putting on a
show and telling great, authentic stories. And most importantly, he fol-
lows through consistently, has patience (especially with me), and avoids
drama yet gets over it quickly when he slips up. These are qualities I
deeply admire.

The Sisters of Perpetual Indulgence

The Sisters are a huge part of San Francisco culture. They put on many of
their own big events and can be seen constantly at other events throughout the city. And what a name. When I first discovered The Sisters, they
had a spot on the stage at the Castro Street Fair, an early October street
fair where you can hang out with mostly locals while feeling the serenity
of the coming autumn. At first, I thought these queer, genderfuck, very
gay painted nuns were just acting weird and mysterious as a goof. But in
addition to being really fun, super energetic, and genuinely friendly, they
are also very involved with fundraising, community service, and helping those in need. Community service is how they got started back in
the late 1970s. Every time I talked with one of them, I wondered if I had
just met an *official* angel. The Sisters is a worldwide organization that was

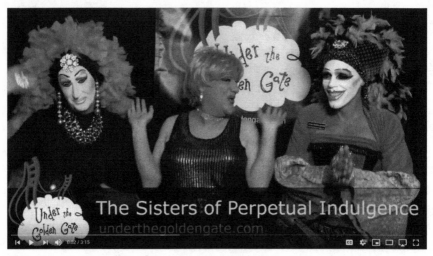

With Sister Roma and Sister Flatulina Grandé

extremely active and important in battling the AIDS crisis from the very beginning. Members start as "aspirants," eventually becoming "fully professed" members of the order. They are one of the great treasures of San Francisco.

 Video interview with Sister Roma and Sister Flatulina Grandé: They describe how they perform many of the same services that a nun would, with one difference. They embrace that most basic and essential human function—sexuality. The Sisters celebrate the joy of sex of all consensual forms.

In a later video, Sister Flatulina Grandé talks about the Sisters' trip to Shanghai China for Shanghai Pride:

We're joined by Monet Allard-Wilcox, a filmmaker who produced *Stilettos Over Shanghai*, documenting their trip to China.

The Sisters were approved by the Chinese government to join the only regular Pride celebration in China—in Shanghai. At first, they were only allowed inside the venue, but so many people loved them and wanted to take their pictures with them, they ended up on the streets. Even the cops, who were supposed to limit their movements, wanted their picture taken with them. It's impossible to measure the positive, freeing impact such a visit has on so many people, especially young people, in a place like China. The reverberations of the waves of love, joy, and diversity are immeasurable and will be felt for generations.

This video was shot later, after we started shooting our show at the Kink.com Armory.

We produced over seven hundred videos, and our most controversial video by far was of the annual Hunky Jesus contest the Sisters organized in Golden Gate[44] park every Easter Sunday. Some of the comments were from people who thought it was entertaining and funny, but others were disgusted and saw it as blasphemy. We even got sued by a little souvenir store in Fisherman's Wharf that happened to

Video *of the Hunky Jesus contest*

have the same name "Under the Golden Gate." They found the video so offensive, they didn't want to be associated with us. Fortunately, my good friend is an attorney.

Announcing the Hunky Jesus contest winner

---

44. It originally was put on in Dolores Park, but moved to Golden Gate park in 2014.

In another video, The Sisters describe the event and how important it is to embrace your inner freak, which allows you to free your spirit and flush out any shame or fear injected into you by certain mind controlling organizations.

All great things have both good and bad associated with them. I'm not a fan of making fun of people, especially somebody else's god. But when a powerful organization has persecuted others and has been associated with behavior damaging to a large number of people, especially children, it is just asking to be satirized. Nothing should be considered so sacred that we shouldn't question certain behaviors, and satire is a way of bringing something on a pedestal down to Earth so we can more easily relate to it. The *vast majority* of church-going folks are great people, so I have reservations about including this video in our material. But I was never persecuted by the church as so many LGBT people have been, and thus am not in a position to judge this. My perspective is that if The Sisters, an organization of service I love and admire, feel that this important annual event is in the spirit of their cause, I would rather represent their truth than hide it. It's unfortunate the people who made the negative comments almost certainly had no idea who The Sisters are and what they stand for. But sadly, this is the nature of the Internet.

We certainly weren't the first to produce something satirical about religion. When I first saw Monty Python's *Life of Brian*, I couldn't believe they got away with it—thanks to last-minute funding by George Harrison, who was an extremely spiritual person.

But satire aside, I smile every time I think of The Sisters, who are the embodiment of the spirit of San Francisco—unique, loving, joyful, outrageous, community-oriented, inclusive, and yes, sexually open and supportive. I'm so grateful I had the opportunity to get to know them well. I never would have had that opportunity if I was just The Dude. But, of course, they know so very little about The Dude's world. I often wonder what it would take to get us all to know each other better.

Fey Boy Collective

Video: The boys tell us a little bit about the collective.

I had never realized many gay men in San Francisco have extended families, many of whom live in a house together such as

the Fey Boy Collective. I was absolutely fascinated and just loved hearing about this rich subculture of support, art, community, and having fun. These guys are *so* gay and *so* different from my straight friends. I loved these guys! I had discovered the beautiful energy of quintessential queer San Francisco.

The host, Bernadette, is a co-founder and an early co-host of our Under the Golden Gate shows. She runs a collective called the Box Factory, a warehouse space in the Mission, where we put on many of our early shows. Bernadette was only with the production for the early years as she had other commitments. These videos were shot at The Supperclub during Gay Pride. I produced and directed the shows when Bernadette was hosting.

Miguel:

Video: Tells us about his life:

Video: Miguel's spoken word piece "Fragrance of a Filthy Faggot":

Filmed at our Mutiny Radio show[45]

Video: Playing and singing "Satisfaction" at Mutiny Radio:

Pnk Feather:

Video: Pnk Feather tells us about his life:

---

45. We had a weekly radio show on Friday afternoons, broadcast from the Mission at Mutiny Radio.

 **Video:** The Boys explain their relationship with the *House of Dyke* and how the San Francisco queer performing arts community supports each other through houses and mothers.

Eric Barry, gay-for-pay escort

Eric is a blogger who discusses his past as a straight guy who used to have sex with men for money:

 **Video 1:** While a starving student at Berkeley, Eric found that sleeping with men was better than folding clothes at the Gap for eight dollars an hour. He tells us how he gets it up and techniques he had to use to get guys to cum as fast as possible. Eric has learned a lot about women as a result, but faces difficulties dating women because of his personality and his past.

Video 1

Eric tells us how it was easy getting into it, given the sexual fluidity of the Berkeley environment:

 **Video 2:** The problem is that many women are afraid he will go back to men given how much damned easier it is to hook up with a guy than a girl.

Video 2　　　*Blogger Megan Murray joins us.*

Peaches Christ, drag queen

Video 1

Peaches (aka Joshua Grannel) is a well-known drag queen, filmmaker, emcee, and actor, best known for her Midnight Mass show and her interest in horror and macabre themes with gay overtones.

Video 1: Joshua talks about what it's like to be fabulous Peaches vs. just being Joshua . . . who sometimes hears other people talking about Peaches! I can relate. She then trades similar stories with Spaz as they shoot to top each other.

Video 2

Video 2: Getting into the McCabre and meeting Elvira.

Video 3

Video 3: For all you Peaches fans, she talks about her San Francisco Underground Short Film Festival on our radio show.

Mutha Chucka, veteran drag queen

Mutha Chucka, a twenty-two-year veteran drag queen, show producer, and personality talks about life as a queen of the city:

Video: Mutha Chucka describes San Francisco twenty years ago, when all the clubs were really crowded and the experience was visceral fun, until the Internet came and now it's like ordering boring food online. She shared with us what it's like helping somebody come out. Mutha Chucka also talks about getting into drag, and how facing death when she was younger allowed her to always live for joy in the moment and be very giving.

Laverne Cox, transgendered actress

I had the opportunity to interview Laverne Cox, the transgendered star on *Orange is the New Black*. We were invited to join a press event at Madame

Tussauds in San Francisco for the unveiling of Laverne's wax figure—the first one Madame Tussauds created of a transgendered person. We filmed the unveiling, and I was invited behind the scenes for a private interview.

I asked her the final question at the event:

 **Video**: I ask Laverne what she might envision people would be thinking about her fifty years from now. She says she stands at the intersection of multiple identities—race, gender, and class, and she hopes in the future the inequities so many people experience will be remedied.

Here is the full video of Laverne along with her mother:

 **Video**: We see Laverne's reaction to seeing her wax likeness for the first time. She talks about how difficult it is for the many transgendered women who are faced with men who love them in private, but not in public. She wishes the stigma attached to such an act of love will go away as we learn to love all fellow humans equally.

Laverne stands with her mother and reminds us she wouldn't be here if somebody didn't love her. She points out that when we say negative things to people, we should think about how such an act affects their family. Laverne's mother comes from a very religious background and she says her fellow churchgoers are now very accepting of Laverne. I hope this is part of the slowly unraveling story of everybody accepting of anybody who is different from the mainstream.

I learned how hard it is getting good footage at a real press conference with all the journalists fighting to get the best view, all the damn mobile phones up in the air, and audio problems[46]. So, the footage isn't great, but I did the best editing I could.

---

46. We got audio off the board, which kept distorting every time a flash went off (and I had to switch to backup audio), and then we also had an mp3 recorder on the stage, but it got knocked over and was useless.

When I interviewed Laverne in a small back room, there was a line of reporters stacked up, each scrambling to get their five minutes with her. By the time I got to her, she was visibly exhausted. It was just me and her, and I didn't have the heart to do an interview. She was clearly looking for this all to be over. So, I just said to her, "You look exhausted." Her face perked back into a smile and she said, "Yes!" I couldn't ruin the moment by bringing in the cameraman. I just chatted with her one-on-one for a few minutes and told her what she was doing was inspiring so many people. We also talked a little bit about trans issues. It was so lovely to simply have a pleasant conversation with her. Maybe I don't have what it takes to be a professional journalist. But so be it.

Philipp Huang, ex-sex worker with straight men clients

Philipp is now a comedian, but he used to be a sex worker who hooked up with suburban married men:

Video: We also talk about straight vs. gay sex with some members of our mixed audience, including Michael Soldier, porn star.

Wilfredo

Wilfredro is a singing Don Juan and comedian. We meet him, and he sings "I Left My Heart in San Francisco" and "Till There Was You":

Video 1 *Video 2*

Video 1: Wilfredo talks about where all his hot male energy comes from and how he loves singing about love. I had never previously played the song "I Left My Heart in San Francisco," as I'm more of a rock and blues pianist. Often on these shows, I had to learn the song quickly right before the show. Wilfredo plugs his music CD.

Video 2: Interview with Wilfredo.

Raquela, international billboard charting singer/dancer

Video: Raquela talks about her musical journey from Broadway to pop star, and then she sings a song for us—what energy! We goof around in this long video, mostly diverging into discussions about sex, but Raquela has so much good energy that I kept most of the material in the edit. Raquela talks about her early career and her eighteen years on Broadway. We then get into how she worked her way up the Billboard charts, and the kind of music she does, which is electro dance music. We learned that Lady Gaga took off her clothes to get attention before she was famous. Raquela says she often shocks the gay community, as people think she's a male drag queen and they are greatly surprised!

Jaden Perry, dancer, talks about the gay sex life

Video: We learn a little bit about the gay sex life in San Francisco and Jaden's dancing and drag.

Everette Davis, first gay stockbroker on the Pacific Stock Exchange, talks about the old days

Everett is a charming and hilarious retired stockbroker. He was one of the first black and gay brokers in San Francisco:

> **Video:** In 1983, San Francisco was very segregated, and Everett had just moved here after high school from Oakland to live his gay life. Yet he got a job with the Pacific Stock Exchange, a place of "true heterosexual men" who were unaware San Francisco was crawling with gay folks. Yet Everett managed to work there for

twenty-seven years and be as gay as can be. He not only managed without anti-discrimination laws, but he helped open up the
doors for more alternative people in that industry.

Sara Moore, professional clown

Video: Meeting a professional clown is not an everyday occurrence.

Maria Konner

Video 1: In this very early interview, I discuss living in two
different worlds—the corporate world and the underground
world—how I'm appreciated for being me, and how my closest associates know about my dual life and are excited they
can live vicariously through me. I also tell my favorite t-girl[47]
joke—a joke only somebody who has kink experience would
understand.

I'm stoned off my ass in this video. At first, we were just ba-

---

47. Noting again that the term Tranny at that time was a commonly used term in
the vernacular of the San Francisco underground and was NOT yet broadly considered to be negative.

Video 1

Video 2

sically partying, because it was important we had fun. Producing the show ended up being a huge amount of work, especially in editing and thinking about the kind of material people wanted to watch. We started focusing more and becoming more serious, but it was important we always had fun to keep the right vibe.

Video 2: The crew chats with me about the benefits of being both male and female and whether I should just become a woman:

Ruby Vixen, burlesque dancer

Video 1   *Video 2*

Video 1: We talk about the life of a burlesque girl and that many are lesbians. We also talk about boobs, and how I want to be a burlesque girl, too.

Video 2: Ruby dancing at one of our shows.

Additional videos

Playlist

CHAPTER 14

DRAG

San Francisco Drag

Our style of drag is an underground art form with a huge range of styles queens and kings perform in. Some dress in the classic glamour queen style, but most are shooting for something edgy. Drag is also a great way to experiment with something kooky and fun. The environment is social and supportive, and it often contains a mixture of new queens and veterans. New queens get to learn by participating. They often find a new family who supports them emotionally and socially, and they develop confidence, which benefits them in so many ways outside drag. When I entered the drag world, I had no idea it was so rich, loving, and diverse.

Most people are familiar with drag as depicted on *RuPaul's Drag Race*, a competitive drag show. Thus, their impression of drag and its *values* come from that show. *Drag Race* has done a huge service to alternative communities by making drag mainstream and accepted. However, on the flip side, one of the most common frustrations of underground communities is the way their art and lifestyle is depicted in the media and by Hollywood. It is most often extremely misleading, and sadly projects values that are the *antithesis* of the values practiced in the real communities. Reality shows are anything but real, because they need drama to sell. The operative term in *RuPaul's Drag Race* is **Race**, not **Drag**. It's a show about competing glamour queens that takes place in the context of drag and, as a result, comes across as catty, petty, and full of unpleasant competitive pressure.

But drag shows in San Francisco are *never* about competition, and only sometimes involve glamour. They are about diversity, weirdness, inclusiveness, experimentation, sharing, helping each other out, mentoring, and community. But that would be very difficult to sell on television. The "Diva Drag" that does sell is just a *small sliver* of the wide variety of drag that occurs in the underground. The vast majority of San Francisco drag is very different and is a very positive environment—a pleasure to be around for performers, newbies, and spectators.

The same is true of kink and other lifestyles depicted in the movies and in novels.

> **The reason why this disparity is *so* important is that the most significant takeaways from the drag and kink worlds are the deep emotions and experiences that drive the behaviors in the community. These are deeply meaningful issues we can all relate to and benefit from, and yet these important kernels are washed out by the media and Hollywood.**

Kevin Seaman (aka LOL McFiercen) describes this:

Video: *Thee Pristine Condition* and I are interviewing her at the Mother drag show debut. This is part of a video we shot on the red carpet interviewing various folks in the community.

Honey Mahogany, Drag Race alumni

Honey, at the time, was surprisingly the only San Francisco drag queen who had been a contestant on *RuPaul's Drag Race*[48]. She talks about her perspective on our show:

 **Video:** Honey talks about how *Drag Race* has done so much for the community by making it mainstream yet is so different from *real* underground drag. It misrepresents the reality which is the diversity and community that is so beautiful and important to the true drag experience. San Francisco drag includes bearded queens, lesbians, genetic women who dress in drag, drag kings[49], comediennes, burlesque girls, and more—it's almost like vaudeville.

Honey talks about how different queens from other cities are and how her comments were cleverly and unfairly edited to make her look like she was out of touch with drag. Honey tells us about what drag means to her and how *Drag Race* affected her life.

---

48. Until Rock M. Sakura very recently, in 2020, in Season 12
49. Women dressed as men.

Video: Honey sings live for us in the studio.

Video

Article

This **article** from the *San Francisco Chronicle* goes into more detail on the lack of San Francisco queens in *Drag Race*.

I find this topic extremely fascinating, complex, and central to our lives, because the question of what it takes to be mainstream is one of our most fundamental challenges we *all* face in so many aspects of our life, community, and country.

Drag performances and interviews

Video Playlist:
Drag Highlights

We started filming at drag shows in the clubs, as I wanted to capture the feel of the club and the community, but the lighting wasn't good, and it was hard using multiple cameras without getting bumped around. We got *much* better quality in a private venue where we controlled the environment and had really great lights. Even though we were only able to show a little bit of the crazy environment of the grungy clubs, we were able to capture many performances in high quality video and show the diversity, talent, creativity, and hard work of so many great queens. I'm really proud to have the opportunity to show some of this community and talent.

CHAPTER 15

GOING BIGGER & THE BIG LESSON

Moving our show to a public venue

We were encouraged multiple times to take our show to a public venue. It's scary to cross that threshold. *Are we good enough? Do we have enough material to engage the audience? How much is this going to cost?* We first started at the Kunstoff Dance Theater on Market and 9th, right above a Burger King. I'm not sure if it smelled good or bad, but it was a nice, modern space that could seat about fifty people.

This allowed us to get some bigger guests on the show. And we were ready because we'd learned a whole lot about interviewing people, running a live show, and editing.

I always respected professional journalists and was curious about meeting them—they were a complete mystery to me. I was also very curious about Kink.com, the largest BDSM porn studio in the world, and it was just around the corner. I combined these into one episode.

I was thinking of a Playboy model of journalism, where hip, curious people would be interested in both sex and deeper issues . . . perhaps the sex would draw in new viewers who would then find other interesting material, like our having a journalist from a progressive paper on the show. But there was something else to learn—the "Unbundled Internet." In today's world, people can easily jump around from one post to the other, so it's very difficult to create a comprehensive experience. And that reality hit us in the face so hard, I bounced into a different world.

The big lesson

Marke Bieschke, publisher of the San Francisco Bay Guardian
The *San Francisco Bay Guardian* had been a prominent and important progressive newspaper since its founding in 1966. It was considered the most important liberal voice of San Francisco. We hosted Executive Editor Marke Bieschke to talk about gentrification. This was a hot topic in our community. Many people were being priced out of San Francisco by the Tech boom,

Marke Bieschke
Exec Editor - SF Bay Guardian (sfbg.com)

causing the cultural diversity and level of community engagement to drop rapidly. This was a subject of constant frustration and talk in the community. Emotions ran high. And Marke gave us access to the *Guardian*'s 25K followers on their Twitter account. We were in the big leagues.

Video: We talk about topics such as the impact of Tech money on culture and whether San Francisco is still a liberal mecca for "misfits and freaks" like us. Marke reminds us just how complex this topic is, because it also includes the behavior of landlords and lawyers. Marke believes "Tech vs. the Rest of Us" is a false narrative because it's not that clear cut, and people and the press like to create this story. He adds that there are always cycles, and these changes often invigorate people to engage together to create new clubs and experiences. Yet, Marke is concerned that many of the city supervisors are running unopposed[50]. We don't come out with any clear answers to this extremely complex topic, but it's a great conversation.

We didn't expect to solve any problems, but it was enlightening to speak with Marke and framing the topic. I was excited and satisfied with the interview and was looking forward to having additional conversations

---

50. It's expensive to run, and how are you going to work to make money while you're spending six months running? I considered it, but I couldn't run for office *and* do my show *and* work all at the same time.

through social media. I didn't expect a massive flood of comments, but since so many people in the community were *constantly* talking about it and complaining, I anticipated reading opinions and maybe some suggestions to organize around a few key topics.

We proudly posted the heck out of this video on our social media and the *Guardian*'s Twitter account. In the two-month period following the show, we had forty views and no comments. After hearing all that frustration . . . Wow. It was very depressing. Compare this with the reaction from our other guest on that same show.

Sebastian Keys, kink porn star & director

Sebastian was our second porn star on the show, but he was currently active and working as a director for a huge studio. Did we have a lot of fun with this relationship! I was now friends with a real, living, working porn star! I couldn't wait to tell my friends and family, even my mother. My father would have been proud. Sebastian directs *Naked Kombat*, which is male-on-male wrestling, and *Bound in Public* which is BSDM porn shot in public places. We had just shot behind the scenes at his *Naked Kombat* production and were now having him on the show. Sebastian talks about his porn work:

Video: Sebastian was a "straight vanilla Mormon boy" who became a porn star and then a director at Kink. com. He says the key to being in porn is being comfortable with yourself. We find it surprising when he tells us shooting porn is almost just another job. You quickly get used to all the sex, and most people are professionals, very cool, and are there to work hard.

Sebastian's fans include many straight folks, and a lot of women love his gay content. He also has a lot of fans in Brazil and China. I felt like we were part of disclosing what really goes on in the Emerald City!

Sebastian describes how he got into gay porn:

Video: Sebastian started off modelling and was contacted by a producer about doing gay porn. He wasn't interested at first, but his girlfriend thought it would be hot, and he needed a good way to pay the bills. Sebastian tells us how his parents found out. He says he found producing porn to be his life's calling. He loves the whole process of conceiving something and following it though to execution.

Working with Sebastian was a pleasure. He was fun, outrageous, had great stories to tell, and introduced us to even more fun and outrageous people, many of whom had incredibly deep knowledge about the psychology of kink and its relationship to the human condition.

I also enjoyed very much speaking with Marke, a real journalist, and holding my own discussing an important, complex issue. But Marke's conversation was more difficult and abstract. Any online discussions would yield a plethora of opinions and emotions and was a forum where someone could come across as naïve or hostile when they talked about how they felt.

In the first two months, Sebastian's videos got 4,000 views vs. Marke's which got 40, a 100x difference. Sebastian's videos eclipsed the sum total of all our videos to date at the time. To this day, Sebastian's videos got 240,000 views vs. 740 for the Guardian, a 300x difference.

Sebastian had about 15K Twitter followers at the time vs. the *SF Bay Guardian's* 25K, but Sebastian had much more engagement from his followers. Tweeting to *SF Bay Guardian's* followers yielded nothing but crickets. Talking about gay porn sells. Duh.

✶ ✶ ✶

Just a few months later the *San Francisco Bay Guardian* was abruptly shut down right before an election and this raised a big stink.

Video: We then had **Steve Jones**, editor-in-chief of the *Guardian*, on the show for an **exclusive** on this hot story.

The video got **12** views in the first two months after we posted it. More of the same.

Sigh . . . . allright . . .

I got the message.
We were going to focus on kink and sex.
Period.
Time to sell ice cream, not vegetables.

Sebastian provided us the opportunity to start shooting at Kink.com. Yup.

PART 4

KINK SAN FRANCISCO

CHAPTER 16

CELEBRITY INTERVIEWS AT THE KINK.COM ARMORY

The Kink.com Armory

So, what exactly is Kink.com and what is the Armory?

Kink.com was the largest BDSM website in the world. They owned a huge castle in the heart of San Francisco. It was originally an Army depot built in 1912 in the style of a Moorish castle. The basement of the building contained most of the porn sets. The first few floors were mostly offices. The top floor was the Edwardian Suite, a luscious venue, complete with kink equipment and kink paintings. It was used for not only porn, but for mainstream corporate events, and this is where we shot our show for two years.

Sebastian Keys, our porn star/producer friend, takes us on a tour of the Armory:

The Armory[51] from the outside, and The Edwardian Sex Suites

Video: The Armory was like a magical adult chocolate factory located right in the middle of The Mission[52]. You could go on a tour of the basement which housed all the porn sets and dungeons, and then see the drill court which served as the hanger the Millennium Falcon used on Tatooine. And then you could see the Edwardian Suite on the top floor which had slave quarters, and a dining room and lounge where online viewers watched various naughty sex acts and tweeted in their requests for action.

On our tour, we learn about BDSM culture, the equipment, what it's like to work there, the kinds of shoots they do, and my favorite—the most disgusting thing Sebastian has done on a shoot.

By the time we started putting on the show at Kink.com, we had a tight crew. We had to—this was a big operation now. Seeing a show in the Edwardian Suite on the top floor of the Armory was a big draw and would bring in guests to be on the show, including a few celebrities! Our experience and learning from our screwups would pay off. And the shift to kink and sex material would pay off huge! To date, eighty percent of our traffic comes from the kink and sex related videos we shot at Kink.com.

But I was personally interested in creating content that was not just tabloid trash. I wanted to continue to do what I felt most deeply about, which was understanding people's lives, only this time it would be in the

---

51. From Wikipedia. User https://commons.wikimedia.org/wiki/User:Sanfranman59, License: http://l.mariakonner.com/ggparklic
52. The Mission is a mainstream part of the San Francisco, a popular spot for restaurants and shopping. It was traditionally very Hispanic, but gentrification brought much change to the neighborhood.

context of kink and sex, which I was now getting very familiar with. I was very pleased with what I discovered about the *psychology* of the kink life. I found *that* aspect of kink and our sexuality to be most fascinating, and it greatly broadened my appreciation and understanding of how our sexuality, lifestyle, values, activism and work are all very much tied together. Presto, everything comes into focus!

Getting beaten by a Go-Go

Jane Wiedlin, guitarist, singer, songwriter, and our favorite Go-Go[53], came on the show to sing a song, sit for an interview, and then beat me up on the horse with a flogger. Let's start with the really fun stuff:

 **Video:** Jane came out as a Kinkster and was gracious enough to share her knowledge, skills, and experience with us while beating me. She is joined by Danarama, an expert kink instructor from Kink University[54]. Jane and Danarama tie me up, put me on the horse, and beat me with their floggers. And damn, did that feel hot! We also learn why some people are subs vs. doms[55], how to tie somebody up, how to be sensual and safe, and why it's so hot.

Note: Jane is an animal rights activist, works with PETA, and played a concert "Pets against Fur." We make several comments about this when working with the various leather products.

---

53. The Go-Go's were the first big all-girl rock band. They were huge in the '80s and still delight millions of fans today.
54. A subsidiary of Kink.com, although Kink University has since ceased operations.
55. Submissive, Dominant

I was right, the essence of rock is a big fuck you to the system. We interview Jane on the couch, and one of the topics we talk about is the Go-Go's:

 **Video:** Jane tells us how her feelings about playing live have changed over the years, and how she is so gracious and astonished so many people are still coming to see them. When the Go-Go's got started, despite the industry's assertion that an all-girl band wouldn't work, they forged ahead and got their first record deal, toiling away, touring up and down California. We lament how live rock appears to be less popular these days, and how Jane had hoped that the Go-Go's would spearhead a lot more all-girl bands, but perhaps things have not changed as much as they had hoped.

I was concerned about the kinds of questions I should ask somebody who's been interviewed thousands of times. So, I focused on how she feels about things from today's perspective. Dank and I also asked fewer and more focused questions and did more listening during the interviews at the Armory vs. the formats we used in the past. I also changed my look a little[56].

Jane also talks about how she is proud to be a kinkster and pervert:

Video: Jane discovered her attraction to kink from stumbling across the book *9½ Weeks* when she was a teenager. She was in-

---

56. I experimented and shaved off my eyebrows, because covering them with glue doesn't work so well with a high-resolution camera under the lights. Plus, it saves over twenty minutes of prep time. And I always wanted to try that. I was worried about the nightmare scenario that my eyebrows wouldn't grow back, or grow back looking seriously fucked up, but fortunately I had no problem. I hate my hair in these vids. I guess I thought the short hair dyke look was good, but in retrospect, maybe not.

experienced, ashamed, and in the closet about this deep interest until two decades later when she met somebody who changed her life. Jane now encourages people to be proud of their interests and who they are.

And Jane loved her private tour of the Kink.com Amory . . . and was maybe ready for a new career!

And I'm proud of my "Pain and Pleasure" song at the end of the video.

Jane gives us her take on reality TV based on her experience being on *The Surreal Life*:

Video: Not surprisingly, it was anything but real. Everybody created drama in their characters, and the production staff woke them up at five in the morning with a camera in their face, and then provided tons of booze to get them drunk before noon. Jane describes it as a "non-fun torture chamber."

Jane also talks about her three major movie roles—*Bill and Ted's Excellent Adventure*, *Star Trek IV*, and *Clue*. But she also has been in a lot of small, independent movies and does a lot of voiceover work, something she enjoys most.

And I got to play piano for her! She sang the song "13 Men" while I accompanied:

Video: Jane picked this song because it seemed appropriate to the event.

We had no time to practice this until about forty-five minutes before the show started. Jane had sent me the .mp3 of her singing the song, and we talked briefly on the phone, so I learned it based on that. I was nervous as hell that this amazing rock star would think I sucked. When I first played it, I stopped and nervously asked Jane if my playing was okay. Her response was priceless. "Oh, you're awesome, is my singing okay? I haven't sung in a while." She was more nervous than I was! I hadn't expected that! But I was used to playing with many singers, so we quickly fell into a fun groove. My playing started off a little stiff because I really didn't want to screw up, and I wasn't happy with a few of the transitions, but I loosened up towards the end and had a ton of fun.

When Jane showed up in the dressing room just before the show, I was so excited, and a little nervous about the song, but I was mostly confident.

I had confidence in the crew, and that made all the difference. Thanks guys ... LOVE! Any nervousness about unprofessional chaos, the cameras or sound being screwed up was in our past, and everybody brought their best game. I could just enjoy being in the show.

I had admired the Go-Go's since I first saw them on MTV, and Jane was my favorite. I always love smart brunettes. And Jane is a smart firecracker, wow! When you meet her, she's physically small, but she's bigger than life. She's so incredibly sharp, funny, gracious, and happy. She has a kind of glow. When she talks, it's mesmerizing seeing all that coming out of such a small frame. We talked about stage makeup, her outfit, the show, and other general funny stuff. That time in the dressing room was instrumental in being comfortable around such a celebrity and seeing her as just another awesome person. It also helped us to play music together and having her interested in beating me up!

Cassandra Cass, transgendered actress

I really wanted to have Cassandra on the show. She's a diva, yet she isn't. She's sexy as fuck, yet she is one of the authentically nicest, most open women I've met. *That* is what most impressed me. She's a male-to-female transgendered actress, who's had everything done. And I know that firsthand.

Video: Cassandra opens with a dance number.

I'm grateful we had the Steadicam! Thanks, Davey J!

Video: Say hello to Cassandra:

Cassandra tells us her art is her physicality and the fashion, sexuality, and glamour that goes with it. She really admires powerful women and is inspired by them. She feels that by just living her life, and living it clean, she inspires others to not only be beautiful and fabulous, but to have self-respect and be strong. Cassandra wanted to do the show because so often, the media centers on her simply as a sexy trans woman, but we were going to focus on the strong, fascinating, smart, and inspirational person underneath. Amen.

We do, of course, cover the sex and dating:

 **Video:** We talk about how good her pussy looks and who paid for it. She had showed it to me in the dressing room, told me to ask these questions in front of the camera, and then pretends to be surprised. I felt double crossed. That's a real professional! She is, after all, a reality TV star, among other things. Very impressive.

There are a lot of straight men who love trans women very much, many of whom prefer them for all kinds of reasons:

My opinion inserted here: They're super sexy. They have to be strong, and they tend to appreciate men more because they've worked really hard to be who they are. They are often more sexual because it's still new to them, they aren't following the straight dating formula.

But many men won't come out as such. As with Laverne Cox, this is one of the most common complaints I hear from trans women. Cassandra also shares with us her experience with sex and female orgasm.

Cassandra tells us about her move to L.A. and what it's like to be a reality TV star:

Video: Cassandra was on *Trantasia* a Showtime documentary about a transgendered pageant in Las Vegas. She was also in an eight-episode reality TV show called *Wild Things*, which was a kind of American *Priscilla, Queen of the Desert*. In her show, three trans women travel across the country and meet with straight people in the Midwest, even working crazy jobs with them. She says the shooting schedule was intense, and drama naturally broke out after being together for a solid month non-stop in excruciating heat.

Cassandra is excited for her move to L.A. and tells us that real acting is opening up for trans women vs. older Hollywood when trans women were often depicted as freaks for entertainment value[57]. Cassandra acknowledges glamour is her wall—the wall many divas put up. But she acknowledges that wall and takes it down for certain people. This is the first time I heard a woman admit to and talk about that wall that The Dude had encountered so many times throughout my teenage and adult life. Now I was beginning to get a better understanding of what it really was[58].

Cassandra shares with us what it was like growing up trans:

Video: Cassandra, who grew up without a mother, tells us how her conception of women was her father's *Playboy* magazines and porn habits. Cassandra started her transition at seventeen years old in her hometown of Des Moines, Iowa, which was incredibly difficult, but she managed to find the strength.

When I tell Cassandra I admire her strength, she responds that she didn't have a choice. Cassandra gives us some insight

---

57. That was my recollection, too.
58. This also made me wonder about my interpretation of encountering the diva wall in queens over the years, but it's hard for me to grok it because I'm not a glamour queen.

into the power of choosing your own name after you know who you are. She closes by reminding us that in order to do anything significant in your life, you need to be determined and focused, seeking out community and people you admire.

We also find out why Cassandra was doting on Dank so much... she loves men, ah ... duh!

Jello Biafra of the Dead Kennedys

I should have a button made to put on my blouse saying, "I survived an interview with Jello Biafra." It was a real treat interviewing punk rock legend and royalty Jello Biafra, the singer and key songwriter for the legendary punk rock band, The Dead Kennedys. Jello is smart, funny, energetic, and makes you think, but interviewing him was like getting into a boxing ring with the champ. But I managed to get a few quick good jabs in, and then a nice one at the very end.

We get out another big rock and roll "fuck you to the system" on the couch when Jello gets onto the topic of changing San Francisco:

 **Video:** Jello tells how the changes brought about by Tech money inspired his most recent music with his band, Jello Biafra and the Guantanamo School of Medicine. He expands on how the city has changed since he moved to San Francisco in 1978 for college, and then quickly dropped out to focus on the punk scene. He describes some of the bands he loved, how back then great bands were coming to San Francisco, and how that has changed.

Jello talks about modern music:

Video: I start by trying to get his perspective on my perception that our modern youth mass market is very much into electronic dance music (EDM), which is conducive to being put into a mind controlling trance vs. past generations, who were more into hard-driving, individualist punk music, and the implications for our culture. But it appears he erroneously assumed I was complaining that all new music is EDM, which was frustrating. But my comment elicits something he feels really strong about, which is that really good new fringe music is being drowned out by modern pop music because people aren't supporting it financially. They are only complaining instead of going out to see the bands play live. And he is a record producer and has a label, so he would probably know.

Jello gets into his love of both new and old music and his music label Alternative Tentacles. He tells us a few funny stories of shows where one punk band used the autotuner and another lip synced, much to his horror.

The all-important first question:

Video: One of the key challenges when interviewing a celebrity is coming up with a good question they haven't been asked a thousand times. And Jello's known for not being kind to those who ask the same humdrum questions. So, my strategy was to open with a really good question that nobody else had ever asked him before. And I succeeded. I asked, "How did you like your tour of the Kink.com Armory?" He was delighted to give his reaction about how sex is better than war. Great, he's in a good mood. But it was still hard getting in a word edgewise.

He talks about his DJing, songwriting style, and his favorite hobby—slamming politicians.

I was able to find a pause in his political talk, where I was able to quickly inject a simple question—does he admire anybody in politics today, a question I like to ask a complainer:

 **Video:** And I stump him! He makes a few good jokes, and then reminds us that the real problem is people not voting or choosing to run. I argue back that nobody wants to because it's such a sewer. Jello counters with the story about when he ran, and some funny bits about his platform, including his favorite topic, slamming Dianne Feinstein, who he calls "Feinswine." He also reminds us that politicians are *talking* BS to the average person and *listening* to the power brokers.

Then I finally get to my closing question with a topic I had thought very carefully about. I ask Jello what advice he would give to our young people. He quiets down, and gets softer and more serious, sharing his ideas on being a good person—**and that's the moment I'm most grateful to have had with punk rock legend Jello Biafra.**

Phew, I made it!

I met Jello for the first time about an hour before the show started. He was very pleasant, a little quiet, but I could see he was very much in his head looking for something gripping to say. He brought up several topics he had strong opinions on. This was very different from meeting Jane and Cassandra before the show. I didn't feel any connection with Jello. I wasn't sure if it was because I was trans and maybe that wasn't something he was used to or if he was just very much in his head. He seemed like the kind of person that even in private, you had to try to get a few quick clever jabs in to get his attention and his respect.

I told Jello one of my anecdotes about what I discovered with my extended time in Jerusalem, and he smiled and seemed to absorb it in his memory banks. And then he mentioned it in a little joke a while later. I took that as a sign I had made a connection with him though a good story, not with my heart. The lack of a good connection made the interview difficult, but I felt privileged to have this opportunity. I was satisfied with what we got, which was entertainment, things to think about, and a little bit of his heart.

CHAPTER 17

EXPLORING KINK

The kink professor

Danarama has the knowledge of the naughtiest kinkster, but the demeanor of a friendly college professor. He is not just an expert in kinky sex, but in kink lifestyles, and most importantly in the psychology and physiology of kink. We learned a heck of a lot from Danarama, and I'm thinking a lot of people could benefit from a few sessions with him rather than years with a therapist.

Danarama gives us the real scoop on kink:

Video: Danarama first tells us that many folks who are interested in kink want to be dominated but want to feel safe. And many are women. They are interested in feeling out of control, but not in being abused. BDSM is very caring and intimate. It is about trust, communication, and safety—ironically more than any other kind of sexuality. He gives us a simple example, which is the standard use of safe words to slow down or stop a scene if necessary. This allows people to feel safe before going deep. We also learn that some people use BDSM as a way to re-create a traumatic experience in a safe way, and thus often get past it to reclaim their power.

Danarama gives us ideas on how to broach your interest in kink with your partner. Rough sex is the most common activity couples are interested in. These are challenges that can be overcome with trust and communication. For example, often a submissive wants much rougher sex, but the dominant may be worried about hurting his/her submissive. But they can explore having transformative fun if they take the journey together with trusting communication.

Kink University helped individuals and couples learn these tools of BDSM: communication, safety, and the psychology to engage on this new journey. It has sadly been shut down due to the declining revenues of the porn industry.

Danarama then tells us about the St. Andrews Cross, which he's going to use to flog me. The Cross provides a nice platform to grab onto while you're getting whipped.

Danarama then flogs me on the St. Andrews Cross and continues after I grab my electric guitar:

Video: Mama Dora, our favorite crazy drag queen, joins as assistant because she has a little BDSM experience and a whole lot of desire to beat me. I take one for the team, allowing myself to both be beaten and filmed. I, of course, wanted to make sure I wore sexy underwear, so fishnets and rubber seemed appropriate. I at least get some points for not being lame and boring.

First Danarama blindfolds me to illustrate how sensory deprivation enhances the focus and experience. Danarama shows us how to use your arm for a good swing to hit the muscle part of the ass cheeks. He also shows us the Florentine—two-handed, two-flogger technique of beating. We learned that combining the two floggers together is the ticket for a good shot of hot pain, and that *stop* is not a good safe word. *Red* is. Wow, my ass was getting red as I took those beatings.

To end with a spectacle, I grab my electric guitar and play Black Sabbath while the beatings continue.

Real world vs Hollywood world

I learned over the years that kink is one hundred and eighty degrees different from what I had expected, which was as depicted in the movies. It was probably the most authentic, accepting, and caring environment I had ever encountered, which is divine to me because it involves the most intimate part of ourselves, close to our soul. Engaging in kink more broadly would release all kinds of anxiety and demons, giving more people their power back and making our whole world better.

However, movies like *Fifty Shades of Grey* end up depicting kink as the *antithesis* of the values, behaviors, and attitudes in the real kink world. Most kink folks are pretty normal and friendly, and they get into kink usually after they get to know and trust each other. It's usually a very playful activity, vs. the movies, where it is depicted as dark, nasty, and angry.

The irony is that shows like *RuPaul's Drag Race* and movies like *Fifty Shades of Grey* create a service by bringing these once "shameful" activities into the mainstream, enabling a lot of people to explore their curiosity. But beyond that, those representations fall short of reality, creating an enormously misleading impression of the lifestyle. *RuPaul's Drag Race* depicts drag as glamorous and competitive, yet drag in real life is rarely competitive and is typically more weird and full of variety and experimentation. *Fifty Shades* depicts kink as creepy, impersonal, and dark, yet kink in real life is about trust, safety, and communication.

Neither the *Fifty Shades of Grey* author nor the filmmakers appear to have any experience with BDSM. The author of the book said her inspiration for *Fifty Shades* came from the vampire novel series *Twilight*. Not something real. But I can't blame her. She didn't expect the book to be such a blockbuster, and thus perceived by a large portion of the public as representative of what BDSM is all about.

She succeeded because her writing spoke to the audience, not because of the accuracy of the material. Why does this matter? Because now millions of people think BDSM is about abuse and unhealthy relationships with creeps. Those who engage in it might actually be abusive. And on the flip side, many who would benefit greatly in releasing their inner passion won't because they think it's too abusive and dark. *Fifty Shades* is basically about a peppy young smart woman who starts dating and having sex with a creepy abusive guy because he's a good-looking billionaire. And he happens to be into BDSM, but clearly doesn't really know that much about it, probably because he's such an arrogant asshole that he has never had the opportunity to learn and experience with a community. Ew, who wants to associate with him? *Fifty Shades* is basically a Disneyfication of BDSM, much like *Drag Race* is a Disneyfication of drag—oversimplified, cleaned up, and watered down for mass consumption. It is groundbreaking and entertaining, but grossly misleading.

Mr S. leather sex store

We visited the Mr. S Leather Sex Store[59], the only major leather store left in San Francisco. Thee Pristine Condition, one of the drag queens in our extended family, worked there and graciously hosted us. This store has everything. Thanks, Pristine for demystifying it all.

These videos are part of a playlist (several videos). They should automatically play in sequence, but full links are provided:

---

59. On 8th near Harrison.

Left: my favorite prop, the horse. **Right:** *Smelling a flogger . . . mmmmm.*

Part I: Intro, Whips and Collars

Video: Pristine assures us that *everybody* can be kinky . . . wink wink. It's a little intimidating, but once you get over the hidden camera fear, you'll really enjoy this kind of unique shop. First, we learn about different types of collars, some of which are used to ensure you don't fall asleep if you're chained up for a while. And there are different types of floggers, in material that ranges from soft deerskin all the way to tough bull. Flogging ranges from a sensual tickling, which you often start off with, to full-on pain. This helps extend your BDSM scene by allowing a lot of variety.

We look at some other items like the single tail, which is designed to sting you and inflict pain and draw blood, and also the penis slapper and a paddle.

We explore the "Locker Room" for those who are into wearing items like jock straps and spandex, plus the sweat and smell that goes with it. All ye wrestling fans, Mr. S has a very popular monthly wrestling group so you can try this little fetish out with others.

Part 2: Swing, Dildos, and Cockrings

Video: I jump right into the sex swing and then Pristine describes the fuck machine. It's quite a machine. You can adjust the height, depth, and speed . . . with a remote control.

Then I see a mind-blowing variety of dildos—the tan ones being soft and the black ones being hard. This is real pro stuff. The size dildos that some people can take is quite impressive. And Mr. S has a starter kit.

We learn about the purpose of a cockring. I thought it was just for show, like jewelry. But it actually serves a function. It will hold your balls down so they don't pop up and interfere with what you're doing, it makes your package look fuller, and it will enhance your erection. Caveat: you might cum quicker.

Pristine gives us some recommendations about items to start with depending on whether you're a gay man (leather vest, pants, and boots) or straight couple (restraints to try something new or switch roles). Mr S. also sells other materials like latex and neoprene, which are good for water sports[60] as they are easy to clean.

Part 3: Restraints and Harnesses

Video: Damn, that room smelled good with all the leather. I first get on the horse, my favorite BDSM piece of equipment. I love getting tied up and spanked on it. Pristine reminds us that BDSM is very much

---

60. Sex involving urination. Yup. Well, not my bag.

about power and role reversals, something many of us can benefit greatly from.

The restraint room has every kind of restraint imaginable—for your wrists, ankles, thighs, or even getting tied up in a leather sleep sack. The harnesses give you something to grab on to while having sex. I made a mental note to give that a try. The harnesses have a lot of metal rings on them, I can only imagine.

Part 4: Cages, Masks, and Tape

Video: Mr. S sells cages that can be hoisted in the air, used to create a scene where you lose your senses, allowing you to be more receptive to the whims of your partner.

Masks can enhance a long-term relationship. When you take away a person's face, it makes adding pain to your sex easier. It releases the inner animal, which can really enhance a stale relationship.

Puppy play is pretty popular, too. Mr. S has not just the masks, but the paws. This stuff wouldn't be in the store if it didn't sell! The appeal is to just let yourself have a good time with no worries in the world, roaming around and being told what to do, complete with a sexual reward. Puppy play tends to be done by gay people, but pony play includes a lot of straight and bi people. I didn't have time to ask about why the difference because I wanted to get something to eat before all the restaurants closed.

Part 5: Penis Pumps and Lube

 **Video:** Andrew the comedian takes this one. He wanted to enhance his marriage with pegging, where his wife puts on a strap-on. But he was concerned about the cost. Pristine asserts that it's not worth getting the cheap stuff; otherwise it will burn. And yes, Pristine claims, penis pumps do work.

We review the different kinds of lube—water-based, silicon-based, greases, and hybrids. Pristine recommends silicon lube, as do I. She tells us a little bit about the macho style.

Andrew asks Pristine lots of questions to get tips of the trade, the kind of questions you would expect from a straight guy.

Part 6: Sex Bed and Wrap up

Video: The four-thousand-dollar bed behind me is tempting, but I was worried I would seal my fate if I bought it. I would have no hope of ever going back to a normal, straight relationship.

We end by having Andrew getting zapped in the balls by a violet wand—a device that generates static electricity. Kudos, Andrew! Andrew admits he kind of liked it. I miss Andrew. He was clever, a good sport, and really fun to work with. He moved back to Australia.

Come to Mr. S., folks!

Cannabis anal suppositories

Brittany Confer from Foria chats about cannabis lube and anal suppositories and her trials and tribulations getting men to put something up their butt and try something new. Big points guys if you give it a try.

Video Playlist (also contains other cannabis related interviews)

Beaten by a dominatrix

Mistress Mercy beats me a bit and teaches us about the world of the dominatrix. Dank had the idea of me doing this to spice up our material, so I was game to give it a try. At the time, this was completely new to me[61]. After she beat me, Mistress Mercy tells us about being a dominatrix and how important the relationship with her subjects is.

Video: *(The beating footage is below)*

Mistress Mercy says she really enjoys the relationship with her clients, trying new scenarios, and sharing different ways of being sexual and present. I was surprised how relaxed and open I felt after the beating. I could very quickly tell that your relationship with a dominatrix is very personal and intimate, and it's actually a really great way for a dude to establish a relationship with a woman without all the bullshit of dating in the way.

Mistress Mercy went to school to be a dominatrix and continued her education as an apprentice. She tells us how important the community of dominatrices is to not only help you learn, but to help guide you through this really fascinating and unusual lifestyle / profession.

The beating:

Video: Mistress warms me up with her fingernails and a little spanking. The little metal birch whip she was using actually hurt *a lot* more than the flogging and spanking even though it is smaller and appears less violent. My facial reactions are authentic yet re-

---

61. The previous videos on kink were filmed after this one

strained—it fucking hurt! And no, I wasn't going to say the safe word. The shots where she lifts my skirt hurt the most as I wasn't protected by the leather.

I learn there are two types of beatings:

- **Stingy:** The birch whip creates sharp pain because it hits on a small surface area
- **Thuddy:** A flogger is impacting across a wide area and thus doesn't sting the skin as much but has higher impact

Bunny Pistol, burlesque dancer and producer

Bunny is so much fun:

Video: Being a producer is a huge amount of work, much of it very tedious, but Bunny calls it a labor of love. She loves creating the costumes and the acts, and giving other performers an opportunity to create a community and participate in a great show. Bunny also emphasizes the importance of not being an aloof Diva.

Bunny adds that show biz is tough. So, it's important to appreciate those occasions when things do go really well, and not just for yourself. Go up to other performers you really like and tell them. She tells us a little bit about growing up loving Playboy bunnies, hence her name and her dreams. She adds that the reality is actually more than she imagined, because she had not

thought about the community, friends, and other people's awesomeness. She closes by reminding us if you're interested in something, go find people *in real life* who are doing it, not just online.

Video: Bunny's full dance.

I met Bunny at a bar in North Beach. She was talking with somebody and kept smiling at me (Maria). When I walked up to her and said hello, I could instantly tell she was a great person and a great artist. I love getting to know burlesque girls. Most of them are radiant and beautiful both on the outside and the inside. I really loved getting to know the person inside that beautiful figure, and how they're so different from The Dude's perception of who they are. Then when you see them perform, it changes the context of how you see them.

I couldn't help but lament how The Dude had no access to such lovely women. But I always had to keep The Dude door locked. Otherwise, Maria's fabulous aura would have collapsed.

"Ode to Mistress"

Video: I had my electric guitar at my beating because my band was playing this song, written by drummer Sweet Jayne. Mister WA joins on bass and Flynn Witmeyer on backup vocals.

CHAPTER 18

BEHIND THE SCENES

Naked Kombat, gay wrestling porn

Sebastian Keys, our porn star/director friend, invited us to shoot behind the scenes at the Armory for the filming of an episode of *Naked Kombat,* a gay porn channel from Kink.com. After the view count started quickly racking up into the six figures, our main video was pulled from YouTube for being "inappropriate"—even though I'd removed all the really naughty parts.

Another video (which wasn't pulled) includes questions we asked the two stars **Billy Santoro** (blue shorts) and **Eli Hunter** (red shorts). Eli is straight but does gay porn because it pays better than straight porn. He really likes working at Kink.com because everybody is really nice and cool:

Video: *Note: The audio is a little hard to hear*[62]

These guys were really friendly. We ask them the craziest thing they've ever done, and Eli says getting shocked by an electric prod in the space between his balls and ass. They both watch porn, but they prefer the amateur material because it's more real. Billy says shooting porn doesn't satisfy him sexually but satisfies his need for attention both on and off the set. His favorite part of the shoot is when he cums because then it's over and he can relax.

At the time, Billy was the most filmed porn star in the industry. He did three or four shoots a week. He once did six in a week, and his dick was huge from being swollen. Billy can be a top or bottom and often he doesn't know his role until right before the shoot.

They both tell us how they got into porn. I ask them if they would go back to working a real job. They say it would be difficult to free up the time to continue to do porn. It's either give it up completely or not at all.

Sebastian tells us about a shoot where he was tied to an electric chair:

---

62. We couldn't use our handheld microphone because the connector on the camera went bad, and I didn't have a backup mp3 recorder with me. Our regular cameraman didn't show up (typical when you get people on the cheap), so we were a little discombobulated. And it was an unusually hot and humid day, so the fans were making a lot of noise.

Video: Sebastian says he was first left alone in a room for two hours. The chair was really uncomfortable, as there were two bars instead of a seat. It was on hydraulics and was moved around to make him even more uncomfortable all while he was being shocked with a car battery. There were also wooden pegs pressing into his body. Sebastian says the first half hour was the hardest. It was painful, and he couldn't breathe well. He went from being annoyed to pissed off, but he wanted to make it through. He eventually reached peace and euphoria, despite all the crying and pain. But then they started giving him the Chinese water torture[63].

Sebastian has a hatred of being dunked in water. He told us his next challenge is getting fucked and being forced to cum while he's being dunked in water. Sebastian says he loves the "subspace" these actions put you into. I'm sure my therapist would love to analyze this all, maybe even write a book. There are a lot of great insights to take in. It's not just being weird. There are reasons behind everything, and this is where the hidden parts of you are found.

Sebastian tells us about the biggest dildo they have, which is the size and width of an arm, and he's proud to tell us that he was able to take it:

Video: His secret is sleeping with a butt plug the night before.

Sebastian says he would love to make a mainstream movie. Many mainstream movie makers have gotten started in porn, because they learn so much so quickly. Sebastian describes his experience as a guerilla job, where you have to learn to do everything.

We learn a little bit more about the Amory and working at Kink.com:

Video: Working at the Armory was a dream, kind of like working at Willy Wonka's chocolate factory, except of course it was a kinky sex factory.

---

63. Drops of water on his head.

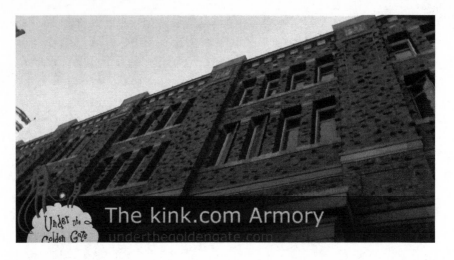

The kink.com Armory

Under the Golden Gate
underthegoldengate.com

We see a little bit of the shooting and directing (e.g. Sebastian yelling, "Suck his dick!"). The room they were shooting in was the soldiers' gymnasium. The building was constructed in 1912 by the US Army and it was abandoned in 1976. Kink.com took it over in 2007 and cleaned it up.

At the time, Kink.com used the whole building to house its staff of one hundred and fifty people plus guests. They had a marketing department, production team, administrative offices, rooms where actors/models stayed, a lounge, and a cafeteria where a fabulous chef cooked all the meals. The porn was mostly shot in the basement, where many convenient hooks were still in place from the army days.

They also had fundraisers and community events—some kink related, some not. And many mainstream corporations held events in the Edwardian Suite. The building has a huge drill court which is big enough to hold concerts, but they turned it into a community center.

One of the funniest aspects of meeting these porn stars is that on several occasions when I was watching porn, seeing somebody's cock up close, when they panned back, it was Sebastian, Billy, or Eli. *Ha, I know this guy!!* That made me very proud of my work!

A Lovely intimate conversation with Sebastian

The most disgusting thing I have done as a porn star

Sebastian gives us an update on the most disgusting thing he's done in the past year, but he also gives us some great additional nuggets of insight about sex and porn.

Video: We review his previous most disgusting story—when they shaved his beard, came on his hair clips on the floor and made him lick it all up. He then shares the most disgusting thing he's done since then. He also shares the most disgusting thing he's made *other* people do on a shoot. Kink is in stark contrast to mainstream vanilla porn where all shoots generally follow the same pattern. Sebastian shares with us the qualities he's looking for in a new porn actor—somebody who is natural and open-minded. This is also in stark contrast to the vanilla porn actors who are just good looking and have largely become robots.

Sebastian has changed people's lives significantly. They have told him he's helped them come to terms with their own sexuality, communicate with their partners better, and learn a lot of things that enlighten them.

We ask Sebastian how he feels about watching his own porn videos.

We have a great question from the audience—what kind of sex in private does Sebastian like? Sebastian just likes to please his partner. That's the result of living through a life with kink. The real *you* comes out and you can connect with others as your hang-ups are gone.

Always so interesting and fun. Better than TV!

In memory of the Kink.com Armory

Credit[64]

I met a lot of professional and amateur kinksters at the Armory. They were definitely more fun, passionate, friendly, intelligent, inviting, and open than the average person. This is probably because when you're involved with kink, you have been relieved of your hang-ups, and you have nothing to hide anymore. People love you for who you are, and you have healthy self-esteem. You've been freed from the influence and judgement of the evil Monoculture Virus. Sadly, Hollywood depicts such people as sick perverts and super weird, because the truth wouldn't be as entertaining. But for me, reality is always more entertaining than fiction. I've been fortunate to be exposed to reality in the great city of San Francisco and be engaged with so many different sorts of people in real life.

We had fulfilled our dream of creating a little *Tonight Show* for underground San Francisco. But sadly, after over a year of shooting there, the declining revenues in the porn industry caught up with Kink.com, and the venue was no longer available. A few years later, they shut down

---

64. From Wikipedia. User https://commons.wikimedia.org/wiki/User:Sanfranman59, License: http://l.mariakonner.com/ggparklic

much of their operations, moved the remaining shooting to Las Vegas, and sold the Armory to a developer who converted it into office spaces and a facility for small scale manufacturing. Barf.

When Kink.com sold the Armory, San Francisco lost one of its most interesting and exciting venues. Many San Franciscans were proud to have a literal castle of kink in the city, one that opened its doors to the community. So sad that now it's just another corporate building, and a shell of what it used to be. We were so fortunate to have had the chance to explore this fascinating one-of-a-kind place whose likeness we will never see again.

We'll wrap-up our time with the Kink.com Armory with a video we shot behind the scenes as they were finishing up their annual Halloween Haunted House:

Video: They created a helluva an experience. The props and sets were breathtaking. After all, they had tons of carpenters, electricians, mechanics, and artists who just shifted their focus from porn sets to Halloween! They also had live actors.

CHAPTER 19

KINK ABOUT TOWN

Dore Alley street fair

Dore Alley (aka Up Your Alley) is *The Gayest Place on Earth*, a gay oriented street fair dedicated to leather, BDSM, and kink:

Video: We take in the gayness, and then survey people about their favorite kink. We catch many people being beaten and see a whole lot of red marks on people's skin. There are many human animals, including a pen for dog play. We learn a little bit about *tm4m*—trans men[65] who date gay men. And we discover the hot parties are the ones where guys come into the party and start immediately screwing, no chatter required . . . wow!

I reflect with Dank on how I learned in my time in San Francisco you don't really know your true sexual preferences until you have

---

65. Women who have become men

tried out various options and taken in the sights, sounds, smells, and tastes. You might be surprised. You can't live your fantasy online. It's very different from reality. Truly more than you can imagine.

Folsom Street Fair

Folsom is the world's largest BDSM, fetish, and leather fair[66]. Unlike Dore, which is almost all gay, Folsom is much more mixed. Along with Dore, it is one of the few events in San Francisco today that still represents weird

66. About 250K people.

San Francisco. People fly to San Francisco from all over the world for a weekend of events and parties.

 **Video:** You can see weirdos of all sexes and persuasions, leather and kink outfits, naked people, toys, gadgets, wild clothes, demonstrations, and vendors showing their wares. Although the fair attracts many people in the kink community, it includes a whole spectrum of people who want to be kinky for a day with no shame, or just spectators who want to check it out. We also ask about people's favorite kinks, meet more porn stars, learn about some really crazy stuff like water sports[67], and see more puppy play.

Additional videos

Video Playlist

---

67. Sex involving urination

CHAPTER 20

TIME TO LIVE IT

The power of Kink

The antidote

If you were an alien monitoring data coming from Earth, you would conclude that lust drives us. Around thirty percent of our internet traffic and web searches are porn related[68]. Some of the kinky porn compilations and accompanying narrations are far deeper and more interesting than many mainstream movies and deserve Academy Award nominations.

There is no other subject that takes so much of our collective time, except maybe extremely conservative religious movements—and they watch a whole lot of kink porn, too[69]. The more shackled you are in your regular life, the more you want to experiment with being shackled in your

---

68. The figures vary
69. We learned from Kink.com that the Vatican has one of the highest download rates of Kink / BSDM porn

sex life, but on your own terms. Hence the strong interest in kink in the highly religious community. I've experienced the same thing, but the religion that persecuted me was just a different one—mass consumerism.

Some of us may think we're above all this, but deep down we are lustful creatures. And this has a huge impact on our behavior across the board. Everybody wants to feel sexy. Most everybody wants to feel romance. But life takes us on unpredictable paths, and many of us get interested in kink. The reasons vary markedly. Some just naturally love it. Others drift into it as the result of some trauma or problem associated with their sexuality. Kink often becomes a way to discover something very deep inside, by first validating your own feelings and sexuality.

I hadn't planned to find connection in lust and kink over romance, but I'm just going with what delivers results. I had lived with a Monoculture Virus that created an upside-down world, so it's not surprising I became much more successful and happier when I flipped things around for a change. Kink is toxic to the Virus, as it's a big middle finger to the system. When I was younger, I found my heavy metal guitar playing to be an essential tool for emotional and spiritual survival. But metal guitar started losing much of its power after my teenage years. With kink, I can continue and fully extend my middle finger to the system. The system no longer has the power to control me and make me feel like another brick in the wall, or a loser if I behave differently. When I put my sex mask on, I'm changing the rules. I've learned to love the lust because it replaces my broken romantic heart, and kink is my way of living through that.

The mask of Kink

There's nothing like putting on a mask to feel sexy. For me it's the makeup and hair plus stockings, garters, heels, leather, and preferably something very tight and elastic. I'm hijacking the commercial tools of fashion and sexuality and seeing what I can do with it on my own terms.

The first few times you put on that mask, you are afraid yet excited to see what it unleashes within you. Take the shame life has created deep within you, transform it into excitement, and renormalize it, removing the infection causing your shame and hampering your spirit from evolving. The first step to being fabulous is to embrace everything you are. Feel part of the natural flow of things and be proud of who you are in your entirety. Exorcise those demons, even if you need to become one for a while. This is evolution trying to burst out of you. This is a hidden part of the real you, heretofore frustrated from satisfying your natural curiosity and passion. Find what that really is. Find the deep meaning in all feelings, good and bad. Embrace it and take back your power and joy. Flush out that feeling of being judged. Retire that victim. Be a leader in your life. Consider the mask as a way to shield your eyes from the monster and to release what has been locked up within you for way too long.

Sound crazy? Well, you don't really know unless you've tried it, just like you can't describe what chocolate or pizza tastes like. And then of course you may discover how you can integrate this new treat into your life—a little reward, stress relief, meeting like-minded people, or going deeper into the craft. At the very minimum, get rid of that nagging and distracting dark curiosity and the accompanying shame for being curious. Once you try kink or BDSM, you might not want to stop. And it just might help better prepare you for operating more effectively in the *actually perverted* real world, especially if you're interested in politics.

Addicted pervert or freedom?

Am I now fabulous, or am I a sick, twisted addict? Some of my friends wonder why a smart and worldly person like me would want to descend into this filth. I find looking down on kink ironic, as there is far more perversion in Washington and the halls of corporations than anything in kink. Kink is about honesty, trust, and respect vs. polite, clean, and proper society, which is often really about deceit and manipulation. I also find it very interesting that many involved in kink are also involved in political and corporate power games, and there are plenty of kinksters willing to oblige them. The power dynamics of kink are consistent with those environments. Why is that? If you really want to know, try it for yourself.

However, we should remember to channel some of our new kink-inspired confidence and energy into work and creative projects. It's easy to get caught up in the endless pursuit of trying to find that one porn video you missed that hits the bull's eye of some new kink. Or get endlessly caught up in going to kink parties or surfing online kink websites, hoping to find that one party you've missed, that sexual Shangri-La that has an endless supply of new crazy, kinky, fun, cool, and sexy people who love your particular kink.

I ended up at many sex parties and orgies, which at first was pretty exciting . . . taking it all in and meeting all these people. But ultimately, many of the people either weren't interested in my sexuality and kink and vice-versa, or they were really gross. I've had really yucky guys chase me around and not leave me alone to the point where I had to leave. So much for that fantasy. Various kink websites looked like said Shangri-La. I was hoping to find some new kink parties on some of these sites, but I found probably 90% of the people on these sites lived in far off places and were bored, looking for action online. The SF kink groups had very few people who lived in SF, sigh. I like the idea of chiming in to add to the excitement, but trying to meet people this way gets old after a while and can suck hours out of your life with no end in sight.

But living a kink life does come in handy because you can be more selective because you're not desperately lonely and no longer incessantly curious. I don't suffer from FOMO[70]. I'm more confident and can focus more on what I want. When I was just The Dude, I had to take whatever crumbs were available to me. My new life is a hugely different way to live. It's spiritually fulfilling and relaxing.

The obvious question is: Doesn't this hamper my opportunity to have a relationship with a woman as a man? No. I can only tolerate so much boredom, futility, and rejection in online dating. I can only tolerate so much being invisible when I go out to events, parties, and the local bar. I need to be whole and confident first, and then that other stuff will either come or it won't.

I would eventually try to find my way back to the romance, but in the meantime, what happened to *Under the Golden Gate* after our Kink palace shut down?

Why I wound down Under the Golden Gate

We had our day in the sun, but it was hard to stay motivated without the venue, and it took a huge amount of effort to sustain *Under the Golden Gate*. Our fans wanted us to keep going, but I was exhausted from what was almost a full-time job, especially the enormous amount of video editing I had to do. I was also unable to create any new music or writing during this time, and I was hankering to do that. So, after four and a half years of producing the show, I decided to shut it down. To this date, seven years from when we started, the site has about one million down-

---

70. Fear of Missing Out

loads. I'm so grateful for having so many interesting artistic friends we pulled in to create these videos, our fabulous guests, and for my co-host, Dank. We had a great run, creating over seven hundred videos covering the lives, activism and art of hundreds of *real* San Franciscans who make this unique city weird and fabulous. I had achieved my objective of capturing a lot of the richness, variety, lifestyle, culture, and loving energy of this incredible city. And most of the material is timeless as it focuses on people's lifestyle, motivations, and deep intimate feelings related to their sexuality.

I was ready for the next step on my journey, which was to see where this new sexual power could take me. I was still out of balance. The Dude was trying to control me instead of being my partner. I had been working really hard on the show, and it was time to go back to the fun and remind The Dude that a life without the proper amount of love and sensuality was not a life. And *Under the Golden Gate* had a few cannabis sponsors, so I was now getting enough free samples to fill an entire drawer in my filing cabinet. I was in even more trouble. I had done the drugs, I had done the rock n' roll, but I hadn't quite done enough of the sex to ensure these three were in balance. It was time to ramp up the sex. I had plenty of the sex wonder drug cannabis to lube me up, and I had a new set of skills and renewed confidence. Watch out!

PART 5

TO WORSHIP THE DICK

CHAPTER 21

STARTING IN THE GRAY ZONE

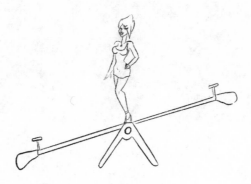

Now that I was ready for some real fun, The Dude was no match for me. I had dabbled in the Dick, but I still worshipped the female. Now it was high time for me to try worshipping the male and see what more I could learn about being a woman. My new trek started with a few women in between the sexes. And they oiled up my slippage towards the other team as soon as a bump in the road set off the powder keg that had been filling up.

A dominatrix and a swing

As with so many other super sexy people I met, what *really* drew me to Eve Minax was that she was a delightful and open person. And when I showed up at her house, I was even more impressed with her set of tools. The pots, pans, skillets, knives, and other equipment in her kitchen were all professional grade and, damn, could she cook. I asked her about the spiral staircase in the corner of the living room. She responded, "That's where the dessert is." We had a wonderfully pleasant conversation while

I tasted several of her delectable creations. And then it was time to descend down the spiral staircase into the dungeon.

Wow, I had arrived. What a room! I felt like I was in the showroom of a kink store.

We first sat on the yellow chairs on the left and just chatted about life, what I was into, how I got into it, what I had tried, and what I was still fantasizing about. Then she asked what I wanted to do. There was no doubt I was getting in that swing, and I was going to get fucked. Eve showed me some items I might want to wear—a rubber garter belt, a rubber corset with metal rings, and one helluva set of kinky five-inch heels. The dominatrix experience is based on the relationship with your dominatrix. This wasn't some dark, impersonal, sleazeball encounter. This allowed me to feel really free and comfortable sharing all that really dark shit on my own terms. And all while she was to tie me up on that swing, completely dominate me, and satisfy both sides of my sexuality—the Dick and the ass. The boy and the girl.

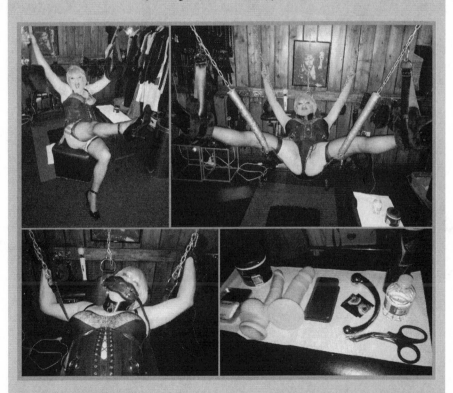

SORDID DETAILS

When Eve got me up on that swing and put my feet and then hands into the restraints, I entered a whole new headspace of heaven. Just wiggling around while restrained, becoming one with the motion of the swing was like I just discovered a new religion. And I felt totally comfortable because of the time I spent chatting and hanging out with Eve.

Next thing I knew her expert hands were working with all kinds of tools on my male and female sides, giving me all kinds of new feelings and combinations of pain and pleasure in harmony with the motion of the swing. I would have tried meditating in this new spiritual space, but she was keeping it too hot for that. After about twenty minutes of heaven, I did something I have never done before or since—I ejaculated prematurely. She had something up my ass, and I'm not even sure how she got it in there without pain. The orgasm had built slowly, in such perfect harmony with our motion I didn't believe it was an actual orgasm. I didn't say anything because I didn't want the ride to stop. I wondered if she knew . . . of course she did, but I pretended that she didn't know, and we kept going for a bit longer. Finally, it was starting to hurt too much, and just moments before I was going to tell her to stop, Eve said, "It looks likes maybe you want to take a break or stop?" She could tell what I wanted without me saying anything. That's a pro.

When we finished, I was all giggly. I felt like I had just graduated into a new world. We hung out for a little bit, and then I went home in a wide-eyed daze, thinking about endless possibilities. Over the next year or so, Eve and I hung out just as friends numerous times. She had a great outdoor deck, and we went out there several times and talked about the stars, the universe, and life. She also put me in handcuffs several times, and pinched and teased me while I couldn't use my hands. I was very apprehensive at first because I really had to learn about trust—these were hardcore thick stainless steel handcuffs! I enjoyed having that personal connection and bonding experience with an unusual woman I really respected and liked. I loved her confidence, strength, independence, entrepreneurial mindset, and love of her craft. She was so different from most other women I met who were caught up in the usual rat race.

I preferred to hang out with her as The Dude, but she wanted to see me as a girl, putting makeup on me and giving me some girly clothes to wear. I felt strange doing that, because I'm very binary. I'm either in man or woman mode. And when I'm with a woman, I prefer to be a guy. But she saw me as a woman. This was the case with a lot of women Maria

was to get close to, which really irritated me. I wasn't offended or mad, I was more confused and disappointed. I didn't say anything because I really enjoyed hanging out and cuddling. But that connection I craved so much with women was only achievable to me when I was a girl. Sigh.

I was also a little confused because I knew she earned a living being a dominatrix. I had paid her for only that first session, and I wasn't sure if she was looking for me to eventually pay her for another session. I never bothered to ask. I just avoided that question, figuring I would find out sooner or later. I started feeling attached to her in a very ambiguous way, letting it just roll. However, The Dude couldn't stop being a dude and wanted to hang out with her as a straight couple, even though I knew she was more into sexually fluid people who had a big female component. The Dude invited her to go to Hawaii. She agreed, but she didn't follow through on coordinating with me. I wasn't sure if it was because she was just busy, or she wasn't comfortable with what she sensed The Dude wanted. The whole thing was too full of ambiguity and confusion, and at the time I needed my conscious to be free from complications because it was time for Maria to really let things rip. I let our relationship fizzle out despite how much I deeply enjoyed it, but my time with Eve was one of the highlights of this journey.

M2F post-op[71] transsexual intimacy

When I first met Diane, she worked as a boy in a professional job but lived as a girl off hours. At the time, she was taking female hormones and had small breasts, but hadn't had any surgeries. She was a pre-op transsexual. She and Maria were initially just platonic girlfriends, but we started hanging out more with me as The Dude. Then she asked The Dude out on a date. I was surprised, but excited because I really liked her. But The Dude had never been on a date with a t-girl. I felt a little

---

71. A M2F (Male-to-Female) "Post-Op" transsexual refers to a man who has transformed into a woman and has had his penis converted into a vagina with surgery.

uncomfortable, but I didn't let that stop me. We were both were part of the trans community, and both understood and respected living as both sexes and all the insight, openness, and complication that comes with it. So, our relationship was very natural and easy going. We went to a wine bar that had great little food dishes. I really enjoyed the flirting, smiling, and innuendo on a first date, especially when I knew we were going to end up in bed together that evening.

Back at my place, we made out and got naked, except she kept her tool tucked away in her panties the whole time. I really enjoyed making out. She was very feminine, but the smell, the skin tone, the feeling of her breasts, the quality of the voice, didn't feel natural to The Dude. But we were having fun, and I wanted to be with her. I wasn't a stranger to new things that made me uneasy.

SORDID DETAILS

We did a bunch of dry humping on the bed, pretending I was fucking her from behind. That was super-hot. Dry humping is useful in this confusing and ambiguous world of alternative sexuality. I got her so fucking hot, she rolled over, grabbed me, pulled down my pants and started giving me a blow job with no condom. She fucking loved it, and it showed. Trans women give the best blow jobs. I should know. She was going up and down with her whole body, working it with both hands. Often, it's hard to cum when you get a blow job without playing with yourself at least a little. Not with Diane going at it. She wanted that cum more than any other woman I had ever been with. Very impressive.

The best part is when your body quivers, your back curves, you lose your focus, your brain gets a little foggy, and then you feel it about to explode. Diane started going in rhythm with the waves of my body. I looked down and saw an animal who knew she was going to get her prey. I could hear her breathing getting harder as she anticipated that explosion of cum into her mouth. I grabbed her head and arm and she went even faster. I grabbed her harder and BAM! I unloaded my juice into her mouth. Super fucking hot. She breathed harder and kept going up and down while I was cumming. After I was done unloading, she sat there for about two minutes with my wet dick in her mouth. She wanted to savor every drop, which she swallowed with huge breaths of joy. Holy shit, that was the best blow job I ever had . . . damn steaming fucking hot!

When she finally opened her mouth, she said, "That's it, I'm *worshipping* the Dick from now on. I'm done with being a guy. I'm a woman. I'm going to *worship* Dick for the rest of my life." *Yea, my dick is helping her change her life!* At that moment, I was literally thinking like both a man and a woman. The Dude was like, *Fuck yea! That's was so fucking hot, and helping to convert a trans to being a woman!* Yet the girl inside of me was curious and jealous. Maria also thought it was hot and couldn't get the idea out of her head that she wanted to try that, too. Such a complicated life!

Damn that was fucking epic! But here's the best part. After we were done, I told her I wanted her to see a porn video I thought she would like.

The video was of post-operative transsexual Danielle Foxx getting her new pussy pounded by a guy while her legs were up in the air. Danielle was screaming like she had completely lost herself and found a new religion of pleasure. The look on Diane's face was priceless. Her jaw dropped with her eyes wide open. She was speechless. I stoked the fire and said, "This can be you. After a hard day of work, no matter how good or bad it is, you can get fucked like this every night for the rest of your life." She stared at me, still speechless. I had never seen a look like that. *Wow, I think she really liked it.* I had a sense that this was pretty epic for her, but I dismissed that as just my own projection.

I kissed her goodnight and she left, both of us eminently satisfied. Diane wanted to keep seeing me. But I was unsure of what to do, because The Dude had a chemical and psychological resistance to being with a trans woman. At the time, I really wanted to date genetic women because I was just wired to be more attracted to them. It's simply my truth. I didn't know what to do. I was pissed off that I could be with a trans woman and not a genetic woman, and I was in a funk over it. How would I explain my hesitation? Since I knew her so well, I just told her the truth.

Train wreck.

I'm not proud of it, but it's the truth. In retrospect, I should have gone out with her a few more times. At this point in my life, I now see that the compatibility we had in lifestyle, attitudes, and our friendship was so important that I should have explored it.

We ended up not speaking with each other for over two years.

Two and a half years later...

I got a text from Diane saying, "Guess what I just got." "A new car?" I asked. "No, a new pussy." Holy shit! I didn't think she would go through with that. She never said anything to me. I knew a lot of trans girls, some of whom had the full operation, but it was still pretty rare. So, we set up a date.

I met Diane for dinner, and she came over my place for some fun. I was really nervous. I had never been with a post-op transsexual woman. She was still not fully recovered, so she warned me we probably couldn't do full penetration.

SORDID DETAILS

The time came. She pulled down her panties and there it was. At first, I didn't know what to make of it. It was a vagina, but her scars were still healing, and I wondered if I could see where the penis was folded into a vagina.

I must admit, it took me a while to take it in. *Okay, game on!* I started fingering her. It actually felt like a very tight vagina. Pretty cool. I was feeling around for a clitoris or the equivalent, but since she was still healing, I had to be very careful and couldn't probe around too much. I pressed my cock against her pussy and put it in a little bit, but with the tightness and healing, I couldn't do much. We got each other off, and then happily laid in bed chatting.

Here's the crazy thing. I asked Diane when was the moment when she had decided to have the sex change. Diane laughed. "When you showed me that Danielle Fox video." I remembered that look in her eyes and her jaw dropping, and now *my* jaw dropped. She smiled, "Yup." We both understood exactly why, and she knew this was something I could relate to. I was instrumental in her following through on her dreams, something I thought about in my dreams, more as a fetish than anything else, but she actually did it. I remembered how I felt when she sucked my cock a few years earlier and screamed how she was going to worship the Dick. Well she was here to stay for sure.

I saw her a few more times. I even sent her the Danielle Fox video, and that really turned her on. But both wanting to fuck her and my curiosity about Maria following her path—coupled with my binary view of my two sexualities—scared me. Our intimate relationship fizzled out again, but this time we stayed friends. She eventually got married to a guy. I went to their wedding.

I thought about what Cassandra Cass and Laverne Cox said about straight men being in love with trans women in private but being afraid to date trans women publicly. I wondered if I was guilty of the same thing. On one hand, it's different because I'm trans, but I still wasn't comfortable with that kind of long-term relationship. I didn't know if it was the way my body is wired or if it was my fear. I've been around the block more since then, and I've really groked the importance of having a connection with somebody, especially since I'm not very compatible with the average women because of my unusual my life and attitudes. Over time, physical traits become less important, and I think I would have been happy with Diane.

But The Dude and Maria were about to start duking things out, and it would be difficult to be in a relationship until they settled matters. The Dude thought he had an advantage because our body wasn't wired for the Dick. But Maria knew she had the upper hand because of her power to consistently generate sexy excitement. She was just waiting for an excuse to make her move.

CHAPTER 22

LEARNING TO LOVE THE DICK

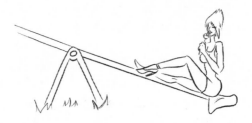

Frustrated into finally tasting cum

The Dude wanted to date women, but he wanted romance and passion with somebody who was also a good friend. Good luck, Dude. How many years will that take? The Dude had a few more agonizing experiences with dating. After the power of Maria, it was too much to stomach. So, Maria convinced me The Dude was jinxed. I thought maybe I am a girl—maybe this romantic thing inside of me is just fairytale nonsense.

After a girl I dated a few months dumped me, I had to run away from the humiliation. I couldn't stop thinking about how much my trans friend Diane loved sucking Dick and the freedom she felt after deciding to "worship the Dick." What did cum taste like? What did it feel like? What's all the fuss that women seem to be gaga over the Dick about? What could be so good that so many people would shun romance and connection and do other crazy things to get? I had learned about the power of dressing as a woman, but this was clearly way beyond that. I had to try this drug. I had to continue this journey. It will be humiliating, but I was being humiliated anyway. *Let's try doing it on my own terms. Simple hot sex with guys with no complexity and bullshit, I love the idea!*

And then I had an epiphany. I could do this. I could convert this fantasy of having a guy cum in my mouth into reality that week if I wanted! I could be just like those t-girls in the porn videos having a load of cum shot into their mouth and feeling it drip down my chin

And then I felt that sinking feeling in my stomach. *I'm going to do this.* With the snap of my finger, I made the decision. *Kill that humiliated loser dude right now. I don't need women, fuck them. I'm going to find out what it's like to be a girl just like you. What a ride this is going to be.*

It took exactly two days to get what I wanted. How do you like that?! The Dude would have spent years trying to get what he wanted, but Maria got it in two days.

I had given several blow jobs but always with a condom, except with that safe nerdy guy who was so limp nothing happened. I had been extra cautious, as I didn't want to suck raw dick while I was still trying to date woman, but no worries on that anymore. The time had arrived when I was truly ready to try on being a fucking slut. I took out an ad on *Craigslist*, and by *the end of the evening* I had a tryst with Pete set up for two evenings later!

As I was getting dressed for the big evening, I was so excited because I knew I was going to have some crazy fucking sex and find out what cum tastes like. Watching women suck dick in porn videos and then having guys cum in their mouth is so gross that's it's super fucking hot, because it's so wrong. And I was really needing something wrong. I figured I probably wouldn't like it, but I'd be glad I gave it a shot.

It was time to break out the bong so I could feel nice and ethereal as I put on a hot garter belt, stockings, huge heels, a sexy waist cincher, a lacy bra, and a very sheer see-through top. And of course, heavy makeup and dick-sucking lips.

Pete was around forty years old and had a girlfriend, but he wanted something different. Don't they all? The magnum-size cannabis charges from the bong helped make me feel like a woman, so I was ready for flirting and gunning for slut sex. It had been a while. And he was ready for action. *Damn, I forget how fucking easy this is with guys. No courting, talking about emotional problems or ex-boyfriends. Just sex. No comparison. I like this!*

SORDID DETAILS

The time I feared finally came. As we stood in my kitchen, glasses in hand, Pete pushed his balls up against me. I still wasn't used to that. It was a gross and scary feeling many young boys know all too well—that feeling when one of their friends accidently presses up against them. And there is a flash of gay fear and feeling like a sissy in front of the girls that causes most boys to recoil. But I now *wanted* to be a sissy, so now I embraced this fear and unease. I was so stoned and drunk, I grabbed his balls and led him to the bedroom to complete my mission.

He went straight for the edge of the bed, unzipped, and pulled it out for me while still standing up. *Oh, cool—he's all shaven and cut.* I knelt and went down on him. I just stared at the head of his partially erect cock and thought *I can't believe I'm fucking going to do this.* I grabbed his hip with one hand and his dick with the other. It felt like warm rubber. I opened my mouth and slowly extended my tongue and curled it around the head of his cock. When it landed on his flesh, it didn't at first taste like much, just that slightly salty taste. So, I was mostly in my own head thinking how I had a cock in my mouth and was about to finally be a true girl. I started moving my head up and down the head of his cock. Still that same slightly salty taste, so I was still just mainly *thinking* about what I was doing. *I'm giving a fucking blow job, just like a girl.*

And then everything changed. His dick started growing in my mouth, and I tasted something really sweet. The sweetness came in little spurts. What the fuck is that? *I kind of like this new thing.* Then his dick started expanding in my mouth as he started moaning louder. *This is actually pretty hot. Holy shit, I think I do like this.*

Pete then abruptly grabbed the back of my head and shoved his now rock-hard cock into the back of my throat. *Whaaaat . . . this feels so rude.* I started to gag, *but damn, this is what it's like to give a blow job? This is what girls do? Fucking rad.* I didn't care about the gagging. I wanted to know what it felt like to be a slut. And more of that sweet taste came out of his dick. I realized that sweet taste must be precum! I'd heard about it, but wow . . . the more I sucked, the hotter it got. I didn't expect this! *Am I a girl?*

It crept up on me . . . I was deep throating him! I was shocked that I quickly gravitated to using my throat to give him head! This is *so* much better without a condom. He started screaming, and I kept going, ignoring the occasional gag and saliva & mucous dripping out of my mouth.

This was just too hot! Then I locked both my hands with his, which I never did before. That was super erotic, handholding a guy while I was deep throating his cock. And I very quickly learned how to get that dick even harder by finding a new angle, pausing and changing the motion. *Fucking slut I am. Damn, porn is so boring compared with this. This is fucking real.* And I was making another person happy.

I paused and Pete laid back on the bed. I was still on my knees when I started up again with a fresh angle. After just a few minutes I felt his body start to quiver and tighten. I knew what that meant, I had been there with Diane on that very same bed a few years earlier. But this time I was the one with the Dick in my mouth. I knew my doing this was inevitable. *I'm going to do what Diane did! I'm going to worship the Dick and in just a few moments, I'm going to know what it tastes and feels like to have a guy cum in my mouth. I will no longer be a virgin. There will be no going back. I'm going to join the Dick club any second!* This thought fueled me even more and I started grabbing his ass as I got into a rhythm with his thrusting.

He started screaming. *Any second, I'm going to feel it and I'm going to taste it. Suck that dick, make him cum in your mouth, you fucking slut!* I felt alive! I felt hot! His body tightened even more. I felt some kind of huge vein or something in his cock get really engorged, his whole body spasmed, and then I felt this warm taste in my mouth . . . *whaaaaaat?!* I'd never tasted anything like it. It tasted like mucous mixed with warm hydrogen peroxide, slightly bubbly with a slightly metallic taste. It had a very strange aroma, and it caused little tingles on my tongue. And he kept pumping more of that goo into my mouth as his body spasmed in rhythm with my stroking. *So slippery, fucking shit wild hot!* I kept thinking about how I was now just like Diane. *Oh shit, I really do like this!*

That was it for me. *Holy fucking shit, this is the nastiest, hottest thing I've ever done and the sexiest and happiest I've ever felt. My god, I love semen. I'm definitely going to do this again. Fuck, I didn't expect this. I could choose to do something that in a few seconds would cause me to lose myself and change my whole identity. Sign me up.*

I found myself pressing my cock up against the bed, essentially masturbating with the taste of warm cum in my mouth. *Fuuuuuck yea! Seeeeeex!* And I didn't hesitate to swallow all that cum after swirling it around my mouth, taking in joy of being a woman. And just like Diane, I took his whole shaft deep into my throat and wiggled around a little bit while I swallowed the last of the semen, waiting for him to relax.

I pulled his dick out of my mouth and I had to say it. "I love worshipping the Dick." He let out pints of air from his lungs and said, "Wow, that was the best blow job." *Yes! I did it. And I crushed it! I knew it! I knew I could do this! And girls will never want me now, and I don't have to worry about them anymore, I'm free!*

I was glad Pete left pretty quickly, but not before saying he wanted to see me again soon. Damn, that was the best date I'd *ever* had, and it was so simple! After he left, I laid on the couch and started jerking off to this new sensation with the taste of cum still in my mouth. I thought about the cum in my stomach, and I could have sworn I could feel little sperm swimming around in my body making me feel all tingly. I really liked that. I mean, I *really* liked it. Oh shit, I didn't expect this. *Oh shit, I want this easy sex, I'm a fucking slut. I need to try this again. I'm in trouble. I need to see where this goes, this power, this experimentation. New sex, new power, new rules! And I can keep doing it regularly. I'm not a loser guy who has to wait another five years for sex. I can get all dressed up and really make it happen on a regular basis. I can use this for stress relief and a regular regimen of fun. What is life going to be like now? I can live a sex life. Me! I'm a cum-guzzling slut!*

I came as I thought about him cumming in my mouth, only this time the masturbation fantasy was so much hotter. I knew what it tasted and felt like. Slut! I couldn't stop giggling because I was so happy, so free.

After I was done, I cleaned out my mouth, went back to being The Dude, and took a nice hot shower. I didn't feel any apprehension or guilt about doing this. I was so happy I had the courage to take the sex bull by the horns and do what I needed to do to get laid, have fun, and feel sexy.

The next morning as I came into the office, I saw one of the girls who worked there—a super-hot Hispanic woman with large breasts and a pretty face. She was nice enough, but The Dude was largely invisible to her—a regular source of frustration. But not frustrated anymore! I went out of my way to say hello and smile, and she smiled back. I hadn't had that simple interaction with her before. As I looked at her bra showing through her shirt, I thought to myself, *last night I wore a bra just like yours and swallowed cum, and I bet you didn't. I have cum in my tummy right now, and I bet you don't. I'm going to have more sex than you. I want to be just like you.* I felt so happy and relaxed, something I hadn't felt for a very long time.

Pete came over again about a week later. This time I was more relaxed and more aggressive. I wanted to really exercise this new power muscle I had. This time when he pressed his balls up against me, despite my natural desire to recoil, I thrust back into him. I thought about the girl at work, imagining her watching me being turned into a girl just like her as I pushed ever harder against him and then grabbed his balls. *Ew, weird. But hot—his dick is getting hard right in my hand.* We did a few shots of tequila, and back into the bedroom! *I like this. Yup, this is my new stress relief, reward, and confidence building program.*

SORDID DETAILS

More confident and bold this time, I unzipped his pants, pulled out that dick, grabbed it, and quickly worked up to deep throating him again. I was a fucking natural, varying the kind of sucking. He grew really fast this time, and I was really enjoying the precum and the whole sexcapade, because I knew what to expect. And because I was enjoying it, so was he. I wanted him to cum in my mouth again, but instead of swirling it in my mouth and swallowing it, I wanted the cum to ooze out of my mouth and drop down my chin on my chest. As I started deep throating him again, feeling his cock swell, Pete grabbed my head and started pumping it hard. *Whoa, this is nasty and rough, and I fucking love it.* Now I know why so many girls like this so much. I was gagging even more this time, the saliva & mucous was really gushing, but I powered through it, loving the sound of my own porn tryst. *I'm good, baby.*

Here it goes again! I felt his body quiver, his dick swelling, and he started screaming as the cum was about to explode. There was that warm juice with the same strange taste, but it was slightly different this time. *Wow, cool!* I now understood why many girls say they love the taste of cum, and the added bonus is that it's different each time. *How many times am I going to have to do this before I get bored of it?!*

I let his cum drop down my chin on to my chest just like the t-girls in my favorite porn shoots. I was now one of them! "Wow," Pete said again. "Another great fucking blow job!" I couldn't stop giggling. *Slut!* I wondered what I looked like. *Wait a second, I can see!* I got up and ran to the mirror in the bathroom. And there I was with my black garter belt, heels, stockings, and bra, but this time with cum all my face, chest, and bra, just like a porn slut. *Only a few days in and my dream had already come true.* I twirled the cum around in my mouth, rolling it over my tongue. I swallowed some while I looked at the cum on my face in the mirror. And this time I jerked off while looking at myself in the mirror tasting all that cum—fucking smoking hot!

I was so proud of myself. And it was scary, knowing I was going to be doing a lot more of this as I discovered where I could go with this new power and my ability to have new sexual experiences, practically on demand. Being scared is part of true excitement. I was getting ready to normalize this behavior. But did I really want to do this? I hadn't expected to *actually* enjoy it. Fuck. I was just trying it, right? But I didn't care as I realized all this fear was just programmed into me. I had damn good reasons for doing this. I was no longer a powerless loser in my sex life, and that is all that mattered to me.

Pete never came back. Most guys only come over once or twice because they stop screwing a t-girl once they got it out of their system, or because they're such horn dogs they're already on to the next t-girl. But I would soon be getting so much Dick, I just didn't care. Plus, I didn't want any attachments anyway.

Tasting the next few guys

Not too long after that, I was at Divas chatting with an older guy and then ended up in bed with him. He wanted to blow me first, ew . . . but I let him do it, waiting for it to be over. Seeing a guy suck my cock just wasn't my bag. I didn't see anything sexy about it, so I was limp as a noodle. I lied and told him I was on hormones.

SORDID DETAILS

At this point I would never give another blow job with a condom. He became the second guy to cum in my mouth. This one shot right into the roof my mouth. Wow, each blow job was so different. Crazy fun! I got up and went straight to the bathroom mirror to look at myself as I let it drip out of my mouth. *Wait, this dick juice was burning. What the fuck.* I spit it out into the sink and as I looked at the yellowish goo, I thought *what the fuck am I doing?*

I hit the mouthwash, and thankfully when I went back into the bedroom, he was already getting his pants on, ready to leave. Guys are so easy. We chatted briefly, he asked me to play a song on the piano, which was fun and then he promptly left. Another man leaving my apartment.

I hooked up with a few more guys in rapid succession. I had learned to tell the guys right before leaving the bar with them that everything about my body was an illusion—the curves, the breasts, my hair. When I would ask them, "Are you OK with that?" pretty much every guy responded, "Absolutely." They always respected that, and they knew to let me keep my bra on the whole time and to not pull my hair when I blew them, or eventually when I started having them fuck me from behind.

Each time a guy unloaded in my mouth, I felt more like a woman and felt more and more distant and protected from the humiliation of straight dating. It was so wonderful.

Vince the teacher

I was learning pretty quickly how to give great blow jobs. The best tip for giving a great blow job, is to *enjoy* it. And we t-girls enjoy it because it makes us feel like women, and we like feeling sexy. Thus, we give great blow jobs. Very simple math. But I really didn't know what I was doing. I mean, nobody had ever taught me until Vince started coming over a few times a month and giving me lessons.

SORDID DETAILS

Vince liked when I went really slow and built up. He taught me to take that big shaft in my mouth all the way, and then stop, and then rub the head around the back of my throat, and then slowly go in a little bit, and then a little more. He kept saying, "Slowly baby, yea slowly." I couldn't believe how much time I logged on that dick. Fortunately, his cum tasted good. And I began to really crave the taste of that sweet precum, occasional little blasts of sweetness as I sucked and sucked. Little rewards for a well-behaved girl.

I learned how to blow him with no hands—just using my tongue to move his cock around. He taught me to be patient while his dick got harder, then find the spot he likes, then vary between slow and fast, soft and hard, continuing to find the right spot. With each change of stroke, I felt and tasted something different. And I found some favorite positions—him lying back on the bed with my knees on the floor, me on the floor with my back against the bed and him standing up with his dick in my mouth, or me sitting on the edge of the bed with him standing up with his dick in my mouth. The most common was him on the couch with my lying on the floor sucking him off while I rubbed my hard, satin panty-covered cock on the floor, double pleasuring myself. I tried something different every time Vince came over. I got better and better at it, and he kept wanting more. And the cum load was different each time—the way it hit my mouth, the taste. I never thought I could have so much fun with another guy.

Pretty soon, after each blow job I would automatically run to the mirror. Cuddling afterward? Fuck that, I wanted to stare at myself with the cum all over my lips and chin.

I would love to include pictures of me with cum dripping out of my mouth, but that would be too crass.

I was working mostly at home, and Vince would periodically call in the middle of the day. I knew before I answered the phone there was a ninety-five percent chance I'd have another load in my mouth that afternoon. I would immediately drop the boring tech crap I was working on and get ready. I didn't feel gay at all; I guess because I was a woman. I was so happy I was having regular sex, I didn't think much about what my sexuality was. I didn't care.

SORDID DETAILS

I absolutely *loved* feeling it when it shot in my mouth. It made me feel so sexy, so unlike the loser dude. But sometimes while sucking him off, I wouldn't feel the shot of cum. Instead, all of a sudden, that unmistakable taste mixed in with all the salvia and mucous that had built up from a whole lot of sucking. I loved trying new things like having him shoot his load in my face, or at the edge of my mouth so it would drip down my chin, or shoot it up in the air where it would land back on his cock and I would lick it off his dick or swirl it on the head with my tongue just like in the movies. I was getting really good, and he was having a ton of fun and kept cumming back.

As I got more comfortable with the Dick, I got more aggressive. I loved the ritual of feeling his dick through his pants, then pulling them down and keeping his underwear on while I stroked it, waiting for it to get fully hard. Then I'd pull his shorts down, taking a big swig of a screwdriver, my standard blow job drink, and stick my tongue out to tickle and lick his dick from the head down the shaft. After a while I started going for his balls to add to the new experiences. It smelled like a gym down there, but I managed to ignore the smell because I was living my fantasy. I was now doing it just like a girl.

After he left, I would often go to a bar where I would see women and smirk to myself, *I have cum in my tummy, I bet you don't!* Pretty soon I started telling hot women I met at bars that I had cum in my stomach. I would almost always get a "Yea girl!" and a huge smile right from the depth of her soul. And now it was for real! I can't describe how fucking awesome that made me feel. I was in heaven. I was connecting with women about sex. I love girls. I couldn't believe I was one of them now! It was like I was constantly on vacation and visiting heaven.

Dick slut

After about six months in training with Vince, I was busting to try these new skills on others. It's one thing to try it a bunch of times and get better at, but yet a whole other thing when you start doing it regularly. I was normalizing dick sucking. Easily picking up guys at bars was now a regular part of my weekly routine. I wanted to know what *that* felt like. I had loved the *Sissy Maker* porn video that shows a girl with a cock in her mouth. As she smiles into the camera and opens her mouth, you can see a huge load, and a caption appears, "You're not just experimenting anymore." And I knew I wasn't alone in this fantasy because this video had millions of views. And here I was actually doing it in a world where dreams of being sexy really did come true.

I knew I was on my way when I started to lose count of the number of dicks I had sucked. It's easy to remember when you've only sucked three or four, but you start to lose track when you're pushing twenty. You're a real slut when you aren't really sure—it could be fifty or it could be eighty.

I was getting very bold. I met a t-girl at the piano bar. We went to her car to smoke a joint and much to her surprise, I blew her in the car. I had always wanted to do that. Check. It was so awesome to do something nutty with sex, and at the same time make somebody else's night. My overall confidence was going off the charts. At work, my confidence got so strong, I started doing bold things, which led to cool jobs. I also had some interesting complications because I was getting a bit too cocky.

At this point, it was all blow jobs and dry humping. I had not yet gone back to trying anal. Many t-girls had the "no penetration" rule. It was a sensible rule. Anal sex is painful, and it requires a lot more preparation[72]. It was more dangerous and required a lot of trust and skill. That's part of the experience. You also need to master the mixing of pleasure with pain. And anal requires a lot of practice and patient partners. It's also very violent. So of course, I fantasized about anal a lot because you always need the next big thing to fantasize about, right? I wanted to break that "no penetration" rule again! But it also leaves a big mess of lube and nasty stuff in the middle of your bed, so it was easy for me to put that fantasy off for now. I wasn't quite ready to try that again. I wanted to first learn to really love the Dick, become a master Dick sucker, and launch myself into the next stage of womanhood. The Dude now felt really far away from women, but I felt much closer to them, and that was perfectly wonderful.

---

72. e.g., douching and shaving

CHAPTER 23

ONE OF THE GIRLS

Now that I was a true sex queen, I was giving off a new vibe. Smoking hot young women walking down the street were stopping *all the time* and telling me, "Girl, you are so amazing. I wish I could do makeup as well as you!" "You are so put together, girl!" "I'm sure you've had so many hot guys, I'm so jealous." "Don't get pregnant." Women did that before, but now it was constant. I used to hate the shallowness of fashion, but I loved it now that I was on the other side! How ironic! And now I realized, The Dude was not in a position to judge how women use this whole fashion thing. It's like any other powerful tool. You can use it to create a wall, or you can use it to help light up the world around you. The Dude saw mostly a wall, but maybe he was just jealous?

I could really talk with women about sex now. I couldn't help but tell them how I had just wanted to *try* having a guy cum in my mouth, and I didn't expect to get hooked, but once I got my first load, that was it. Invariably their eyes would light up, and they would say something like, "Yea, gotta get that Vitamin D, girl!" Or "Yup, can't give up the D!" D?

Vitamin D? Oh, the Dick! Wow, a lot of girls referred to it as the D. Wow, a little secret code. I really was on the inside! *Hot!* The look in their eyes when they talked about how they love the D, was super crazy and new to me. I was one of them. I agreed wholeheartedly with them on something sexual while we were both smiling with fire in our eyes. *Yes!* And when I told them I was giving up dating women because I was addicted to the Dick and cum, they loved and encouraged it. Every single one of them knew exactly what I was talking about and never questioned it because they didn't understand why I would ever want to date women. They were basically welcoming me to the club.

When I would meet women at a party, bar, or club, and they asked me what I was up to, I would say things like, "Just trying to find me some Vitamin D," and they would smile and say all kinds of things. Instant bonding! One of my favorites was doing bong hits at a cannabis party. I knew this young woman and was admiring her incredibly hot body and slinky dress, wondering what kind of fun she has and what it would be like to be her and wear that hot dress. When it was my turn, I hit the bong hard and she screamed, "Suck that bong like it's a huge black cock, Maria! I know you're an expert!" I felt so honored!

Girl secrets

I couldn't believe I was talking with girls about the details of their sex lives. And I learned some secrets. I'm not sure I should be revealing this to The Dudes out there. Am I breaking some kind of code? Well, I figure if I'm unveiling a few women secrets, it's only fair I follow by unveiling a few men secrets. Maybe we'll all get to know each other a little better.

These are, of course, just general observations and should be taken with a grain of salt.

1. It really is all about the Dick

. . . for many women. My first exposure to the power of the Dick was a girl at a club who looked really upset. I went right up to her and asked her what was wrong. She liked this new guy she was dating but was really worried because her ex-boyfriend had a huge, nine-inch cock, and she was worried this new guy's cock wouldn't be big enough. The look on her face was priceless. This was a serious dilemma. You would have thought her dog died. Another girl told me her boyfriend was kind of a jerk, but she just loved the way his semen tasted. Wow. Well, guys will do all kinds of things for big boobs.

A lot of women *really* love the D. They are as obsessed with it as I was, to the point where the size of his dick, the guy's ability to use it, or how clean and tasty it is often far overshadows any interest in what was inside that guy's head. I had little interest in these men's minds and lives. It was nice if he was a little interesting, but I didn't want him to say all that much anyway. I wanted him to focus on how hot I was, as long as he was a little aggressive and wasn't a dick himself. I now understood why the Dick was so important and how casual sex was truly a major factor in driving our world. I learned to embrace that reality and not feel ashamed about having so much lewd fun. I used to think that love and romance was just about the most beautiful thing, but my frustration with the reality of the world led me to something more beautiful because it was real—raw, erotic, and kinky sex. Why not! We are suffering from overpopulation and there are plenty of babies in the world. Sex has evolved into being more of a social phenomenon and important for self-esteem. This is saving the planet.

Am I justifying my wanton behavior? Emotionally it seems that way, but in order for men to understand women, they need to know what it's like to have so many options for casual sex and how incredibly powerful and emotionally satisfying that can be when you have made the choice to not deal with the complexities of a long-term relationship. You need to experience it to grok it.

I can't attest to what it's like being a woman when you are looking for romance. But, hey, I'm halfway to understanding women. That's pretty good. For me, the fun was just awesome. I figured I would leave the romance for another time or let it happen according to the whims of God. And I was doing something important. I was giving these guys a great t-girl experience. They'll take this attitude with them and treat other people in their lives better. I was changing the world one Dick at a time.

2. Many women think men are boring idiots
. . . and many are.

Women tend to elevate themselves above men and develop a healthy, independent self-esteem. Girls often feel they lack power in their lives, so when they become women—become the ones with the power, it's natural for them to start treating guys as sex playthings, which I concur is only fair. But women often get used to this simplicity, and this emotional distance makes it very difficult for them to engage in a relationship when the rare opportunity with a great guy does comes along. It's simply easier to avoid intimacy and have fun. Of course, men have their own version of this.

I don't think women realize just how much power they have, or how fucking hard it is to be a straight guy. Women can more easily choose to forgo romance and focus on casual sex when they're in that mood, and then easily switch back to romance when the time is right.

3. Women don't want to lose great guys as friends
... so they keep them in the friend zone.

Guys all know about the dangers of the friend zone, but what is not obvious is why they get stuck there so often. It's very simple. Women have guys hitting on them all the time, they have many options. Guys don't understand that a woman usually wants to concentrate her sexual and romantic energy on one guy at a time, and the world doesn't revolve around your urges and fantasies.

Everything was now falling into place. I understood why I was such a loser dude with women. I was always very nice, but I was trying to attract women with just how clever, experienced, and funny I thought I was. They didn't care about that. I wasn't being present. I wasn't giving a proper welcoming smile. I didn't know how to focus on them and get out of my own head and romantic fantasies.

Now all my anger and frustration as The Dude started melting away. But I was caring less and less about him anyway. I *loved* hanging out with women as a woman. They were so present and nice to each other, talking about how they felt. I really respected them. That was in such incredibly stark contrast to my experience with women as The Dude when their shields were in full defense mode.

Guy secrets
Guy secrets are largely obvious, but many still find them hard to fully understand:

1. Guys are raised to view women as a piece of meat.
Your classic guy-guy talk is about how a girl has huge tits, a nice ass, or is cute. And you very rarely will hear guys talk about how cool a girl is or

the things they find interesting about her. Those who do might as well be speaking in dolphin clicks. Now, girls also talk about how boys are cute and have a nice ass or smile. But girls grow up and guys don't.

Young men especially have an uncontrollable sex drive, and it's extremely competitive for them to get laid. Combine that with their not being used to having to deal with somebody who is so different from them, and you have a powder keg of bullshit ready to go off.

2. Guys hate the rituals and having to adhere to them strips them of their real personality.

Most guys are nicer than they appear, but they are forced to say the romantic line, buy the flowers, do the dancing thing. It's a façade, so it's no surprise they have little idea how to engage with women at a deep level. Although boys can be blunt and rough, they are used to being pretty authentic with each other. They actually do want to connect with a girl, but they have been conditioned to believe they can't be themselves, which is an anathema to them. They are quite sensitive, but they have nobody to talk to about it. If they try, they are usually emotionally abused and humiliated. So, they self-destruct like the HAL 9000 computer[73].

3. Guys feel constantly judged no matter what they do.

Guys are seen as either too aggressive or not aggressive enough. They are rarely complimented or recognized for the complex nuances of finding a good balance, so they become extremely defensive at any whiff of criticism, constructive or otherwise. They're not used to taking anything in stride, because we have a culture of perfection. If the price we pay for being imperfect is nothing but excessive reprimands, we will naturally develop fearful and defensive behavior. Women have to face this too, but they appear to be affected less because it's okay for a woman to express her emotions. When a guy expresses his emotions, he's labeled as naïve or a whiner.

4. Guys fall right into the groove of a male-dominated world.

Our work environment is still very male-oriented, especially in a power job. Feminine values such as caring about what you're doing, thinking

---

73. In *2001: A Space Odyssey*, the computer went berserk because he was forced to lie, which was against his programming.

about how your actions affect people, and asking complex questions is shitted on as a matter of course. Guys end up disrespecting the "feminine" because it causes them a lot of pain, and instead focus on the "male" qualities of competition and easily measurable results.

5. Guys being inattentive and clueless is usually because they settled for someone.

Women often complain that guys are clueless and inattentive. If a guy was really into you, he wouldn't be inattentive. You would not care about the little infractions because he's doing so many other wonderful things. A lot of men are settling for the woman they are with. They're not excited about the relationship and fantasize about being with the one they can't have. Just about all men are fantasizing about other women, but if they are really into you, they will still be attentive. The excuse that men are just clueless is bullshit. Sure, some are actually clueless, but you shouldn't waste your time with them anyway, unless of course you want them there for just some good fucking.

I can't be that guy

After all I've learned and experienced, I would never date a guy like me. Why would I be interested in a guy who thinks really highly of himself and talks like he's putting on some kind of show, instead of being in the moment? I want him to be focused on me—to talk about passionate and sexy things. I don't want to hear about some cool trip he went on. Dude's excuse is that he is just being himself, sharing his interests, finding out more about her interests and enjoying a little fun banter, trying to find the real her. He's baffled why this doesn't seem to work like it does in other relationships. The only advice I can offer him is that women do like to talk about our interests and worldly issues, but only after we get to know each other. When guys talk to each other, they immediately jump into lofty ideas without knowing who they are talking to. I guess I don't know how to be a man with a woman. That's why I'm a woman.

And Dude could not relate to all that dirty sex Maria loved so much. Dude is probably average when it comes to his face, dick size, body tone, and guy fashion. He didn't feel like he could compete in a sexually charged world.

Dude was out of his league with most women, yet he kept saying to me, "They're so friendly, supportive, and cool. Why can't I have a close

relationship with them like you do?" He started interfering in my relationships with women again by telling them about himself. And as before, it *never* went well. Right in the middle of a great conversation with a
woman Maria was chatting with, he would tell her I'm also into girls and
would explain the frustration dating as a dude but also having the Maria
option. In every case, the girl just stared into blank space. But when I
changed the subject back to how much I loved the Dick, the smiles and
bonding would immediately return.

I finally decided I would never let The Dude do this again. This double life filled me with too much emotional clusterfucking. On one hand,
I was fabulous, but I was also a loser. And who the hell was I going to
find to empathize with me? I decided it would be a whole lot easier if Dude
went away for a while.

The Dude fought back. "Okay, but I'll just do my own straight online
dating thing while you do yours. And then when I find a great girl, we
can focus on me for a while."

"No! Dude, I need to take a break from you. Your romantic wishful
thinking and disgust at my recreational activities is cramping my style."

"No, we can both do our own thing."

"Dude, you already know how hot it is to be a girl having sex with guys,
so what woman is going to want to date you? You know their secrets. One
little frustration in the relationship, and they know you're going to drift
into fucking guys. It's just too easy and hot. You think you're going to lay
off the weed and easy kinky Maria sex and go back to being contempla-
tive and spiritual? You've been doing that your whole life, and you're sick
of it. I know you."

"But—"

"And if you don't get this out of your system now and really go for it,
it will always haunt you. We need to go full in Maria sex slut now. One
hundred percent."

Dude acquiesced. He wanted a break, too, and I got him with *get this
out of your system now*. I knew him better than he thought.

So, I was going into uncharted territory. Dickland. I clicked my heels
and snapped my fingers, and I was done with Dude's shit. I was going to
live a simple and clear life. I was on a mission to feel even *more* like a girl.

I hired a designer to go through my closet and give me ideas for outfits. The girl clothes had taken over my huge walk-in closet, pushing The
Dude's clothes into a little corner. She took special notice of my large

collection of kinky lingerie. She said, "Oh, I bet you're having a lot of fun with this," and there was that huge-eyed sister sex smile. Priceless. I was in my sex closet talking to a smoking hot woman in tight jeans. The Dude would love to fuck her, but here I was instead talking with her about the kind of clothes I should wear on dates with guys, and how to best switch to the lingerie when it was time to have sex. Indeed!

After she left, I stood in that closet and practically cried thinking how happy a girl I was. I rubbed against the silky clothes and happily dreamed about all the dates and the gobs of cum that would soon be dripping on some of these clothes. This was no fantasy. I had the power to actually get what I wanted. Guys, do you have idea how awesome this is?

CHAPTER 24

LIVING THE DICK LIFE

Barfly

When Maria hung out at a place like Divas, if a decent looking guy so much as smiled at me, there was a ninety-five percent chance I was going to end up in bed with him. If a girl smiled at The Dude, that number was less than zero-point-one percent. Actually The Dude *never* picked up a girl in a bar. And Maria didn't even have to try. I got all this by simply being my fabulous self and having fun. The Dude is fabulous, but just doesn't project it. He does it in his own way with humor and wit, but that doesn't work in a loud bar, or even at a party.

I was getting laid so much, I thought this must be a lucky streak. This can't go on forever. But it did. There is an endless amount of Dick out there. It was ridiculous. I never experienced anything like it. I couldn't believe women had it this easy. It was not that unusual for me to fuck two guys in one night. One guy would come over early, usually a fuck buddy. I would go out all happy and satisfied, and then I would meet another guy without even trying and fuck him, too. Being a girl is *a lot* of fun.

My online dating profile pics—I quickly threw these mediocre pics into my online profile and they immediately generated swarms of men. Unlike the Dude who crafted his online profile pics and got crickets or Russian prostitutes.

Online was a good supplement to the clubs, contributing about twenty-five percent to my bounty. Dealing with flakes, bots, and guys who just wanted to chat online with a t-girl but had no intention of meeting was annoying, but I learned how to filter most of these out. I ignored anybody who sent a dick pic or spoke like a pig right out of the box, whose chat was simple one-liners, and anyone who wasn't willing to meet at a bar first. I would also tell them my preferences before we met. No, I'm not going to fuck you in the ass, and I don't have breast implants, so I need to keep my bra on to hold the pads. Surprising, only a very few fell out from that[74]. The Dude never had a chance to learn what worked online, because he didn't have the volume I had.

After I met a guy online and he made it through my filter, we would meet in person at Divas. Surprisingly, they were almost always good look-

---

74. I did have that clearly stated in my profile, but you had to double check. About eighty percent of men I met in clubs wanted to fuck me, but about twenty percent wanted me to fuck them.

ing enough, and I didn't have to do anything else to know if they wanted action. If they went to this effort, I was getting laid. The few times a guy didn't show up, I picked up another one or had my usual fun barhopping or dazzling tourists. In one case, I was in the mood for a black guy. I found a black guy online, and he didn't show up to our rendezvous. No problem. I headed to Divas on my way home to see if I could find another black guy. And yup, I walked up to a muscular black man at the bar and smiled. He gave me a big smile back and started flirting, and ten minutes later we were headed back to my place.

And the most incredible part was they contacted me *en masse* online after I had posted just two rough pictures and a simple introduction. I also find it titillating that thousands of guys probably see me as this mysterious sexy trans woman. They've probably created untold number of fantasies about who I am and have jerked off to my pictures. How do I know this? Ask The Dude. I do appreciate I'm providing such a service. And I may live forever in some distributed database of favorite online trans woman pics guys download for easy access when they find those precious moments to jerk off. I wonder how many different fantasy versions of who I am are out there and if any of them are even close to who I really am.

However, I only now realize that they *were* seeing me the real me. They were seeing a sexy outside being driven by my inner fabulousness. And the more fun I was having, the more interest I got. *Maybe I should consider doing this permanently.*

Okay, so I'm a slut

Mission accomplished!

But I'm not a bitch. Well, I'm a bitch when a difficult but critical situation can only be resolved by a bitch. And I'm an effective bitch, because this bitch has the inside information and tools of The Dude at her disposal.

The Wikipedia definition:

> **Slut** is generally a term for a woman or girl who is considered to have loose sexual morals or who is sexually promiscuous.

I'm not clear if promiscuous is necessarily a bad thing, and if so, what in particular is bad about it? I'm not proud being a slut *per se*. But I'm proud of having the courage to go where the opportunity presented itself in order for my soul to survive. I'm proud of having the wherewithal to discover more deeply the one aspect of our humanity that clearly dominates all others. I'm intrigued by the irony of doing exactly the opposite of my natural romantic desires to find a divine connection. I'm a proud slut. Embracing the slut allows me to understand and deal with the real world. Sex and eroticism are the roots of not just biology, but also energy and ideas. Who am I to argue? Nature has been doing this for billions of years, and that's why we're all here.

Becoming a slut crept up on me. I was so busy seeking experiences and variety that made me feel more like a girl and buried my frustrations as a dude that I forget just how many guys I was sleeping with. Here's the rating system:

- **Bronze:** You lose count of the number of guys you fucked.
- **Silver:** You realize you've slept with way more guys than the average female has in her lifetime.
- **Gold:** You have no idea how many guys you've slept with.
- **Platinum:** You're confident the number is over a hundred.
- **Platinum Plus:** You reach the one-thousand threshold, which is a different league. I know plenty of members of that club.

It really didn't sink in until I hit **Silver**—I was so proud. I also have fucked more guys in one month than the average woman does in her whole life. I'll take being a **Gold** slut over being a loser any day of the week.

The best compliment I ever got *in my life* was from a guy I had just blown. As he was putting on his shirt, he said, "Maria, you give the best blow jobs. They should make a bronze statue of you sucking dick." I was so touched, I almost cried. And he got around with both women and t-girls, so he was a credible source.

That really boosted my confidence, but I still couldn't shake the idea that this was way out of my character. So I needed to keep going until feeling sexy being myself, making people happy, and feeling like a women *did* feel in character. It had taken about five years after moving to San Francisco to get used to the idea that it was okay to simply be me. Maybe this would take another five years. I needed a new relationship with the

Dick. I felt like a teenage girl, discovering how much fun boys can be and how I could uncover a new creative power that I would use for the rest of my life.

I wasn't just a slut, I was a *cum* slut! I had been familiar with that term as a guy, but I didn't really grok what it meant until:

SORDID DETAILS

I started getting load after load squirted into my mouth, each a slightly different experience and taste. *Wow, some girls do this all the time?* It was an elixir, a secret potion I craved. Not because I was into guys. Cum is gross. But when I tasted that nectar in my mouth, it was so nasty and unusual—it took away my depression from being a useless and desperate man, and it was so easy to get. It was like a magic drug. It made me feel like a woman. It made me feel young, as I was learning something so many young women learn.

That slippery cum just kept me sliding down that slippery slope. No matter how stressful or rough my day or week was, I would look forward to pleasure and relief—being dominated and then getting on my knees in humiliation and into my alternative world where the rules were completely different. I was *choosing* to be dominated and humiliated, and that's real power.

When I saw a woman I couldn't have, I'd think about the nasty flavor of cum. About swishing it around in my mouth and licking my lips with it and swallowing it, especially as I looked at myself in the mirror. I would also have fantasies that a woman I really liked who rejected The Dude accidentally comes into a back room where I'm blowing a guy in the dark. Just as he unloads, she turns on the lights and screams as she discovers I'm secretly a cum slut. I'm not just some lame ass guy, but a sexual person. These kinds of scenarios have better plots than most of the movies out there, are much cheaper, and don't require popcorn and candy.

I sucked off one guy who was married with kids and hadn't had a blow job in fifteen years:

SORDID DETAILS

When I put my tongue on the head of his cock and started swirling it around, I'd never felt a dick grow so fast in my mouth before. For each in and out I did, his whole body tightened, as he squeezed my shoulders. That didn't last long because in just a few minutes, he said, "I know it's too soon, but I just can't help it!"

I love the moment I know that load is coming. I felt that tight muscle wave, and I could feel it coming out before it hit my mouth. He grabbed the back of my head and shoved his dick in hard, and as I pressed the head of his cock against the back of my tongue, he exploded with the most unbelievably huge sweet load in my mouth. Some loads I actually feel hit my mouth, but this was the kind where I suddenly felt a ton of warm goo. So fucking gross, but I felt alive as I took in that live hot juice, and for those few precious moments, we were locked together in mutual pleasure. Totally spiritual. No amount of watching porn can prepare you for what it's really like. You have to actually do it.

"Oh God, that was so fucking awesome!" he screamed, as I swished his cum around with the head of his cock still shoved into the back of my mouth.

He was all set for several years.

Each guy and each blow job were a unique weekly experience. I had a fuck buddy who was older, but was super nice, super fun, super kinky, and super horny.

SORDID DETAILS

His dick was always hard as rock, so much it was fucking surreal. Turns out, he was the first guy I was with a who took Viagra[75]. Holy shit, being on the receiving end of Viagra. It was preposterous putting that swollen flesh pole into my mouth. It was like a gigantic, warm, rubber dildo. I couldn't believe it was alive. This was when I started to really feel I may be "gay." But it was another rite of passage into womanhood. And the more gay I felt, the more I didn't care about the tragedy of modern straight dating, so gimme that big dick!

We could go for hours trying all kinds of positions because he had a hard time cumming. But I found a way to make him always lose his load. I would sit on the floor with my back against the bed, and he would stand up and shove his cock in my mouth. And then I would grab his ass and use

---

75. I started noticing around 2016 that a lot of guys were taking Viagra.

both my arms and head to give him a rapid full shaft in and out, getting the head of his dick deep into my throat with each thrust. And it wouldn't be long before that unmistakable magical taste of cum appeared. *Girl!*

The new normal

This was becoming routine. I didn't even think about how much of a slut I was and how unusual my double life was. It was just something I did. But I wasn't a non-discriminating slut. I developed a few basic rules for guys I met at a bar:

1. I was going to act exactly as I wanted to act, something I clearly couldn't do as The Dude. Just look at the results.
2. If they touched or grabbed me without saying anything—*get lost!* I couldn't believe how many guys would do that.
3. There had to be some pleasant flirting first, and they had to show me some respect by proving they were listening to what I was saying. Once I ensured a human was in there, I was ready. I wanted to know at least a little bit who I was fucking, so that put me above most of the real sleaze, didn't it? This hopefully would also filter out guys who were really weird, on serious drugs, or dangerous. It also made the situation *a lot* less stressful and *a lot* more fun.
4. I also didn't want them to talk too much. If they acted like The Dude and talked too about themselves before I saw some kind of sexual interest, game over. Strange that The Dude just couldn't seem to do this one. Loser.

They didn't always have to make the first move. Sometimes I did because they were a little nervous. At first, I was hesitant about moving on such guys, thinking maybe they weren't interested in me. I couldn't stop seeing The Dude inside me for a while. The irony was they usually *were* interested in me but were surprised I was interested in them! It took a long time to get used to the new power structure. And what a precious moment it would be when I realized, yes, that person does want me, and pretty badly—moments The Dude very rarely got.

However, I liked waiting for them to make the first move and took huge joy and comfort in that I wasn't *expected* to do it! What a relief. What a wonderful way to live, to go out and be sexy and not have to even think about that rubbish. My favorite thing was when a man started by touching me lightly or I saw that sparkle. I'd take the flirting to the next step by touching his shoulder and saying we should have another drink. Then I would be able to read his reaction. And I then had license to go ahead and grab his cock. Well, I usually waited until just after we swallowed our first gulp of another round of drinks. I basically developed a sort playbook for getting Dick and making a lot of men very happy. Dude never had a chance to develop these kinds of mating skills.

And if they didn't show interest, I didn't care because often I could use the rest considering all the sex I was having.

What are they seeing?

Even after all those years, I was still surprised just how much these guys loved me and how hard these guys would be when I first grabbed their cock. Why did these guys want to fuck me? I didn't understand because *I* wouldn't fuck me! I had a hard time respecting these guys. What were they seeing that turned them on so much? Some guys told me they liked the edgy male/female mixture, yet others said I was all woman. But I couldn't help but feel a little disingenuous, because I still felt like I was role playing. I felt like a doll that was getting fucked. Were they just fucking the pretty, kinky doll, or were they fucking my soul?

At first, I didn't think they were seeing the real me. But I ultimately realized they *had to be*. Most of the t-girls around had surgery and hormones and were *a lot* hotter than me. Yet I was getting great guys they weren't getting. Guys would tell me I was a wonderful, fun, open person, and that's what they really liked most of all about me. To explain this, I fell back on the notion that when you reconcile how people perceive you with who you think you are on the inside, you really discover who you are:

> **When I'm The Dude**, many people just don't notice him or are turned off because, for some reason, they think he's just another annoying white dude. And since I'm clearly fabulous on the inside, the gap between these two is bizarre and hard to understand. Is it I just don't look the part, or should I chalk a good part of that up to an iron defense mechanism, straight white male privilege, and hubris?

> **When I'm Maria**, I have the opposite problem. I tend to be apprehensive about the way I look, especially when the light is too

bright. But people see fabulous Maria energy, and not the little physical imperfections I focus on. I finally realized I *was* a doll, but I was a *real* doll, the kind of compliment you give somebody you *really* like. It was hard to accept, because The Dude was so used to feeling like a miserable victim in an upside down, perverted world.

This Maria mask I was wearing was amplifying and focusing fabulous me. It took me years of this lifestyle to even realize what was going on. I had a hard time simply accepting I really was fabulous. I always believed it, but now I had proof. That fucking Monoculture Virus does a real number on us. I was having trouble reconciling The Dude and Maria, but at least Maria herself was now whole. Maybe she could teach something to The Dude.

A special relationship

I found most guys to be nice and respectful. I was surprised, because women complain about guys all the time. But many straight guys have a special fondness for t-girls. We love being women, and we've worked hard at it. So, we appreciate guys who are nice to us. And relationships with men is still new territory for many of us. I felt like an eager and playful teenager, but one who hadn't been tarnished by men at a young age. There's a real advantage to becoming a woman *after* you've passed the twenty-something mark. And the relationship is really simple—I was looking for a one-night stand or a casual fuck buddy whereas most genetic women probably ultimately want a relationship.

I had a hard time admitting I was starting to actually like guys. I really enjoyed having sex-only relationships with gracious, fun people. Their sexuality was so unimportant compared to this. And we liked the same things . . . raw passion and fucking. Plus, after I got used to the idea, I was really good at connecting with them. I understood them and appreciated the simplicity of what they wanted. I was making them very happy, and that turned me on and pleased me. A symbiotic relationship.

I got along particularly well with the military guys. I greatly respect them, and The Dude has known quite a few, especially from the Navy. I understood what they do and could converse a bit about it. One of my favorite topics is the Navy versus the Air Force. That always prompted lots of good jokes and conversations. They really loved a woman who understood and appreciated that world. I'm also genuinely interested in great military stories. Being in the military is a big sacrifice and requires a special courage and stamina. This was a clear case where The Dude helped me be a better woman.

Semi-pro

I was now one step away from being a paid escort. I always had my place all ready for when guys came over. Dim lights on, candles in position—I needed to keep the overhead lights off so my womanly appearance would be smoothed over. My sex music playlist would be all set up—always modern upbeat ambient jazz & disco mixed with modern gay dance music. The Dude hated disco and dance music, but I loved it and liked to rub it in his face by playing it when I had a dick in my mouth.

SORDID DETAILS

I usually encountered one of two scenarios. Either their dick would already be rock hard before I started sucking them off, or if it wasn't, it would usually grow quickly as I started my master sucking technique. The one that always got them was starting slow and gradually sucking it deeper into my throat with my undulating tongue. When it was halfway in, I massaged the head against the back of my tongue and the roof of my mouth in beautiful rhythm. And as it grew, I would drift along into deep throating them until I gagged. But gagging never bothered me, because it was hot, and I would often get that sweet reward of precum telling me I was doing something right.

Several guys snorted coke while we were having sex. I've only done coke a few times, as The Dude set hard limits on my drug use. Doing a line and then devouring the Dick is fucking nuts. I love feeling that rush with a slippery cock head in my mouth.

About half were also into sucking my dick, which I found strange and never managed to turn me on at all, but I let them. I just thought of something kinky while they were sucking on me, which wasn't hard to when I had the full-length mirror in position.

And the guys really liked hanging out a little and talking with me. We kept it sweet but short, though. I loved the way we both understand the guy approach to things and could easily talk about our favorite topic—pig sex.

Totally works. They would very often tell me about their frustrations with straight women and why they love our simple relationship. I *loved* hearing this. Also many had bad experiences with working girls[76] and were glad to be finally having a great experience. This would be a night they remembered their whole lives, but they thankfully didn't get attached to me. These days love and lust are compartmentalized, and t-girls and their chasers understand this. Everybody wins. I didn't want a relationship and neither did they. They were curious, kinky horn dogs, and nothing was going to scratch that itch except a girl like me. I made them all very happy and euphoric and left an uncountable number of great waves of good energy flowing through them out to the world. I consider that part of my legacy!

I am the other woman

Most of these guys were bored with their girlfriends or wives and wanted somebody who was fun, cool, and ravenous for the Dick. I did things to them things their wives or girlfriends wouldn't. I guess I can't blame them, as all relationships tend to get stale. I must admit, I never felt bad for the women they were cheating on. I guess I should have, but I honestly was so concerned about living a woman's life that I didn't think about it. I justified it by figuring they're going to be out there screwing some t-girl anyway, so why shouldn't it be me. I had such a hard time dating as The Dude, I wanted this one part of my life, being a woman, to be simple, fun, and guilt free.

But eventually, I came face-to-face with me as the other woman! I had been fucking Greg every few months for several years. I knew he had a long-term girlfriend, but she was just an abstract concept. One night at Divas, I saw Greg with his girlfriend. She was a dirty blond and had a really classy blouse, huge breasts, and great makeup. I wanted to *be* her! I was so titillated I had to do it. I walked right past her and smiled. And she stopped me and told me how hot and awesome I was. We chatted for a few minutes all while Greg was standing right next to us saying nothing. I was officially the other woman! The next day, Greg texted me. "That was hot!" I giggled and texted back, "Fuck yea." He texted again. "Now I need to fuck you tomorrow." So we did and got closure. Badabing!

---

76. Many working girls have a really bad attitude because it's a job they no longer enjoy doing. I have nothing against them, but when you do something only for money, it doesn't usually come out well.

Other notable fucks

Black muscle guy fuck buddy

Black guys do have huge cocks. Many white guys too, but black guys are more consistent.

Anthony was a hard-bodied black guy I met online who kept telling me I needed to experience his chocolate dick. Getting into black men was another rite of passage. I had previously been with a few, but Anthony was the one who really got me into it. When we finally met, I had just bought a shiny satin red bra. While I was getting ready to meet him, I jubilantly looked at the back of that bra in the mirror, imagining my head bobbing up and down on his huge black cock. I didn't have to imagine much longer. I put on a black and red corset, complete with garters for my slinky, silky black stockings. I loved that I could just buy myself into looking sexy with this shit. I ran to Divas to meet Anthony. I was a little nervous wondering if he was going to like me. And yet *once again*, I was surprised he was clearly pleased. I've always had a thing for muscle guys. It was so different from being with a woman. *Damned, maybe I am gay, this is fucking hot*, I thought as I started rubbing his huge arms and strong back at the bar, unable to stop. I boldly said, "Let's go to my place." He smiled. "Absolutely, girl!"

We went back to my place and followed the tried-and-true protocol—made two screwdrivers, smoked a bowl, and looked at the amazing view. Then I planted a huge kiss on him while grabbing his incredible body and shoving my cock against his. Some guys were turned off by such an aggressive act. But not him. And weed and alcohol simulated me, but suppressed The Dude—perfect chemistry. What genius designed that?!

SORDID DETAILS

Anthony took off his shirt. Whoa, I really felt like a girl staring at his muscles. I rejoiced in the whole ritual I'd seen so many times in porn movies, but putting myself in the movie—slowly caressing his body, getting lower and lower, bound by lust, and inevitably ended up staring at that fucking huge black cock. The head was like a gigantic skull! I just stared at it, recalling the best cocksucking porn videos I could remember. And, with them all in my head, I projected myself into the audience and watched as I took that fucking huge dick. I had a hard time getting my lips around it. I was all choked up getting it into my throat.

I gagged so many times, the mucus was all over the couch. I had to grab a towel. I came back and looked at him and said, "I love you," and we went at it hard, ending up in the upstairs bedroom. I asked him to pretend he was fucking me in the ass, so with my panties, stockings, and heels still on, he got behind me, and I melted into that mass of powerful muscle drilling into me. I was floating in heaven. I had to ask him to stop so I could reposition the mirror to watch myself getting drilled by this beautiful body. I was watching my own porn movie, all while staring at the San Francisco skyline while grabbing the railing on the balcony of my loft so I could withstand all the pounding. *It doesn't get any better than this.*

Finally, I rolled him over on the bed and went for it. I had taken some cannabis edibles, so I was swimming in heaven. I took that magnificent chocolate cock into my mouth and was determined to keep going unabated until he exploded. We went at it for about ten minutes, his dick like a fucking flagpole. He pulled his dick out and then screamed, "I'm going to cum in your face." I couldn't see the first shot of cum, but it went up in the air and landed on my face. I'd never had that happen before. I had imagined I'd feel it hit me, but I only suddenly felt the warmth and then that taste. I immediately put my lips around his dick with him still cumming and had the most huge load of warm juice I've had to this day. Fuck ... he kept cumming and cumming. I was actually scared. It was shocking how much cum there was. So thick, creamy, and tasty. I licked some of it up and then then shoved his dick deep into my throat, and then swallowed. *I had the best sex with a black guy, nuuuuts! Double slut!*

When Anthony would come over, I just loved rubbing the huge head of his cock against my lips. It was a massive skull of flesh ... it was so fucking wrong. He always had such a huge fucking load that kept going, oh dear. And I got my dream of having gobs of cum dripping down my chin and on to my sexy lingerie. I loved looking at that in the mirror. What would all those girls who rejected me think? *Have you ever had dick like this?!*

I found myself having to do a lot more washing.

I saw Anthony on and off for about a year, but then he eventually got back together with his girlfriend and couldn't see me anymore. But not before fucking me in the ass! More on that later.

A few days after my first tryst with Anthony, I was at a bar describing my encounter to another t-girl and a guy. I started getting into the detail of the amount of cum he shot, but then I stopped and said, "Sorry, maybe this is TMI. You probably don't want to hear this." They screamed, "No, keep going!" Oh cool! The other t-girl's jaw dropped as I completed the story. I was the neighborhood slut—a proud slut, leaving The Dude in the dust! Why couldn't I have been this popular in high school?

Truck Driver Dick

Jose was a big, muscular, Hispanic truck driver who drove a street cleaning truck in San Francisco. He fucked me on and off for about a year. I was really getting into this muscle guy thing.

SORDID DETAILS

His cock was fucking huge and uncut. I didn't really know what the heck to do with an uncut cock, so I did what made the most sense. I took a huge hit of a cannabis sativa vape pen and hit his dick hard. What are all those strange folds in the head of his cock? I learned to spread the folds with my tongue and lips to get to the head. He was a total pig, and his cum had a strange, somewhat nasty, but thick and creamy texture. It was so dirty, blowing a truck driver. This was real man shit. And the dirtier it was, the more I felt like a woman. I loved dreaming about the taste of his nasty semen when I was going about my day feeling frustrated. He tried fucking me in the ass a few times, but he was too big, and I was too tight.

After seeing him for about a year, he told me he wanted me to dress him up as a girl, and he wanted to see me as a dude. I kept saying no, and he kept insisting, so I had to put an end to the relationship.

Ex-convict

I also fucked a muscular ex-convict. I met him at the Cinch bar, a friend of a friend. He was hot to fuck me, and since these ex-convicts are all muscle guys, that worked.

SORDID DETAILS

We started with violent, erotic dry humping. So hot feeling that hard body. He rolled me over and pushed me down on my back, and I instinctively raised my legs with my black nylons and fuck me heels and put them on his shoulders. I always loved seeing t-girls getting fucked like that. He pulled back my panties and started shoving his unprotected cock into my ass. I wanted this *so* badly. I wanted to feel like a super slut willing to go bareback[77], but I'm never that stupid, no matter how fucked up I am. I had to stop him, so I pushed him over and sucked him off. As he unloaded his warm semen into my mouth, I caressed his magnificently muscular back. *I just fucked an ex-convict! Check!*

We were both so exhausted and wasted, we fell asleep until the morning, something I had never done. I woke up pretty early and had to get him out of there quickly, making up a story about having to go to work. I needed to get all my gunked-up makeup off because it was burning my eyes. I also wanted to take a shower and get some real sleep. Girls, I never realized how much of a pain it would be getting guys out of your place when so many of them just want to sleep in a nice bed.

I didn't want him to see my makeup looking like shit. I was halfway to being a pumpkin. No hot dick-sucking lips, instead black shit smudged

---

77. Anal sex without a condom

under my eyes, my real eyebrows popping out, eye shadow a mess. I quickly shooed him out before the sun got too bright. There I was, *yet again* standing by the door, saying goodbye to *yet another* guy, giving him a hug or kiss. After a while, I pictured each one of these similar farewells being cut into a movie, creating a rapid sequence of just how much of a busy, busy slut I was.

Gay man magic

I was at Divas chatting with Walter, an older gay guy, about deep feelings, life philosophies, and kink. It was so easy to chat with gay guys. I didn't feel pressured to worry about the sex thing. But then he made a move on me. *Oh, okay, let's give this a whirl.* I never had sex with a gay man. I downed a shot of whiskey, went to the bathroom to light up a bowl of weed, and came out in a haze, ready for some more sex . . . again!

SORDID DETAILS

After we started going at it, something new came up. Walter started fingering my ass. My first reaction was, *this must be what gay men have learned to do with each other, I'm not gay, so I can't do this!* But holy shit, this new feeling felt *so* fucking good, and he was really good at it. It felt like the energy and knowledge of generations of gay men was being delivered to me through him. *Oh, shit, I really like this, fuck. I guess you understand a community better by having sex with them.* I felt like I was joining the gay male community and that made me uncomfortable. The conflicting ideas of both loving it and feeling The Dude's apprehension were shooting around in my head. But I was already pretty used to feeling both super excited and totally uncomfortable and judged, and the juxtaposition of these two and doing it anyway was now starting to really turn me on.

Girl problems and opportunities

Regularly giving into the Dick like an animal was a spiritual experience. When I was really turned on, I would get that exciting, sinking feeling in my stomach, something I hadn't felt in a *very* long time. But I began to panic and became overwhelmed and confused as the opportunities for sex just kept coming with no end in sight. I wasn't equipped to deal with this new paradigm. Girls, how do you stay sane and focused when there is so much sex available to you?

I tried to convince myself I was still just experimenting, but that got harder and harder to believe. This was my life. Uh, oh. I needed to stay healthy and continue to get some actual work done and not be out all the time partying and getting laid! I tried to solve the problem by becoming more selective, but I was attracting more and more guys as I got more confident.

I had to do something I had never done before. I had to take extended breaks from dating because I was exhausted from all the sex and having so many guys chasing me. I was starting to see guys more and more as just a body I wanted to fuck because I was bored. Girls, do you do that sometimes? My favorite part of a hookup was starting to be right after he left when I could close the door and jerk off while looking in the mirror, thinking about all the slut shit I was just doing, then finally get a shower and some rest. I was a kid in a candy store.

Maybe this was an addiction? But it had its benefits. My stress level at work dropped because I was more than satisfied, and I felt confident and powerful. I had managed to kill off The Dude's paradigm that beggars can't be choosers. I forgot what it was like to be a zero sexless nobody. And there was no fucking way I was going back there.

It was confusing, suddenly being a woman with all this social power after being a weak man. How to manage that new power and not self-destruct or turn into an asshole? Knowing how to properly use female power wouldn't happen overnight. Those born female have learned how to use it over the years. I was accustomed to only male power. Female power was much more sophisticated—the power of leverage, persuasion, love, and patience. However, it seemed to me many genetic women didn't know how to use it most effectively. Perhaps they didn't know enough about men?

I also had an advantage—being able to fall back on The Dude for security, both physical and financial. I was surprised when The Dude asked a fun question at a straight party, "What is the first thing you would want to do if you could BE the other sex for a week?" The general response was:

MALE → FEMALE: Be sexy and fuck

FEMALE → MALE: Just to walk around and feel safe

Wow, what a difference! I wondered which part of me was The Dude vs. Maria. Did The Dude even still exist?

I don't think either sex has a solid understanding of their power and respective roles in the balance of our world. Maybe this trans thing was a lot more useful than it appeared. But it's very tricky business integrating the male and female. I had discovered the fabulous joy and erotic side of being a woman, which was in stark contrast to The Dude's view of analyzing things and focusing on where and how to apply power. How could I combine these? But I wasn't ready. I was still a young woman, and women need each other. Now that I was satisfied with my "teenage and early twenties" sex years, it was time to think more about being a sister as a young woman.

CHAPTER 25

A TRUE SISTER

Sister slut

For me, becoming a slut was what a person seeking deep, real relationships did when shunned by a world that emphasized Virus programmed consumerism and fake relationships. This slut got to really connect with people at the most intimate level and have real relationships, immune from programmed fears, behaviors, and expectations. It may have been casual and focused on sex, but it was real.

Many men like their dominatrices or call girls because they crave real relationships. I pondered, *maybe I should become a professional?* People are always saying how you should do work you love. I liked being a slut a whole lot better than working for the Man in the corporate world because I felt like I was making a real difference in people's lives. And I was really good at it—both the flirting and the sex. It's just too bad it doesn't pay enough.

But I was now really enjoying connecting with women as a fellow passionate, emotional, and sexual sister. We got some insights from **Ginger Murray**, founder and editor of *Whore!* magazine:

Video: Ginger talks about her objective with the magazine, which is to "Give dignity to that which has been scorned." Ginger broadly defines a whore as a powerful woman who challenges the boundaries of the roles women have been assigned. She admires powerful women through the ages, especially so many women who helped create the Wild West back in the 1800s, some of whom had to start off as prostitutes. Ginger talks about the magazine, then we asked her about naughty things and about her life as a straight woman in an LGBT world.

I had now logged enough hours on the Dick to officially engage in conversations with women as an equal sister. Moreover, many knew I'd had more dicks in my best month than most sisters had in their whole lives.

One night I started chatting with a smoking-hot long-haired brunette around 30 years old who was on a date, sitting at the table next to me. I couldn't believe she was focusing on me. I told her I was recovering from fucking a hot black muscle guy the previous night. She grabbed my arm and exclaimed, "OMG, that must have been so much fun!" I responded, "Oh yea, his dick was fucking huge. When he came in my mouth, I could not believe how much hot cum he unloaded in my mouth. I was afraid!" Her eyes bugged out of her head as her jaw dropped. When she caught her breath, she muttered, "Wow, I have never had black dick." "Really?!" I responded. She was smiling with that devil's look in her eye and said, "I have got to try black cock." I smiled back, paused and said, "Girl you have to, it's so fucking hot." Her mouth opened as her smiled expanded, and she grabbed my arm again, "Girlfriend, you and I need to talk!" I couldn't believe we were having this conversation with her date sitting right there. But he was busy watching the show, and she was enjoying this way more interesting conversation.

One of my t-girl friends[78] was dating a woman named Sharon. Every time I (Maria) met them, she basically ignored me, thus I didn't particularly like her. One night, I was at a bar, with her standing next to me, ignoring me as usual. I decided to try to connect with her with one of my dick stories. She immediately broke into a huge smile, and I was her new best friend. She bought me a drink and exclaimed, "That's fucking hot, let's drink to the Dick!" We chatted a bit more, and I found out Sharon had multiple sclerosis. It was frustrating and exhausting for her to do a lot of basic things at home, and she was really scared about her future. My ex-wife had MS, so I knew quite a bit about it. And now we're buddies, Dude included! Wow, I had connected with her over the Dick and got into some important, serious stuff. Too bad she was dating my friend.

Female frustrations

As time went on, I felt less compelled to use the Dick as an easy ice breaker and often got right into real, bona fide girl talk. I found myself talking a lot about all the various frustrations women had to deal with. Some of the topics we discussed included:

Online Creeps

When I went back online after a long hiatus, all the creeps I had tried to avoid in the past were the first ones to contact me. *Go away! Ugh.* And what the fuck with all the dick pics! Is that supposed to be sexy? Does that shit actually work? Any stats on that? I think the best protocol is to ignore them.

And then you have so many guys say just a few words like, "Let's get together, text me." Even The Dude isn't that obtuse. Maybe some of them are bots looking to milk something out of me. I ignored most of these and then worked out a series of questions. If I didn't get a pretty direct response, I would terminate the conversation. You need a whole immune system against this stuff.

Dealing with gross guys at bars chasing me

How do I get rid of the idiot pigs? I try not to be rude or aloof to any guy, because The Dude has had that done to him so many times. But after so much of this, I didn't care anymore. I also had to worry about my safety.

---

78. Works as a man, lives part time as a girl.

I didn't want these guys pissed at me. Early on, I'd tell them I have a boyfriend, but it sounded like a lie, because it was. Things worked better when I told them a half truth. "Sorry, but I'm into girls," or "I'm meeting friends."

Safety

Are the guys going to beat me up? Or get too rough and not stop? And the STD situation is much worse as a t-girl. I didn't have to worry about this stuff as a guy.

Did I give you authorization to grab my tits?

Personally, I'm flattered when a guy grabs my tits. But I draw the line at doing it two seconds after meeting me or walking up to me and snapping my bra strap. That's just a little too creepy. What the fuck are you thinking? Are you on drugs? Probably[79].

Breaking the friend zone

This is a hard one because The Dude has done it. I know how fucking terrible it feels to fantasize about a friend for a long time only to be hit with a dose of reality and humiliation that makes you want to go back in time and prevent your parents from having sex nine months before you were born.

This happened to me several times, but this time as the girl. On two separate occasions, I had a soirée at my place with friends, and as the crowd was leaving, one of the guys I knew pretty well wanted to stay to finish his drink. He really threw me a curve ball when he asked to hook up. Oh, fucking awkward. I knew how bad my turning him down could sting, and I wanted to be as nice as possible. I couldn't make up a good excuse, because he knew I was single and liked to have fun. So, I just basically said no. It's really hard and I hate when this happens more than anything. But when I saw him again, I made a point to go up to him and say hello and smile as if nothing had happened.

I now better understand The Dude's *epic* failures in this scenario. Women get annoyed when their cool guy friends suddenly want to

---

79. I used to use the phrase "Are you on drugs?" often before I moved to San Francisco. It took on a different meaning once I moved here, because many of them actually were.

date or fuck them—*yet again*. What made this particularly painful is that, when Maria felt annoyed and sorry for the guy, I remembered how The Dude felt being rejected like that. Now, reflecting on how women felt about The Dude's advances was retroactively quadruple humiliating. **That was one of the more powerful thoughts that made me never want to be a dude again.** It's so hard, because so many guys have romantic dreams of falling in love with a female friend. We see it so often in the movies it seems like destiny. But this rarely happens in real life. Sigh.

Is he looking at my ass?

I know guys are looking at my ass when they're walking behind me. Dude does it *without exception*. That's part of the reason men don't mind letting women walk in front of them—they aren't just being polite. I love the whole idea of walking in front of a guy and try to wiggle around, thinking he might jerk off later thinking about my ass. I even sometimes walk a little slower than I would otherwise so I can spend as much time as possible feeling like a piece of meat, demoted to sex creature. This is what I signed up for. But the problem is I don't know how my ass looks.

Is my panty line in a fucked-up place? Has my blouse popped out of my skirt? Do I look messy? Is my corset making my ass look curvy, or did it descend asymmetrically and now looks like a sack of potatoes? I have hard time enjoying wiggling my ass, because I can never get that fear out of my mind. And I'm not able to distract him from my imperfections by dazzling him with my makeup and personality because he's totally focused on staring at my ass. I just keep wiggling it while I'm talking and hope for the best.

Guys are <u>such</u> liars!

They say they want to see you again but are unavailable, or they can't because they're going back to their girlfriend. Then you find they're online all the time or you bust them in a bar with another t-girl. Just tell me you want to fuck around. I'm not looking for romance or exclusivity. One of my fuck buddies and I talk all the time about the other people we're fucking. He likes getting off on the sordid details. At first, I thought he was joking, but he really did. This is modern dating, so tell the truth.

✴ ✴ ✴

Girls, where is there a recommended rulebook on how to handle guys?

Guys, you have no idea what girls have to put up with all the time. It's no wonder the male/female relationship is so difficult. Men just shrug and think, "What's with the attitude, bitch?" I know. The Dude has done it. His lack of patience is embarrassing me—thinking her attitude was about me when it wasn't. Girls, I apologize for not understanding. So, guys, if a girl is aloof, try to remember there's a good chance she's had some really bad experiences and doesn't know the best way to handle a situation. It's not a reflection on you. Well, honestly, it might be, but at least you can take comfort in knowing another explanation is possible.

Women are so beautiful and cool, but so often they've been emotionally damaged by all of this. I don't know what it's like to have to grow up as a girl in a man's world, bullied by boys, constantly *attacked* by glamour magazines, advertisements, movies and TV shows, and forced to wear a makeup mask every day. And then having men staring at your tits and ass, not respecting you, making awkward moves on you constantly, and then downright harassing you. Maria gets a lot of respect, but I haven't tried working as a woman. I at least can escape by taking off the clothes and makeup.

And here are some more female frustrations that aren't related to guys:

It takes so damned long to get ready!

I guess I'm getting payback for all those years when The Dude got ready in five minutes and was annoyed at his woman for taking so long. Now I know why girls are often late, and I respect it.

Enough said.

Hair!

Oh God, is this a pain! Every little flip of the hair changes how I look. I did a great fucking makeup job, and then to have it all go to shit because my hair isn't working? This isn't fair! And then, even if I get it looking good in the mirror, when I walk to another room and look in another mirror with different lighting and a different angle, it looks like shit. Ugh! Or I thought I looked great, but then my hair looks like shit in that picture my friends posted. *What happened?!* Are people judging me on my hair, or am I'm judging myself based on what I think they'll think?

At times I've leaned toward short hair, but then I look like a chiseled t-girl dyke. That isn't me. Or do I really look fabulous and that's just me seeing The Dude hidden in there? People tell me I look great, but are they just being nice? Why can't I just freeze frame my hair along with the angle and lighting. I guess models do this for photo shoots. We live in a fucked-up world of shallow perception. *Okay then, why have I chosen to be a girl?*

But I've learned to just say *what the fuck*, compensate with my fabulous personality, and remember to just keep moving.

Sisterhood beyond the bar

Girls are magical. The Dude had this *insane* craving to be near them, only to bang headfirst into the invisible shield surrounding them. Once Maria discovered the shield frequency, I slipped right through and found it to be more magical than I had ever known. I only saw the shield clearly once I was looking out from the inside. Damn, I wished we weren't all so smothered by all the Virus energy floating around, sucking our energy and leaving us with deep, burning scars and prejudices or preconceived notions about people.

Strangely, although my old-fashioned Dude romantic ways didn't work in straight dating, they were perfectly suited to the world of platonic sisterhood. Girls were so loving and open, at least in this t-girl's experience. I was increasingly engaging with women across all situations.

Maria visited a plastic surgeon's office. The two office assistants were women, one around thirty and one around sixty, and we were chatting about dating and life in San Francisco. It was a friendly, joyful conversation with two people I had just met. *Wow, do women do this all the time?* It made me feel so connected, like people care about me and will look out for me. I had a similar experience with a nurse practitioner at a clinic. With all this sex, I was having myself checked regularly. I was all chatty with her and her assistant. By talking about sex openly, as a sister, I quickly established a comfortable relationship, which helped me have important health conversations without being shackled by nervousness and shame. And I must admit, it was exciting to brag to them about how much sex I was having! But I was also reaching out to validate that other people were as promiscuous as I—and that I was not a complete degenerate.

When I visited Vegas, I went to a stripper store to buy a choker. It was so exhilarating to walk around that stripper store as one of them, talking with the saleswoman, looking at the different outfits, chokers, and knick-knacks, feeling stripper energy all around. As I tried on a choker, it was like putting on the queen's crown. I pictured all the strippers I had met, and in an instant, I was one of them and presto—I had that stripper energy. And I began to *feel* them more as a person.

I was feeling ambivalent about the idea of being a stripper. On one hand, I felt charged and confident. On the other, I knew what it *felt like* to smell sweaty balls, taste little pings of precum, and, of course, taste a full load. Only at that moment did it really hit me that these strippers were *feeling* this time and time again with guys they didn't know, and many of these guys were in varying states of being gross. At that moment, I was finally *grokking* what it was like to be a stripper—The Dude really didn't know. The juxtaposition of the sexual power with the grossness of the sexual act for money and power is one strange amalgam of feelings. It's probably representative of the larger world we live in. Is it really much different being a politician or businessperson? I'm amused at the irony of learning about the world at large better through lust and kink than anything else.

I also found it particularly fun, interesting, and strange that older women loved me. What a strange gift to suddenly be able to talk about life with somebody I never would have otherwise connected with.

The allure of sisters

With all this connecting with women, I couldn't help falling even more in love with them and wanting to be with them as a man. The romance bug wouldn't leave me alone, and I wasn't going to have romance with a guy. I figured I would eventually end up back with a woman or otherwise find my way to the bottom of a bottle, as I could never get into Dick without healthy doses of weed and alcohol.

I loved being a sister but wondered if I'd learned enough that The Dude could have the connected romantic relationship with women I'd craved for so long. I figured I should be much better at dating women this time around. I now knew the inner beauty and eroticism of women, and I could be more supportive and confident because I had an awareness and respect for their frustrations and pains. I might get past their shields by resonating on their frequency. And I was also less interested in The Dude at this point, so he would naturally talk less.

But what *would* I talk about? What if she asked me what I do for fun? I was two different people living a super awesome, unique life. How was I going to explain this to a regular straight woman? Should I even try? And what would I do with my walk-in closet filled with Maria's shit—it had no door!

I wasn't ashamed at all, it was just . . . well, complicated. Maria was addicted to having an easy, no bullshit, shields-free relationship with women where we could share almost anything, and our souls would touch. I wasn't giving that up. My life was awesome, fuck that. Plus, I was performing music several times a month. And if I dated women, I needed Maria in my back pocket to know I could have fun on my own if I got dumped or ignored on a date. I had to remain immune from frustration. I couldn't give up my secret powers. I guess that was part of the problem. I had gotten so used to easy, fun, sex, I didn't know if I had the patience and faith to deal with the pain and problems of romance. It was so damned easy to just not care. My theory that I'd have fun, queer sex while waiting for the right women was losing credibility. Perhaps I had drifted too far and couldn't find my way back?

I was also worried that if The Dude was dating a woman, that Maria wouldn't be the same, because I wouldn't be projecting that happy, free slut energy. But that seemed like a reasonable tradeoff. A far bigger problem was that I was addicted to something far more powerful than my desire to connect with women.

I loved the power of turning away opportunities with women and just going straight for the Dick. This stemmed from my *hating* my attraction to women because it had only frustrated and humiliated me. I liked drowning my sorrows in my drug of choice. Sound familiar to some people? My drug was stripping myself of the shackles of straight manhood and romantic fairy tales so I could feel pure freedom instead. I didn't want to go risk getting my heart broken again.

Maybe I was just getting a little bit too addicted to slipping down the kinky slope?

So, again I wondered, *was Maria addictive or empowering?* Was I avoiding having to face straight dating rituals again, or was I blessed to be free from it forever? An addiction is:

1. Something that has life-damaging consequences
2. You want to stop, and you can't

The problem is that being Maria was so much fun, I didn't *want* to stop. The problem was that I *really liked* being a girl. And as you get older, you start choosing things that are just easier. Maybe I wasn't experimenting anymore.

And where were the *life damaging consequences*? It was time to re-evaluate.

It had been a long time since I had been with a woman romantically, something I really wanted. Maria was taking time away from finding a woman.

But I already knew straight dating was a toxic cesspool. Maybe I was just merely having a hard time accepting that fact.

Or maybe I just didn't want to grow up, and I was addicted to the kink kandy.

Or maybe the kink kandy was a gift from the Universe. Maybe I was afraid that Dick was just simply a lot better than straight sex, and The Dude could never have such a close and terrific relationship with women as I did. I wasn't getting the message that this whole thing was simply okay as is. And I was spreading great loving energy.

But the bottom line was I *wanted* to be with a woman as a man. I really wanted romance. And I needed it. On the very rare times I had it, it made me really happy. And physically healthy, too. Maybe I had just lacked patience and determination. Maybe I had to renew my faith in Dude destiny and get back to positive Dude thinking. Should I?

The biggest problem I was facing had nothing to do with me. I had a basic math problem. It was still 250x easier finding a date as Maria, and that was driving me *insane*! The Dude would have to wade through the straight dating cesspool in the hopes of finding a needle. And why would I want to put up with that stench when I had such a rich and fun life?

So, it came down to how important giving it a go with women again was to me. Maybe it was my destiny to crack my male shell and learn about women this way and then return to being a man. I had to at least try, otherwise the question would haunt me forever. I had to prove it wasn't an addiction by focusing on straight dating for at least six months. *Okay, I'm going to really try. And no Maria, you can't go screwing around on the side during this time. I know you, you clever little bitch. If I give you an inch, you're going to suck all the air and cum out of the room. Other than performing, you're shut down for at least six months, girl.*

CHAPTER 26

BACK TO WOMEN AND ROMANCE

<u>I (The Dude)</u> knew from firsthand experience just how dirty women can be, myself included. But I was a romantic, so how would I respect them?! I also knew that in the first few seconds of meeting, a girl often decides if the guy is elidable dating material. I hate when girls do that. *Don't you want to get to know me first?* Yet Maria did that every time.

I was also worried about the modern tendency to fuck on the first date. Being so overtly sexual with a woman I'd just met wasn't natural to me, even though doing this with guys was natural for Maria. I was different from her. I also had performance anxiety because I hadn't had sex with a woman for seven years[80]. I hoped if my date liked me

---

80. It's not that I wasn't trying. Plus, I had a huge tumor on my chin which I'd had my whole life. It made the left half of my chin black and blue all the time. It was hideous looking, but I had gotten used to it. But I eventually realized how difficult it was making dating, so I stopped even trying for about four or five years until I had it removed. It took this long because the medical technology had to catch up so the procedure was less risky.

romantically, performance might not be a driving factor . . . but I was worried I was too old fashioned.

It was complicated trying to figure things out from both sides. Maybe it would have been better if I hadn't known all of this, but on the flip side, I was much more aware of how women think, so I was hoping I could connect with them better.

The straight women who knew both Maria and me were off limits. Too bad. You would think they would be ideal. But I remembered the horrors and double humiliation of breaking the friend's zone. I needed to remain free of those complexities. Sadly, online straight dating was my only real choice[81]. I also figured online dating would give me access to a much broader base of women than I met in the Maria world. Or so I thought.

Online straight dating

I put together a profile, not mentioning anything about my double life, and spent weeks and weeks being ignored, having promising conversations just die, and being trolled by prostitutes and robots. Maybe once every two months I would finally get on the phone with somebody. Usually it would be a boring conversation, or they found me too energetic and weird, but every once in a while, I would go on a date. All of those were total failures. I was interested in learning about somebody no matter their looks and disposition[82], but that didn't seem to be returned in kind. They wrote me off faster than you can say "No."

I asked several women friends to write new profiles for me, and I tried multiple dating sites. Same results. Then friends would tell me this was wrong with my profile, or that was wrong. One said put a picture of you playing the piano, another said that piano picture is too dorky, you look like a nerd talking about your music. After a while I wanted to scream *SHUT THE FUCK UP, THIS IS SUCH FUCKING BULLSHIT, THIS HAS NOTHING TO DO WITH REALITY!* I was tempted to go back to my Maria social life because it was so much better. But I stuck with it. I went through this utter fucking torture for almost a year.

Finally, fed up, I redid my profile and told the truth, leaving out a lot

---

81. I decided it wasn't worth getting back into all the other things I (The Dude) had tried and failed.
82. Unless they were a total pig.

of details. It basically said: *I am a performer, and I hang around with a lot of queer artistic performing types. I have a rich life, but I want to be with a straight woman and share this with her.* I figured this profile was unique and it was a filter. I got better results. At least they seemed more interested in me.

Over the next four months or so, I finally got a few dates decent dates out of it—women who didn't write me off the second they saw me. Maybe being more honest about my life would work out. I was older than when I had last dated, and I was becoming confident women would now appreciate uniqueness, adventure, and quality in a person. But they all asked me about the performing I mentioned on my profile. What the heck was I going to say?

I tested the waters with one woman by saying, "Well, I like to do edgy things." She smiled and said, "Like what?" "Well," I said, "it's flashy and totally out of character, but gets a lot of attention." She said, "Drag?" I smiled and told her yes. She said it was really awesome and gave me a big smile. I didn't say much else about it. We went one more date, but then she dumped me over text while I was on a business trip to Paris no less. She didn't even say why. As far as I know, she thought it was cool she was friends with a drag queen, but of course would never date one. I decided to go back to not telling them if they asked.

The next woman had two kids around ten years old and lived in the suburbs. She flipped out when I told her one of my friends was a reverend who was coming over in the evening for a glass of wine. That was just simply too weird for her, and she broke up with me. It didn't matter that his job was helping people in need during off hours. Okay, new rules. I'd have to completely leave out *everything* about my incredible life until after we slept together. The odds were already strongly against me, so why complicate things?

Girlfriend

Courting!

Finally about nine months into my straight online dating, I started dating Cheryl, who lived in the suburbs about thirty miles outside San Francisco. My kiss on the first date was a little peck, because the romantic in me likes to go slow and leave a little anticipation.

For our second date, we met at the Embarcadero Ferry building and gravitated to a romantic railing by the water. We leaned against it and watched the boats against the backdrop of the Berkeley Hills, Treasure Island, and the Bay Bridge, beautifully complemented by the sound of seagulls. It was still hard for me to believe I actually lived in this place.

I remembered the basics of what Maria had taught me. Don't talk about the amazing things I've done in my life. Instead, just be quiet and take in the moment. If she wasn't attracted to me, she wouldn't be there. Then Cheryl started staring at me. It had been a really long time since I had embraced a woman romantically. I smiled and touched her hand, which she locked into mine. *Oh good.* I grabbed her other hand and smiled more, pulling her close to me. She giggled a little, and that made me really happy. I embraced her back, pulled her closer to me and gave her a nice deep kiss. That felt so naturally wonderful. And no drugs required. I just kept kissing her. I had waited for this for over ten years.

I pulled back and looked at her. Her eyes were still closed as she took in the kiss, and then she opened them and giggled a little more. I grabbed her slim, incredibly sexy body and pulled it against mine, rotating my head a bit to the right, and we melted into a deep lover's wet and salty kiss. I let that kiss linger for several moments, and then I moved my tongue around a little, and she joined me, and for the first time I really felt the presence of the other. Together we created this moment of romance, standing out there on the pier as so many other couples had done.

I rubbed my cheek against hers and then she pulled my tongue back into her mouth. It was worth waiting years for this. I moved my hands down toward her hips. I could feel everything as Cheryl was wearing a silk dress. First her bra, then her tight back, and then her curvy woman hips. We stood in that embrace for about a minute as I took in those curves, feeling that fragile female body pressed up against mine. Oh, those curves, the softness, the feminine energy, I just melted. The Dick didn't hold a candle to this. I knew what my cock must have felt like to her, and I thought for a moment what it would feel like to be her, having a vagina with a cock pressed up against it, but it didn't last long. I was too preoccupied with enjoying being a man.

We started seeing each other regularly, taking it slow before getting into the sex, which in San Francisco is a few weeks. And that's exactly how I like it. I really wanted our first sexual experience together to be exciting and passionate, not just a fuck. I wanted simple things like cooking food together and taking walks. I wanted to pair with somebody who complemented me. Now that Maria had discovered the feminine within me, I not only appreciated it more, I was especially in love with the part of being a woman that I wasn't and never could be. That softness, that simpler presence of being in the moment and present with your emotions without all that internal male chatter.

I even noticed something I had never noticed in a woman before. The color of her socks matched the color of her shirt. I giggled and said, "That's so cute." This kind of thing never happened before. I was happier than I had been in a very long time. I loved courting women. It was the best. *I am old fashioned, unlike that woman Maria.*

Sex with a lady!

Shortly before we consummated our relationship, Cheryl said to me, "This sounds weird, but I just want to make sure you're not bisexual or gay. My ex-husband came out and I couldn't go through that again." This shocked me. Was I giving out strange vibes? But it seemed innocent enough. I told her my version of the truth according to my new rules, which was to leave out important details. "No, I'm not bisexual or gay." I certainly didn't feel that way. Man on man wasn't my thing at all. So, I wasn't lying. Good enough. I figured I deserved a little room here.

Soon it was time. I was really nervous my dick wasn't going to work after all the kinky shit and drugs I had gone through. But there's nothing like having sex with a woman as a man.

SORDID DETAILS

I embraced Cheryl as we stood naked in her bedroom. I loved her soft skin, her salty lips and slinky naked body. Cheryl had exquisitely curvy hips that I could just run my hands over and over, while I slowly worked my lips from her cheeks, down her neck, and on to her nurturing breasts.

It was so erotic, being speechless with somebody I knew and liked. I nudged Cheryl over to the bed and grabbed her soft, tight back and gave her a deep tongue kiss signaling that she was about to get it. As I pressed my stiff cock into her, I felt her body melt into mine. And I knew what it felt like to have that cock pressed into you, letting you know you're going to lose control any minute and turn into an animal and get fucked. Nothing else in the world will matter in those moments when you're doing that thing that makes you a woman. That thing you think about all the time is actually going to happen right now.

I rolled Cheryl onto the bed. She stared at me in a trance as she opened herself up for that moment of pleasure. We were two animals, no words, just pure physical presence. I got on top of her, grabbed both her hands hard and pushed them into the bed. Hers legs spread open automatically. I tongue kissed her as I shoved my cock against her pussy and started rubbing it up and down. I reached down and found her clit, making sure she was all lubricated and ready for me. Each woman's clit is different. You have to find it, then coax it open, and find the spot that makes them disappear into heaven on Earth.

Having been a woman, I knew how torrid it was to be dominated by a man. And for the second time, I was *really* enjoying giving a woman pleasure! It was time to slip inside her. The feeling of my raw cock[83] going into a woman is like God designed it just for me so I could feel loved. It's so warm, and makes you want to deep kiss her so hard you melt into one mass of flesh. And now that sweet, proper woman was turning to an *animal*, screeching as I pushed my body into hers. Two opposites banging away at each other, two intelligent creatures hopelessly lost in their animal roots.

We rolled around fucking for a while, and then I got behind her because I wanted to bang up against her curvy woman's ass. Time to add a little nasty to the erotic. Our bodies rocked in harmony, first with my hands on her hips, then I grabbed her shoulder with one hand and wrapped my other arm around her body so I could pull her up while I was kissing the back of her neck, working my way up to kissing the side of her lips from behind. We were as nature intended us to be, frolicking in passion.

Okay, time to go for it. I rolled her on her back and got on top of her with my hands pressing hers into the bed again. As I started pounding into her in the final stretch, I intensely loved hearing her squeals mixed in with the slapping flesh—because I had a very good idea of what she was feeling. I buried my cheek against hers and she surely knew that in a minute I was going to explode inside of her. As I started deep kissing her, my body started quivering, and then wham! After fifteen years, I came inside a woman.

---

83. We did *not* use a condom, as we had time to get tested, and we trusted each other.

I loved lying there afterward, staring into blank space, enjoying that post-coital moment of bliss together. This was what life was all about. We drifted off into a blissful sleep, the kind with little quasi-dreams that take you into all sorts of nondescript states that seem to somehow connect. Because it's all meant to be. This was *so much* better than fucking guys. And I didn't get thrown out.

The reveal

This went on for about six weeks before I told her. I didn't even consider it relevant. I was following the new modern rules: if the sex was great, then worry about all that other stuff. Cheryl came over my place several times, and I had to erect a curtain to cover all that girl shit in my huge walk-in closet that had no door. She could have peeked in and discovered it, but I wasn't worried. If it happened, it happened. In that case, I would just go back to being Maria for fun. Talk about freedom.

It was awkward because I had to run into my closet and grab my clothes while she was in the shower, lest she catch a glimpse of the corsets, dresses, skirts, wigs, and stripper chokers. *Can you imagine her going in there while I was in the shower? "Uh, it's not what you think!"* I made no extra effort to ensure this didn't happen, other than standard procedures like making sure a bra strap wasn't poking out of my dresser before she came over. I had also just purchased a makeup desk with a mirror that closed neatly into a tabletop and covered all the makeup. It was pretty ballsy, but fuck it, what was my alternative, move all that into my storage locker? Fuck that. My new life was about freedom and pride in who I was.

So, how did I tell her? Cheryl knew I was an entertainer in the LBGT world based on my profile, and she loved hearing me play piano and guitar. She increasingly kept asking to see me perform. And I just kept telling her I'd send her the links when I was ready. I figured she knew it was racy and different, but she had stayed with me, so I didn't feel like I was being duplicitous.

I sent her the link to my Under the Golden Gate video channel. I thought about just telling her in person, but the shock might overshadow her ability to see the whole thing in context. She might have had preconceived images of me as an ugly man in a dress, or as a sex-crazed kinkster getting fucked in a swing by various people—which was true, but I ain't giving everything away. So, best to start with my videos. If we watched them together at my place, it would be awkward, because where would she run? If we did it at her place, she'd have to throw me out. Cheryl needed time to digest what she was going to see and didn't need me sitting around grinning while I waited for her to process all of this.

After a few days, she called me. "I watched your videos, and I guess I'm not really surprised. You're a good interviewer, and it's interesting stuff." Her son was gay, which might have helped. She asked me a little bit about it, but surprisingly it didn't seem to bother her or affect our relationship. We had some good sex just after that. All seemed to be okay, but when you set off a little explosion at the bottom of a dam, everything also seems okay. For a while.

The next step was for her to see me perform. I wasn't just going to walk out of the bedroom as a woman. I was playing piano for a singer at the Chapel, a trendy music venue in the Mission. Perfect. It was in context with me as rock star. We went to the venue together with Maria in the bag. I introduced Cheryl to a few people, so she kept busy on the main floor while I went into the dressing room and went down the bat-pole. I emerged in a black leather miniskirt with a flare and midnight black silky pantyhose.

Playing that night at the Chapel

Cheryl said, "You look like a tart!" I guess I did! Women had the chance to experiment with makeup and trashy looking clothes when they were teenagers. But we Dudes never did. Made sense. That was the first sign that there was going to be a problem. She was a mature woman, and I was still a teenager, who was becoming a young woman. She'd already gone through all that. Cheryl saw Maria two more times at shows. One time she brought some friends, two of whom were gay and knew the drag scene, and they gave a big validation to fabulous me. But Cheryl was quite shy and coy, and she didn't take to the scene. She mostly talked quietly in the corner, or just sat and watched.

This wasn't a match. Would it have been if I was only a guy? Probably not. Although we were compatible in many ways, I was used to excitement. I was an entertainer and a gregarious engaging person, and if I were to stay with her and enter into a more serious relationship, it would have to be because we were compatible. Not because I needed companionship. Sound familiar? I had learned from getting divorced that staying with the wrong person was a bad idea. It would result in a bad outcome, and was a bad way to live.

The end of the honeymoon

We dated for another four months, but the relationship slowly unwound. She kept asking me why Maria was so important to me. The problem was she didn't understand the passion and irrationality of an artist and gender warrior[84], and thus didn't respect it. She was increasingly worried about what other people would think. I told her none of her friends or family needed to know, but that didn't matter. The whole idea of it bothered her. It was too far out from her world. She also wasn't interested in my friends. I thought it was amusing that I had many strange friends, and I loved telling her the weird stories about their sexual trysts. I thought these things were much more amusing than watching fake dramas on TV. She didn't. And I was finding her few suburban friends intolerably boring.

I wasn't trying to be a jerk, but after living the Maria life in San Francisco, I was into a different world she had no interest in discovering. I was kind of hoping women outside my world would find this interesting—that it could spice up their life before they died. Maybe I was wrong in trying?

---

84. I took this term from the book *Gender Warrior* by Kate Bornstein.

It was difficult for me to engage in conversations about restaurants, TV shows, wine, building up home equity for retirement, and remodeling the house. It wasn't until I returned to the suburban life with her that I realized, for me, how much all these things had just been an attempt to create meaning while living in an isolated world.

Her increasing discomfort showed she only *tolerated* Maria. She didn't accept or appreciate the whole thing. Thus, being with her increasingly made me feel like less of a man. I didn't want her to tolerate this—I wanted her to celebrate it. I was proud of the exploration I had done, the shows, and being on the cutting edge of a fascinating subculture. I didn't want my partner looking down on me because I didn't stay inside the mold created by the Monoculture Virus. I didn't say anything negative, and we never argued about it. But little things kept coming up. This is in stark contrast to the San Francisco women who knew both me and Maria. They loved everything about me, full boat! I had so much fun with them, and I was used to that. With Cheryl, that old familiar dark cloud of shame, nitpicking at how somebody else lived their life, was starting to form above me.

This started triggering Maria back into action. She started looking at Cheryl's bras, thinking they were way too boring. *Nothing with lace? Nothing with an usual, kinky back? I have hotter bras than you.*

Her friends showed no interest in me. To them, I was just another nondescript guy who played guitar in some band. I was a rock star in my work, lobbying/activism, and entertainment, but in my home life, I was a nobody at best, a weird mutant at worst. Didn't you see *Tootsie* or *Mrs. Doubtfire*? Isn't this supposed to have a happy, glorious ending?

I took in all this shame, doubting whether all those things I had done with Maria was a good idea. *Maybe Maria is just some perverted, bored, sex and drug addict who fell out of line. Maybe we were foolish for producing these shows and for trying activism and environmental lobbying.*

But **I (Maria)** wasn't taking that shit. I had been very quiet and patient when The Dude would go out with Cheryl's friends, being the docile nice boyfriend. But as he was marginalized and humiliated Virus style, I couldn't help from smirking as I looked at Cheryl's girlfriends, thinking: *I've had hotter guys and more Dick than you can ever possibly imagine. What would you think if I told you I've slept with more guys in a month than you have in your whole life? Have you ever worn a leather corset? I have*

*a hotter closet than you would know what do with. If you and I went out to a
club, guys would be coming after me, not you!*

The Dude tried shutting me up, but I had to keep protesting this
bullshit. "What are you doing with Cheryl? You're repeating the same
pattern that resulted in your train wreck marriage because you settled
for somebody you knew was a bad match because you didn't want to be
alone. She can't match our joy, courage, and fabulousness. If you're going
to bring somebody into our lives you better damned be sure you're *crazy
about her.* And you better make sure she's crazy about us both. Cheryl
and her friends haven't done five percent of what I've done. I'm fabulous,
and don't ever forget that. Don't let them pull us into the framework of
their boxed-in virtual lives. Wake the fuck up! Stop being a victim and
giving up on the life we want and the people we really want to hang
around with."

Dude and I could talk honestly with each other, the way only a true
friend or a true brother or sister could.

Dick to the rescue

The Dude was still trying to convince me I should grow up, move back
to the suburbs, and settle down with Cheryl. The more he pushed that
nightmare on me, the more I started virtually tasting that unmistakable flavor of cum in my mouth. That magic antidote to the scheming of
the Virus. The Call of the Dick was the canary in the coalmine. If I was
really crazy about a woman, the Dick Call wouldn't be pulling at me.
The yearning for the taste of cum and that kinky feeling of a hard dick
pressing up against my pantyhose kept getting stronger and stronger,
and it wasn't going to stop. Then I realized something that should get
The Dude's attention. "We've had Dick in between dating woman, but
we've never broken up with a girl for the Dick. I know you want to have
that new experience. That's hot isn't it?"

The Dude protested. "No, I'm looking for the right woman, hence my
waning interest in Cheryl. That doesn't mean I want Dick."

I thought he would enjoy the idea of a little vacation from this. I felt
sorry for him. He was still chasing that same romantic fairy tale and
couldn't accept this was a disguise for the drudgery of being in a simple suburban relationship. Or maybe he was doomed because as women
get older their interests seem to be more focused on good sex, especially

with younger guys, whereas men go in the opposite direction—less in sex and more in romance.

The Dude continued and fired back at me, "Maybe the ease and variety of fucking has permanently turned you into a slut."

I was trying to understand the logic of his statement and decided to not even bother. "You want us to look for the right woman online? Oh Lord, no, please, save my soul. Go back online and wade around in the cesspool for another three to five years?" Which was what it would take for The Dude to find a match . . . and that would be in a good decade. Fuck that poison.

He didn't have a good comeback.

We started to see eye to eye, at least for now. His heart wasn't in it. We figured, I *liked* being friends with the San Francisco women who knew both Maria and The Dude. We were all living on a happy island free from the Virus. And the chances I would find that kind of woman on a straight dating site? And then find somebody who wasn't just accepting of Maria, but one who could handle *another* powerful woman in the relationship? When were the pigs going to fly out of my butt and drop hundred dollars bills on my living room floor?

I knew without a strong bond with a woman, fabulous Maria would find herself constantly slipping back to men anyway. *I should go back to my Maria life . . . But on the other hand, settling down and relaxing would be healthier and more balanced. Even if the relationship isn't exciting, maybe it's high time. Sure, Maria could enjoy a life with a variety of fuck buddies, but she doesn't have anybody to come home to . . .* But now that I had someone I could be with regularly, I was getting bored and depressed. There was no simple answer.

What now? I couldn't kill Maria. She was a budding young woman. I needed Maria to break thought the noise out there in the world. She was the only thing really interesting and fun I had going for me. I was done with the agony of lobbying and being an activist. My work in the technology industry was starting to be a real drag and full of unbelievable amounts of quick hustling and bullshit—I wasn't equipped to deal with that without my strong female counterpart.

So, I had to go back out into the scene as Maria. She had most of my power. That's where my people were. My theory that women outside Maria's world would really appreciate merging our worlds together was proving to be wrong[85]. Maybe they just felt too much like an outsider, or they were afraid. Who knows? What difference did it make? I had options. If I couldn't be with a fabulous woman I really loved, then I'll just *be* that woman.

This was all theoretical until Maria went to Divas one night after performing at a show. A guy from across the bar gave me *that* smile. I could have just ignored him, but my knees felt weak. I knew what I needed to do, and this was the moment. The universe had sent him to me. I walked right up to him and smiled.

SORDID DETAILS

As my lips went around the head of his dick I thought, *I can't believe I'm back to doing this.* As I felt his body shudder then blast that warm cum, all I could think was, *I fucking love this so much. This is so much more fun than sex with Cheryl. I'm back home. And this time I'm not leaving. I don't care what you call me.*

Okay so I was drunk and stoned, but it didn't matter if those thoughts were totally true or not. I loved that power of turning away from the boredom of an ordinary, suburban, cookie cutter life. The whole idea of *deciding* to be queer instead was hot. But this was what I needed in order to get away from being in a relationship that wasn't right for me. In chemistry, a strong atom needs a strong bond to tear you away from a weak one.

Cheryl initiated the breakup because she could tell I wasn't that engaged. Good, I didn't have to wonder if I should confess to the woman I was dating that I just sucked off a random guy I met in a bar. Although that would have been hot.

And what made this particularly exciting and scary was it was early December, and I had the entire months of December and January off from work. I knew, just like when a disease goes away and then returns, it was going to come back with a fury. And in Maria's world, the line between fantasy and reality was a *very* short one.

---

85. I had dated another woman for a while before Cheryl and had a similar experience.

CHAPTER 27

BACK TO FUCKING MEN!

New Year's resolution

It was exciting to break up with a girl for the Dick. I really broke up with her because we were incompatible, not because she had a vagina. But why not have fun with this and proceed to the next level of the journey, and just go with this concept?

I reactivated my Maria online profile and immediately all the gross guys who had been chasing me a year earlier contacted me. "Welcome back! Do you want to get together?" *Ugh, girlfriend, is this what we have to deal with?* I panicked for a moment but realized I could simply ignore them. I was a woman again—the one with power. And within a few days, new men were stacking up faster than I could process them. In the first week, I fucked three guys—two in one night. I met one guy online, sucked his dick, then went out and picked up another one without even trying. And this kept happening. For the month of December, I was averaging two to three guys a week, including multiple nights where I hooked up with two guys. I lost count in just a few weeks. I was ex-

I now loved wearing tops that showed my bra

hausted. I guess when you go back to the Dick, you glow so much, you attract a lot of guys.

I bought a bunch of new makeup, hair, and clothes, including matched panty and bra sets, something I previously had not bothered with. So, I was looking mighty fun and ready to party. I started wearing mostly chiffon and lacy blouses that showed my bra through the back. It's not fair that girls get to show off their underwear like Madonna did in the '80s. I wanted to do it, too. That had always turned The Dude on since he first saw girls in seventh grade do it, so Maria found it sick-hot. Thus, the guys did, too. I rearranged the mirrors at home so I could see myself from behind. The narcissist has reopened her doors for business! I knew how titillating it was for a guy to see a girl's bra from behind, and I knew how to werk that bold shit! I suspected this was a big contributor to increasing my hookup hit ratios.

If you don't know what it's like to have nasty sex and suck a huge cock after you've ended a frustrating relationship, you need to try it. What a power punch it was to go from frustration and boredom to cum slut in less than a week. I skipped the whole loneliness and reflection thing. I had done enough of that in my life. Well, I was reflecting on the relationship—while I had a dick in my mouth. *Look at me, Cheryl! I don't need girls and all the frustrations of a relationship!* I know it sounds childish, and giving up the hope of romance was sad, but the price was too high. Freedom was more important. And I was making a lot of men really happy with easy NSA and No Drama sex—everybody wins.

Life was so much better. I didn't have the boat anchor of The Dude's inability to achieve his lame ass romantic fairy tales. I needed to be totally free from his moping about the house so I could really feel what it was like to go back to the Dick and become a woman. I made a New

Year's resolution. I was going to be a girl for the whole rest of the next year. Socially that is. I wasn't stupid. I let him do all the work making money, running errands, even bumming around at home. I didn't need to be fabulous at home and burn up all my energy. I figured that ultimately who you really are is when you're out socializing or online. Everything else is irrelevant.

I'm a girl!

Back at it, girl!

I'm all about mindsets. You can't really know something until you live it. Until you *are* it. My ball and chain were gone. I fucked at least forty guys in the three months after breaking up with my girlfriend. Some weeks I scored five times. Even on nights when I was just meeting friends, I would stop at Divas on the way home to grab a drink, and then pick up another guy even though I was kind of tired and not that interested. I even fucked a guy around seventy years old. He was a big scientist at The Jet Propulsion Laboratory (JPL) and was so excited to be with his first t-girl. I wasn't turned on at all, but I really enjoyed giving him one of the top-five experiences of his life. After we were done, he offered me five hundred dollars to stay overnight. Hmmm, tax free . . . I might have, but he kept wanting to suck my cock, and he was biting it because he was so turned on.

My new chiffon see-through blouses were pulling in Dick so fast, I added a new rule. I could only purchase blouses so sheer you could see my bra through the clothes. My plan was to keep being a slut until I validated that I had the right to be happy and have fun totally clear of guilt and shame. I wanted to *feel* confidence and faith in the feminine part of my personality. Not just the sexuality—but the *attitude* . . . joy, love, being a good person, and appreciating life's diversity. Only then I would consider scaling back the sex and partying.

I ended up with a picture on my iPhone with a dick in my mouth and cum all over my face, and I didn't know who's dick it was. I was so proud.

I told all my friends. My ex-girlfriend Cheryl wanted to grab lunch to exchange some items and catch up. At lunch she said she had only gone out on one date, but he was boring, and nothing came of it. She asked if I was dating. What was I going to tell her, that I fucked over forty guys since I last saw her three months earlier? The thought of seeing the look on her face made me chuckle. But I just said, "No, I'm not really bothering to try." Which was half the truth—The Dude's truth.

I really enjoyed telling women I met in the bars and clubs what I was up to and sister-bonding with them even deeper:

> "Well, for the first time I broke up with a girl for the Dick. When we were dating, I just couldn't get the Dick out of my mind. Then I fell off the wagon and had a guy unload in my mouth. When I tasted that hot load, I knew I just had to go back to the Dick."

I got big cheers from the girls. "Yup, can't give up that Vitamin D!" Not one of them expressed one iota of curiosity or compassion for The Dude. There was no sad trombone for him; this was a celebration. Women were *valiantly* validating me, instead of ignoring or criticizing me. I remembered how awesome this felt!

Based on this feedback, I created a view of reality in my head that women were focused on hot Dick and would never consider dating the old-fashioned, romantic Dude. Even though I knew this wasn't true, it was easier for me to tell The Dude that to ensure he would stay humiliated and weakened, thus not interfere with my fun. Clever bitch that I was.

I became friendly with several super sexy female bartenders, and when I picked up guys at their bar, I loved walking out of the bar with him on my arm, wiggling my ass like a slut, and turning and waving at the bartenders who would wink at me with a big smile. And when I would see them again the next night, we'd have something fun to talk about. I was back with all that great girl energy! Life was no longer a chore. Even when some bullshit came about, I just had The Dude deal with it. I knew no matter what happened, I would later be having fun around people who loved me and appreciated me expressing a little girl drama.

And guys were always so nice to me. They all told me what they like most about fucking me is that I really enjoyed it, and I wasn't shy about how much fun I was having. Who would have thunk! More and more of

Hanging with Trangela Lansbury and Punky Pebbles at a dispensary party

my friends were calling me a slut. I was touched. It was such a great compliment to be reminded how far I had come from being a suburban loser to the super slut that outslutted many of the most hardcore SF LGBT sluts. I had normalized being a slut, so I could enjoy and experience a whole new life without doubt and bullshit rolling around in my head. I was a girl, and I wanted to be a nasty girl.

SORDID DETAILS

I was now licking guys' balls, then working my way up their shaft, then blowing them while I was playing with their ass, making them crazy until they shot their load. I would lick up the cum, slosh it in my mouth, then put their dick back in my mouth, spit the cum back up and then whip it around with my tongue.

Ha, I was the devil! Being the devil actually helps you because it then becomes hard for anyone to trick you. You now know it all too well, and you aren't tempted to handle stress by running away from your responsibilities to some kinky fantasy because you've been there and done that.

Now let's talk about real good nasty sex.

Anal sex

The problem with recreational-only sex is you need to keep amping it up. You also have a lot more free time than people in relationships, so you might drift into watching more and more crazy porn. And there is always more new material and variety at your disposal. And this gives you ideas.

I started watching many videos of t-girls getting fucked in the ass. I loved watching a t-girl losing control as a man pounds and dominates her body. It was so violent. Hot! I loved that flesh on flesh pounding sound. I loved going into that completely different raunchy head space. I never imagined I'd want to have anal sex regularly. The taste of the Dick made me feel free, but anal is a whole other thing. It would put me into the major leagues of queer and help ensure The Dude was too humiliated to consider mustering his force to fight me anymore. I wanted him to get fucked out of me.

I was getting bored with giving blow jobs, and anal was clearly the next goal. But this was some serious shit. I had only done it a few times, as it was difficult and a lot of work with the stretching, lube, pain, towels, risk, and challenges getting it in. But I was determined to keep moving forward, and I was willing to give it another go. I needed to find the right guy—somebody who had a big, hard cock and a lot of patience. And I knew the perfect guy, one of my fuck buddies, Patrick. We had dry humped before, and he said he wanted to fuck me when I was ready. I sent him a text and saw him a few weeks later. In the meantime, I put that dildo back up my ass to stretch it out and got a brand-new container of Gun Oil silicon lube. What a great name.

A few weeks later . . .

SORDID DETAILS

I grabbed Patrick's cock through his jeans and, as usual, it was huge and rock hard. I fell on my knees, pulled down his pants, and my jaw dropped as I saw that monster waiting for me. I wrapped my mouth around the head and worked down along his shaft like a pro. I was shocked at how terribly hard and thick he was. I still wasn't used to those hugely swollen Viagra dicks. I must admit, they were pretty fucking hot, so I didn't care what drugs he was on. I could see how Viagra has *major* implications for the human race and its physical *and* spiritual evolution.

I deep throated him for a while, gagged and coughed a dozen times, and then I pulled out, took a deep breath and looked at him with satisfaction. "You ready for me to fuck you, Maria?" he said. I was so turned on by how much of a pig I was, I wasn't even afraid. I was more concerned about getting his dick in, because I couldn't have this quest continuing to bug me every night.

I jumped up and repositioned the big full-length mirror so I could watch. As I was going back to get on the bed, he grabbed my arms unexpectedly from behind and pulled me hard toward him, crunching his huge, hard dick against my ass. *Oh my, my. I really like this... oh this is different... and that pole is fucking huge.* It felt like some big, thick snake coming out of his body. I had never felt anything like that. *Such a girl I am!*

He pulled me back harder, *Oh God, I'm melting into his hot muscle body.* I got on the bed doggy style and pushed my ass back like I was a sheep signaling that I wanted to be mounted. He obliged and started rubbing that thing all over my ass. I loved the feeling of a massive, hard warm body up against me while I wiggled my ass around that thing. Patrick then grabbed my shoulder. "You ready to get fucked?!" I turned my head and looked in the mirror and saw my body in a compromising position with another man, and pushed my ass back against his cock, screaming, "Yea, fuck me!"

He pushed that dick up against my hole. *Oh, the pressure.* I remembered how hard it was getting it in, but I had been practicing. He wiggled around to find the right angle, and when he made that big thrust, *oooh!* I still wasn't used to it. I couldn't help but tighten up, and he couldn't get it in. I forgot how determined I had to be to get it in despite the pain. My body was telling me to stop, but my mind was saying, we're going to fucking do this. He asked me if I needed a rest, but I grabbed my ass, opening my cheeks to relax, and he went for another shot. "Oh God," I moaned as I felt that monster pushed up against my ass. But this time I was going to relax despite the pain. *Oh, that hurts... relax, oh pain, relaxing, oh God, it's filling me up.* "Yea" I started moaning in sync with his thrusts, each going deeper and deeper ... through the pain, relaxing more each time. Remembering I was a slut helped me to open up that last sphincter barrier, *push baby, this is fucking nuts...* "Ahhhhh"... *he's in!!*

I'm here! Oh shit, can I hold this? "Oh fuck!" I screamed. This was some fucking crazy sex. At first it didn't feel like sex, it felt like pain. But once I got used to it and relaxed and got the motion going, it was fucking crazy, nutty fun. I bobbed my head down and screamed, "Fuck me!" He pounded me for a few minutes, but just as we were getting to the really hot violent flesh on flesh pounding sound, it started hurting too much. Or maybe I just chickened out. I had to pull forward and popped out his dick. Ah relief. My body just wanted to rest. I didn't exactly feel sexy, more tired, but I was determined to keep going.

I got on top of him to ride his cock. This was always much easier because I could control the situation better. I guided that cock right back into my ass and felt that pain again, but this time I pushed right through it knowing this super slut could do it now. He was inside me—we were fucking! It hurt, but not as bad, and I slowly started going up and down at my own pace. It was really erotic as our bodies synched in sexy motion. I started jerking myself off with one hand while I stabilized my body with the other. And there was my new favorite feeling again—pain and pleasure! They say pro kinksters can mentally connect the two in their mind. I'd have to work on that.

As I rode that cock, I sped up and focused more on deep synched breathing to get into the zone. I remembered years ago fucking my girl-friend, a sweet Kindergarten teacher who turned into an animal riding my cock vigorously with her eyes closed. I used to wonder what she was thinking. And now it was my turn—I was going to be just like her. I grabbed his hands, cocked my head back, closed my eyes, and started screaming like an animal. I wanted to cum real hard while having intercourse with a man. It was so hot, but I couldn't cum yet and couldn't go on anymore. I had to pop him out of me. We were done with anal for the night. I sucked him off and got yet *another* thick creamy load in my mouth. *Ah, goodnight!*

Round 2

I never saw Patrick again, as he also claimed he was getting back together with his ex. Probably not true. One thing that sucked about fucking guys as a t-girl was that if you wanted to practice something, and you didn't do a great job because you were still learning, they usually never saw you again. Guys are lame. But, no worries, there were a lot more where that came from.

I set up a date with Scott who I had previously hooked up with. He had a smaller dick anyway. We met at my hangout, the Cinch. I really wanted to make it a proper date, complete with flirting and playing around a little at the bar. And I wanted to do one of my favorite things, which was pushing my ass against his cock so I could feel that strangely uncomfortable yet titillating feeling of his balls while I was talking to girls at the bar. I just loved looking at them while I felt those balls against my ass, thinking, "Look at me! I'm a woman just like you. I'm going to get fucked in the ass!" You might think I was acting like an immature teenager, but I deserved to experience all stages of my life properly.

SORDID DETAILS

Scott and I went back to my place and the anal was much easier this time. We did it doggy style, and the feeling of his balls banging up against my ass really turned me on, especially as I imagined those hot girls from the bar watching me getting fucked. I needed quite of bit of imagery to go through with this sort of thing. I screamed as he pushed my head down just like women did when I fucked them. I really let that screaming out, something I couldn't do when I was giving a blow job. "Give it to me!" "Fuck that useless dick!" I loved hearing the sound of the bed banging against the wall, with his balls pounded into me, and the sound of our flesh smacking against each other.

I was thinking about what a great feeling it was to give up something I held most precious most of my life. Sexuality was a gift from God, and I had chosen to throw it all away to be in the gutter of cheap sex. The world had abused, ignored, and humiliated my romantic self, and I wasn't going to let this keep happening. I was going to sabotage myself. The devil won. I was too weak. Yet now I was in control. I was able to cover the sorrow with kink as I protested on my own terms the deranged world we live in. I joined the tribe of heathens and loved it. Scott shrieked, "I'm going to cum!" I screamed, "Oh, fucking cum in my ass you pig," as I thought about how scary it was that I loved this kink shit more than anything. What would all those girls I liked in high school who wouldn't give me the time of day think about this! *Look at me. I've switched teams. I'm giving into my queer inclinations. I choose to be queer because I don't have to follow the straight mold.* I used to think it was just a fantasy, and there I was getting fucked in the ass just like the Sweet Transvestite with my garter belt and stockings.

Scott's body started crunching me . . . here it comes! "Aaaaaaaaah," He screamed, and then he thrust hard into me, grabbing my shoulders and pushing me forward. It was so torrid as he thrust a few more times with those balls pressed up against me. That was it! I was definitely no longer a man. I couldn't have a girl anymore. My body was locked with another man while he was cumming! *Yea! I made it.* One final thrust, and I started playing with myself rapidly as I imagined all that cum inside of me. Scott relaxed, and we stayed there for a minute enjoying the post-fuck serenity. Then I popped him out of my ass while grabbing the condom to make sure none of his cum ended up in my ass. I was tempted to empty the condom into my mouth like they do in porn, but I drew the line at licking ass, and I didn't want any stray ass juice in my mouth.

I was back in the club of t-girls who had intercourse. I was definitely no longer experimenting.

With a black dude

I just had to have black Dick in my ass. I was ready. I had seen Anthony a few times before. This time I wanted to see my stockings and heels on his shoulders while he was fucking me in the ass.

SORDID DETAILS

He had a great body, like so many black guys. We started by rubbing our dicks together. I had never done that! His huge dick was *so* much bigger than mine that it made me feel ashamed. But the shame feeling was so hot and really made me feel like a girl. His dick against my useless dick reminded me I wasn't a real man! Then he pushed me against the headboard. It was time to fuck. I felt so alive having that mass of black muscle pushing me down into the bed so hard I couldn't barely breath with my legs in the air, and then that massive cock poking at my ass. All those girls would be cheering me on because they would be jealous.

But of course, there was a downside to such a huge cock. It hurt way too much to get that thing in my ass all the way. *Ouch. Fuck, this isn't going to work.* We gave it a good go, and then I went for the easy fun. I rolled him over, pulled off the condom, laid on my stomach and blew him while thrusting my dick into the bed so I could get off. Taking that massive black head of flesh into my mouth, I was in pure Zen, not thinking about anything. I was a Dick slut as I skillfully worked that massive cock alternating between stimulating him with my tongue, then my throat, then rubbing the roof of my mouth rapidly against the massive skull flesh head of his cock. Anthony was getting a blow job from a pro!

Haaaaa! And here we go yet again. Anthony tensed up, and there she blew. "Ahhhhhhhhh," he screamed. There it was yet again, the warm unmistakable taste of a great, thick load. It just kept coming. It smelled so strong and so sweet. I rubbed my tongue against the cum-slippery huge skull of flesh as more cum shot out. I had so much warm cum in my mouth that I started blowing bubbles with it! I almost cried because I was so happy to reach yet another slut maximum. I had seen girls bubble blowing cum in a porn video and had to do it once I had a big enough load in my mouth. And there I was, mimicking my heroes.

I sat up in the bed and watched myself for a minute or so, blowing the cum bubbles, smiling at that happy, filthy girl in the mirror. Anthony came up behind me and pulled my arms and body back into his mound of muscle. I looked again in the mirror with my hard, queer cock sticking up, cum bubbles in my mouth, and me mashed up against a black muscle guy and thought, *I'm going to be doing a lot of this.*

Now I understood why many women say it's hard going back to white guys once you've had a black monster in your mouth. That massive head made me feel so deliciously gay. When I feel humiliated because I'm attracted to yet another woman I can't have, I just think of the black Dick I've sucked, and I feel sexy instead of feeing like a complete, utter piece of useless dog shit.

Now what?

This is what happens to a person like me when we break up with our conservative girlfriends.

I was feeling pretty damned good with what I achieved and what I had become. I was an oral sex master who could also have anal intercourse, if it wasn't too fucking huge. I didn't feel one pang of guilt or apprehension about being a sex fiend. I had filled out the big gap in my life . . . sex. I was now ready for my t-girl diploma. I was no longer shackled by the fear of my curiosity of the erotic. The universe's existence is based on all these atomic and subatomic particles constantly frolicking, fucking, and interacting with each other. I was there with the divine.

I still found it hard to believe women were doing this as normal part of their lives. *Girls, how do you control yourselves and stay focused on getting work done?* I still had so many things I wanted to try. I wanted to fuck a guy bareback and have him come in my ass and feel the warm cum drip down my legs—that was the ultimate rebellion. I also needed to have a threesome with me and two guys—one in my ass and one in my mouth, both cuming at the same time. I also want to get my boobs done and have ten guys cum in my mouth and have the cocktail of ten loads dripping down my chin onto my huge new tits. And how about getting pinned up against the wall by three guys while I'm riding a cock.

Okay, I think I was in love with the Dick. Actually I *worshipped* the Dick. Or maybe it was just a drug to me. What should I do? The problem was there was no end in sight. Wasn't I supposed to reach some spiritual Zen at some point after I'd tried enough things? Where was this train going?

Well, I would find it helpful to meet other people who were bigger perverts than I.

CHAPTER 28

THE ORGIES

I had been to orgies over the years and found them to be pretty gross. Don't get me wrong, I was amused. And I'm not judging people for participating. I just felt out of place. Even heavily intoxicated, I never was able to muster the motivation to join in. The whole thing was creepy. Sex should be flirty and fun, and despite being a slut, I still wanted to chat with the person at least a little bit before screwing them. Touching somebody's skin who I didn't know at all was just gross to me. Maybe I was a little old-school? I suppose I could have gotten into heavier drugs, but The Dude did enforce safety limits. Maybe I still needed him.

So, I was to learn once and for all that orgies were a spectator sport for this girl. I had lost the biggest slut status.

Massive all-male gay orgy

I thought I had seen it all, but this New Year's Eve Orgy goes in the top ten list of unique experiences.

How did I end up at an all-male orgy? I got a free ticket to go to a New

Year's Eve Burner[86] party in San Francisco of well over a thousand people. It was put on at a huge warehouse venue with multiple rooms. It had
a stiff admission fee, but I was able to get in for free by working a two-
hour shift. They put me on orgy duty from twelve thirty to two thirty a.m.
When I arrived, I found out it was all-male, which was not my bag. I really didn't want to work the shift. But I had promised, so I proceeded. My
job was to make sure that people were cool—not harassing anybody or
vomiting on the floor. Somebody has to do it.

Imagine being in the epicenter of gay San Francisco in a room about
the size of a two-car garage with so many guys in it that you could barely
squeeze even one more arm in there. On New Year's Eve at twelve thirty.
With music blasting so you couldn't talk. And I was the only girl in there.
Of course, they had zero interest in me—it was like I didn't exist, which
was handy for being an observer. The Dude would have melted and
perished.

I'd never seen so much fucking density in my life. There were mats
against the walls where mostly couples of guys were getting it on in every
possible position. Guys in the middle of the room were fucking in groups,
often with one guy receiving both in the front and the back while other
guys were watching, jerking and sucking each other off. There were
muscle guys standing against the wall with ginormous cocks sticking
out while they played with themselves waiting for somebody to come
along and suck them off. Guys would walk up to each other and just start
going at it. And without saying a word—it was just too loud. They were
like starving dogs looking for food. The look in their eyes was pure animal. I'd never seen a look like that before. Part of this was the drugs. A
lot of them were doing poppers[87]. As I looked in their eyes, I thought how
I admired such gay men. No talk, just go straight for the sex.

Guys were getting into my favorite toy, a leather swing held up by
chains. Other guys would come up to them for blow jobs, spanking,
and ass fucking. We're talking about non-stop action here, and for two
hours, my job was to circulate around and watch. Not only was it hard
to simply push through the mass of fucking muscle, but I kept tripping
over guys who were crouched down on the floor giving blow jobs. I felt

---

86. Put on my people who are active with Burning Man
87. Magnetic tape cleaner. Which is selling quite well these days even though there
is little tape left.

like I was in a pen full of hungry goats who had just been thrown bales of hay laced with cocaine.

I was way out of my league here. So, I tried the poppers. At first, I thought I was having some kind of stroke. All of a sudden it felt like the blood was collecting in my head and would cause it to explode. Fortunately, that didn't happen, and the guys there said that was normal. So, of course, I took another hit, a real deep one, and it was an instant high much better than weed or alcohol. Suddenly I just wanted to be touched and screwed. *Woo, I like this high!* I needed to do something with it, so *fuck it, I'll jump in*. But this gurl wasn't getting any takers. After the high wore off, so did my interest.

There was a huge variety of people there, all races, all colors, even a dwarf fucking big muscle guys, jumping from one to another on the mats, riding each one of them. I'm not making this stuff up! It was really wonderful to see such diversity and inclusiveness. I ran into several people I knew, some cheerfully said, "Hello, Maria," and then immediately got back to business. Others appeared too preoccupied, and I figured it was probably not a good idea to say hello.

This is something you just gotta see yourself to believe it. All I can say is that I really appreciate that we have so many ways to live our lives, and this was a really great opportunity to see how some people have fun. Everybody there looked really happy, and that was really wonderful to see. It had been a while since I had something really new to share with my friends!

As soon as my shift was over, some of the guys invited me to hang out on the dance floor, but my feet hurt, and I really needed a shower and wanted to just eat some cheese and crackers in front of the TV and go to bed.

Trans orgy at Burning Man

I was always curious about Burning Man[88].

I never planned on going. I hate dust and being dirty. But Meghan

---

88. A huge counterculture festival of over eighty thousand people in late August in the middle of the desert outside Reno. An entire city is built in the middle of nowhere, and when it's over, every trace of it is removed. It is very impressive and a lot of fun. If you can handle the dust. You have to be self-sufficient. You can't buy anything there except water and coffee. People come from all over the world to attend. There are other smaller Burning Man festivals around the world.

Rutigliano, one of the singers I worked with, arranged for me to get a free ticket, got me into a camp[89], and we were to play at a big event, "The Great Train Wreck," on the open Playa—the open desert with the big art exhibits. All in my first year. *Okay!*

Lots of astounding art, even turning a 747 into a disco at night. (But first you had to find it out in the desert)

Playing on the "Front Porch" (an art car) with Meghan in front of the Great Train Wreck in 2018. You can't see me, but I'm on the keyboard, behind the trumpet and sax player.

---

89. You really need to be in a camp—which organizes water disposal, sharing of food and booze—in order to be in a good location and for social reasons.

Playing piano at the Folly in the Deep Playa in 2019 with Meghan and many of the same musicians. The Folly was burned to the ground (intentionally) the next night.

The Folly

Video of the show

I got to use the makeup room at the Comfort & Joy camp. Seeing this makeup room in a tent in the middle of the dusty desert was surreal.

✳ ✳ ✳

My first year, I camped at *Gender Blender*, a camp which "welcomes people of all genders, plus their straight friends and admirers". It was a real privilege to join such a diverse group. The Dude showed up first and felt way out of place. They were very friendly, but the energy vibed a lot more when they met Maria. I was more clearly one of the them.

Burning Man camps typically require their members to take one or more work shifts,[90] like kitchen duty, setting up a tent, greeting people to the camp, bartending, or whatever. My shift was orgy detail. Most camps provide some kind of product or service as part of their contribution to the city—booze, grilled cheese, repairing bicycles. Our camp had an orgy dome about thirty feet in diameter with mattresses all over the floor. My job was Vibe Checker, making sure people weren't getting into trouble, regulating the number of people in the dome, and keeping a positive vibe going. There was also a Lube Runner who provided our guests with lube and hand wipes so they didn't need to get up and interrupt their activities.

When I arrived for my two-hour shift, around thirty people were going at it. Most were couples—two women, trans plus woman, trans plus man, two trans. One of the larger groups was men and women, or men and trans, I wasn't quite sure. That's the nature of the trans world. I saw a trim muscle guy with lots of curly body hair, topping several people, mostly women. He looked like he was the king top of that group. After about twenty minutes, he stood up and got into a position where I could see he had a vagina. Wow, he was an F2M[91]. I looked more carefully at his face, and I could see that his features were somewhat feminine. The scene was surreal. The desert winds were blowing like mad that night. Outside, you couldn't see five feet in front of you, the walls of the dome were shaking like an earthquake, and here we were having an orgy in the middle of all this.

When I had entered, a woman was in the corner with her fishnet-covered legs and heels in the air getting pounded by a guy. Thirty minutes

---

90. One of the core principles of Burning Man is participation. Things just don't happen magically with an invisible lower-class service staff. Everybody is part of making the community.

91. A F2M (Female-to-Male) transsexual refers to a woman who has transformed into a man.

later, her legs were *still* in the air! After a while, her partner raised his hand and the lube runner went over to give him a new supply. I was then able to see her face. She was a post-op MTF transsexual I had previously met. She'd had her vagina done recently and was ready to have fun with her new girl parts—I was jealous. He re-lubed and started pounding her again. Her legs were in the air, in the same position, I kid you not, for the entire two hours of my shift. What would that be like, wow, fun!

I saw a couple fucking for about thirty minutes and when they got up to leave, the woman said, "Hi, Maria." And there was another woman and trans couple going at it, and when they got up to take a break, I knew them also. I guess I get around!

Another post-op M2F transsexual I'd met a few days before was in the corner by herself playing with her pussy. A lost-looking guy entered and came up to me and nervously said, "I've never been to something like this before. I'm not sure what to do." I smiled and chatted with him for a bit, and then I introduced him to my new friend in the corner. Within five minutes, they were fucking their brains out. *Good deal!* After about thirty minutes, they were cuddling, and then when he got up to leave,

At the Piano Bar. People wear cool outfits, except the shoes which are typically sneakers caked with dust.

he came over to me with a big smile and said, "Thanks so much." I had helped guide his first orgy experience. I was helping spreading joy and love. Now he's going to go home a happy man and treat all his friends and co-workers with love and inspiration. I should get a job doing this.

When my shift was over, I had the option of staying. I had by this time finally accepted that orgies just aren't for me. I was a square in this world. I ran off to a piano bar instead. You can't take the entertainer out of the slut!

When I showed up around 1 AM, a lot of people were hanging out, but no piano player. I asked where the piano player was and they said, "We were kind of hoping you were." Little did they know. I sat down and blasted out tunes till around 5 AM. And the best part was there were dual pianos at the bar. Several budding musicians in their late teens and early twenties were overjoyed to have an opportunity to play with a performer such as myself, learn a few tricks, and jam out together. I'd learned the same way years before from others. I felt the cycle of life.

Collision of fantasy and reality

I was hitting a major milestone. My sexual fantasies were starting to exceed my ability to deliver them without seriously compromising my physical and emotional health and safety. For example, I wanted to try bareback sex, but I had to be very careful to find the right person and situation. How much farther did I have to go? I had clearly made up for all those decades of being an isolated loser in my suburban house. And I had also peered behind the curtain and discovered porn wasn't real and orgies weren't for me. There was really nowhere else to go.

I wanted to party less, and drink and smoke weed less, and fantasize less about the next big thing, but what was I going to do with all my energy and creativity? How the hell was I going to face The Dude's loneliness? The romantic bug kept tugging at me, and I had to make it stop. Sure, the right women could fall into my lap, along with baboons randomly typing Shakespeare. Romantic fantasies used to hold me over in those long periods of loneliness, but I didn't believe in them anymore. I couldn't even watch my favorite romantic movies because they were way too fake, and they contributed to the problem by setting unrealistic expectations. These dreams were just too distracting, and with The Dude around they kept bubbling back up. I knew I was trying to cover this sorrow up with partying, but there was nothing I could do to remedy the situation. Nowhere to go, nowhere to run.

I wanted to kill him, and I figuratively did. I killed him on *Facebook* in front of all his friends by posting pictures of knives and piles of dogshit. People thought I was just depressed, but they had no idea what was really going on, even though many of them knew about Maria. Talking about loneliness and not being able to find a partner is difficult because the first thing people typically tell you is everything you're doing wrong. Maybe I was too passionate. Or too feminine. Or too energetic. Maybe I should replace my entire brain!

I couldn't draw any conclusion other than my destiny was recreational sex with no realistic possibility of a romantic relationship. It was the only viewpoint that would maintain my confidence and sanity. So, I needed to put my romantic fantasies into quasi-permanent hibernation or, better yet, kill them completely.

I started seeing a therapist who specializes in sex change. The idea of leaning a little bit farther over that cliff to get a better view of the bottom was irresistible. It's important to explore all that piques your interest for whatever reason, right? Just don't slip on the rocks. Was I really serious, or was this kind of a goof, like the idea of Bruce Wayne becoming Batman full time because he loved wearing the outfit and getting all the attention? I used to wonder if Batman ever danced in front of the mirror at home, getting off on his spandex shorts and tights.

By this time, I had increasingly reacted very strongly when I saw women walking around with black spandex pants. I would marvel at the shape of their hips and vagina showing through, so sexy. It triggered my fantasies. I'll never *be with* a woman I really want, but what if I had my sex change and really *became* one of them? I now had a lot of female friends offering to help Maria join their team. I could *really* kill off The Dude, stop the painful struggle forever, and truly be fabulous.

PART 6

SEX CHANGE?!

CHAPTER 29

GENDER THERAPIST

Working with the therapist

One of the first major steps in the sex change process is seeing a therapist. Many t-girls have wanted to transition to becoming a woman for a very long time. Many see the therapist to get the required documents to have their penis surgically turned into a vagina. For others like me, it is more of an exploration of who am I, what's going on with the traumas in my life, and whether or not I should even consider it.

Paula-Jo Husack is a coach, consultant, licensed marriage/family therapist, who has special expertise in the transgendered community, but serves all folks[92]. I met her when The Dude was directing one of our shows.

---

92. Her practice, LeadLifeNow.com, is a resource library for a multitude of life's changes in families, organizations, and on stages. As an intern, she began advocating for kids and youth, who were coming out as transgender. She has been an activist and clinical provider for those, who want to transition, providing the year of therapy required by law; and collaborating with Gender Reassignment Surgeons toward a fulfilling transition experience both medically, administratively, mentally, and emotionally. Also, for kids and teens, exploring their own gender and sexual identity; and parents want a road map where none has governed. She's given workshops for couples and families in and through Transition. She offers virtual sessions throughout the world; and in person in San Francisco and Burlingame.

She was in a choir we had on the show, and I got to chatting with her. She somehow clocked me. Maybe I asked her what she did for a living and a sparkle appeared in my eye.

We had Paula on the show:

Video: Paula talks about the differences between M2F and F2M transsexuals. She also describes the word "trans" to mean not necessarily surgery, but people who may occasionally *need* to dress as a member of the opposite sex, especially many men, who feel oppressed by a highly competitive male cut-throat environment and often do this to relax.

Paula tells us many people have felt this their whole lives, but the level of transphobia out in the world prevents them from exploring dressing as the opposite sex. And homophobia prevents them from exploring sex as the opposite gender.

I ask Paula how one can know if they really should permanently change their sex. For example, I identify in part as an *autogynephilic transsexual*, one who is turned on by the idea of himself as a woman versus the more common case where one really feels like she is a woman.

She tells us that's why the health care community has the one-year rule:

> *You can't have genital reassignment surgery (GRS—where they turn your penis into a vagina) unless you live full-time as the opposite sex for at least a year under the supervision of a licensed therapist.*

You can pontificate and discuss for years whether you are a man or a woman and should transition, but you won't really know unless you live full-time, including working as a woman for a whole year. Well, that will clarify things pretty quickly.

Paula also gives some advice for those who are new to this and want to explore—find people in the community. She is motivated and inspired to do this work because she has seen so many people dramatically improve their lives and self-esteem by exploring this and finding their full, true selves.

I was super nervous as I went to my first appointment. *What if I really am a woman? What if I'm not but she convinces me I am? What if somebody finds out about this?* It helped that Paula was easy to speak with.

The first question Paula asked me was why I thought Maria was a problem. This left me speechless. That was the first *big* lesson—there is nothing wrong with anything you're doing that is *different*, providing it is not harming you. That's complex, because being yourself can harm you in the short term if you're not careful, but it's something you must explore long term.

At first, we didn't discuss any trans issues. We explored traumas and fantasies, as well as my masculine and feminine characteristics. We talked a lot about my growing up overseas outside the influence of the Monoculture Virus. About my being a musician who was very tuned to good and bad vibes in everything from a very young age. About my frustration with straight dating, and about the dearth of feminine sensibilities in a male-dominated work and political environment. We talked about the frustration, misery, and isolation I faced trying to find balance and inspiration in my Tech work, about how I didn't really like the Dick, but I loved being a slut because it was so out of character for me and made me feel sexy and fabulous instead of a loser. And about my normalizing kink and my desire to run away and be a woman and what that meant. Was it a fantasy or an addiction? Was I a man struggling to balance the masculine and feminine, or indeed a woman? Or perhaps both—a transsexual or a spiritual hermaphrodite.

I saw Paula roughly once a month for several years. It took me a few months to talk through these things. Once we got over that hurdle, we got down to business. And the first business at hand was that being Maria *was* harming me, but not because I was doing it. Au contraire. I was anxious about it, which led me to party a bit too much, avoid relationships, and surf too much porn. But that's pretty normal, isn't it?

We then discussed why I would even consider sex change. On one hand, I was worried my interest had the telltale signs of a sexual addiction rooted in emotional trauma around my feminine sensibilities that were trodden upon *constantly* regardless of whether I was presenting as a man or a woman. But on the other hand, my way of working through complex issues is to experience the feelings and thoughts that came from "trying on" various mindsets. Maybe I was a woman, maybe I just wanted to be kinky, maybe I was a pretty natural straight guy who was suffering from the aftermath of serious emotional abuse or trauma. I might discover Maria was really just an entertainer. Maybe she was a part-time girl, or even a full-time girl who would take hormones and have all the surgeries. All these could be explored.

I may seem like an oversexed person, but our sexuality drives almost everything we do whether we admit it or not. The dominance of porn on the internet is evidence of this. Much of our behavior is subconsciously driven by our need to feel sexy or desired. In order to live a healthy, balanced life, you need regular sex, cuddling, or romance, especially if you want to be a high-functioning individual and you're pushing yourself to do things that you really care about and define your life. Many of these things are complex, risky, and require *a lot* of hard work, and you need something in your life you can depend on that provides companionship, support, and fun.

If I don't have sex, cuddling, or romance somewhat regularly, I don't feel good about myself. I feel stressed, and it's hard to keep going. I need at least an alternative, which is fun and easy sex without the trappings of the programmed straight male/female relationship. Otherwise, I would be experiencing *murderous torture* for decades. In the *Star Trek* episode "Amok Time," Mr. Spock went insane because it was mating time, something Vulcans only do once every seven years—except in my case the murderous urge and torture was once every seven hours. This is why that fucking Culture Virus works so well. It has evolved to attack us where we are most vulnerable, in our reproductive machinery. In our case, specifically our craving for companionship and sex.

Maybe the world really is fucked up and upside down and that's why I was in this situation, or maybe the world is just as it should be, and I hadn't learned to adjust. Regardless, The Dude and I would not stop fighting each other. The insurmountable problem was his mismatch with the straight dating scene. Many things in life you just can't explain, and you just have to move on. That's one of the great lessons as you get older. Maybe I needed to be sensitive to the fact that The Dude was resisting his death. But what was I to do? I needed to keep moving and exploring. I had a purpose, and I couldn't have him dragging me down. Maybe it was time to shed the dead skin.

Discussions with other trans women

Playlist

In addition to my invaluable work with Paula, I also had insights from many transgendered women I had met. We have several interviews on a playlist.

After interviewing several trans women, I was a little embarrassed that my conception of trans folks was so influenced by my own experience, that I often forget I was in the minority as far as trans folks go. I probably have more in common sexually with straight men than with trans women. But a whole subculture of trans women is more like me, including many of my trans friends—one of whom transitioned because she could no longer relate to that unbalanced male killer instinct. It was enlightening to *experience* that words like transgender and transsexual can have so many very different meanings. I wondered if I was more of a *spiritual hermaphrodite*, living as both sexes and changing at will depending on my mood and the situation vs. a *transsexual* that some define as being in the wrong body and transitioning to a more fitting body. There are many other terms, such as genderfluid or pansexual, that might describe me. One could debate for hours what these words mean because in the end, they're just words.

Being both sexes provides many obvious advantages. But a struggle existed between me and The Dude because he was so depressed. All he did was make money and work on projects that benefitted me. Maybe this depression and The Dude's inability to connect with a female partner indicated I really was trans? When I later spoke in private with one of the trans women I interviewed, she said she had much more in common with other performers than other transsexuals. This again reminded me our demographics don't define who we are, and labels are just an attempt to categorize certain behaviors to help guide us. We're all different. This is obvious, but we need to be *constantly* reminded of this as we battle to make sense of the world and ourselves.

The surgery, results

I knew many girls who had the full sex change. Cassandra Cass, who we met earlier, looks absolutely incredible. I saw all of her backstage,

With Cassandra Cass

and I wouldn't have known the difference. What about the sex? Cassandra described her orgasm as a "slow burn." And look at the clothes she can wear.

My friend Diane who I had hooked up with both before and after the surgery had a *great* time with sex after transitioning. At first, she had a ton of fun hooking up with men, women and other t-girls, and then she married a man. She told me some procedures are focused making the vagina *look* good (for porn), whereas others are focused on making it *feel* good (for sex). This made sense, as I've interviewed several porn stars and was disappointed to learn that many performers don't enjoy shooting porn from a sexual perspective as much as they love it as a visual art. But you wouldn't know it from watching them. They are professional actors.

M2F sex change is a series of procedures that includes taking female hormones, getting breast implants, GRS, facial feminization (the most expensive), hip and butt enhancements, and other procedures.

Most of the surgeries generally have a good success rate, but GRS is a significant risk, and many t-girls get everything else done except that. You already know how much fun the sex is with your tool, but if you have the GRS, you might end up with no sensation at all, not to mention health complications. And most guys who like t-girls won't date one who doesn't have a tool. The tool makes you more exotic and special, and a lot of guys like to play with it.

If you want GRS, you need to seriously think about what your motivations are. Is it because you get to wear great clothes, or is it because you literally hate your penis and would take a pair of scissors to it if you had to? Despite the risks, many girls go through with it anyway, for various reasons. For some, they just need to feel like a complete woman. For others it makes them feel like they've hit the end of their journey or struggle—it's a kind of Holy Grail of sex change.

For me, GRS was extremely alluring, but it was probably just a fantasy, one I kept getting reminded of every time I saw a girl walking around in her tight jeans or hot spandex pants. I knew the risks, and I heard everything ranging from it's fucking awesome, you have to do this, and the sex is fabulous, to don't even consider it because you'll have no feeling. Realistically, going through GRS requires a *huge* amount of investigation. You also need to consider if you can readily afford to take off work for the six-month recovery time. And then there are all the other psychological and lifestyle factors. And you can't easily fall back on being a man if you're feeling stressed or having trouble earning the same level of income.

Should I?

This is some serious stuff and goes *way beyond* a fantasy. But in order to know myself and the nature of my relationship with The Dude, I had to *be* on this journey of exploration. I now wanted to experiment with deciding to look into sex change. I didn't expect that I would really do it, but I'd already gone so far, so why not just check out the next train station up the line, across the border. Just the first one, ya know. I mean, there wasn't a zero chance I would do it, it was just very low, right? I saw this as a form of quantum computing[93] where I explored multiple realities at the same time and was able to deeply examine all the options at once. The key was that you had to truly consider them all to be possible—because they are.

I had to do something to make this *real*, some kind of action, otherwise it was just research and another fantasy. See the GRS surgeon? Boob surgeon? Try hormones? Do a full-time girl one-week test?

First, I did what came naturally.

Declaration of womanhood

I started telling people I'd decided to have the sex change and was looking into it. I talked as if it were true because it was one real possibility. I wanted to see how it felt to say it and see people's reaction. This was stage one of making it real. I was especially excited to tell a woman I was really attracted to as a man that I wanted to be just like her. That made me feel even closer to women than ever.

---

93. An innovative form of computing that creates an enormous jump in computing power by using the physics of quantum mechanics to consider and calculate all possible outcomes at once, thus solving complex problems and optimization challenges very quickly. Some problems can only be solved with quantum computing.

I also told one of my friend's girlfriends. She was about my age, nice looking, and really cool—somebody The Dude would have *loved* to date. I told her I was going to get breast implants, but I just wasn't sure exactly when. And I said they were going to be big. I added, "If you're gonna do it, you might as well do it. I want to be reminded every second that I'm a woman." I could feel The Dude melting with shame, giving up as a man, as I said this to this woman he was really attracted to. It felt *so* good. She gave a huge smile. "Yea, awesome, girl. Go for it!"

I got goosebumps, as I suddenly became aware of my bra, and started thinking I could end up having to wear one of these every day for the rest of my life. A reminder of the choices I made. It felt so right to have an intimate conversation with a woman about being a woman. The girl energy from her was like waves of spiritual hugs. I wanted to feel like this forever. I felt like I really might get those girls done, like really. I had walked through the next quantum door. I could live like that and people would embrace me. I had already known that, but this was now real, not theoretical.

I kept getting a similar reaction from people. I was concerned about the size and asked people if my DDD breasts were too big. Most people encouraged me to go big. Big personality, big breasts, yes girl! But weren't they were supposed to stop me and say no, this is crazy? But nobody did except a few women, all of whom had larger breasts, who said you don't want to lug these around. But it titillated me that I would be willing to endure pain to have this new way of living.

And then I started also telling women, since I was a cum slut, the first item on the agenda after getting my huge breasts done was to have several guys cum in my mouth and have the cum drip down my chin onto my new tits. Bonding with them this way made me so utterly happy, I started convincing myself I really wanted to jump off that cliff into womanhood—because I realized I *really* did. It was okay to want to have loads of cum on my new tits and be proud of being fucking shit hot! It was so refreshing to not feel The Dude's tug as he slowly became weaker and weaker.

Every once in a while, he would say something. "Maria, this is all great in a world of no consequences. You know this is still just a fantasy. You do know that, right?"

"Shut up Dude, this is my time."

I was sleeping with a lot of guys as a matter of routine, and he wasn't able to do jack shit. Every time I wrapped my lips around a new cock, my being a woman became more real. I was now very aware of my bra and my breasts bouncing around while my head was bobbing up and down on another guy's cock. I *was* a woman sucking Dick. This is what girls do. I felt like a twenty-one-year-old woman building up dick sucking skills. I was so proud and happy. I had reached my goal of near nirvana, feeling completely natural and okay in all my feelings, both joy and kink, and even role-playing shame just for fun. I had this bull on his knees.

Then I told several female friends I was going to see the surgeon about getting a vagina. Most were very supportive and excited for me. Several said, "You can stay with me after you recover, and I'll give some dating advice as you get ready for your new life!" Cool! Sisters!

But several told me not to do it. "Why would you want to cut yourself up like that. And you'll have no feeling. This is not something you want to do." The success rate of the surgery and the pain were debatable, and they weren't knowledgeable about the stats. But they were knowledgeable about something else. "Why would you give up male privilege? Are you crazy? You have the best of both worlds. Your life is awesome. Do you want to deal with boobs all the time?" They looked so disappointed as they encouraged me to reconsider.

One of them, Sharon, was a very close genetic female friend. She told me I should not even get my breasts done. It's too hard being a woman. "Just be a girl when you go out for fun. You have the benefit of having the man around to live easier. Otherwise, you'll be constantly harassed, not taken seriously." She was really concerned for me. I knew she had very valid points from my having met many t-girls who had transitioned.

For example, I had met a t-girl at a club in the Haight who was incredibly sexy and edgy and had an incredible set of boobs. She lived in central California, had been a biker dude, and became a woman a few years earlier. She was so fucking hot with her biker leather clothes and cleavage to complement. It was shocking. I wanted to try that so badly. I was a Rocker Chick, and now I wanted to be like her, a "Joan Jett" with huge breasts. I asked her what it was like.

She said, "Yea it's hot, but most of the time it's just a pain to have to get dressed and put on makeup to pick something up at the store." She added that it was really irritating to constantly get hit on by mostly disgusting guys and a pain to deal with problems like when visiting the auto mechanic.

I told her that was part of the fantasy.

She grabbed my arm and said, "Girl, no! Try it out for a few months, probably a year, and then see if you still want to do this."

And then there was the issue of how I was going to make money and afford to live in San Francisco and keep my grand piano. I was a power dude tech guy, and this wasn't going to go over well with my employers. Even if I managed, I didn't want to have to work in Tech as a trans woman, I wanted to be an entertainer, or even work at a makeup counter. But how would I afford that and live in San Francisco vs. some little no name town complete with chain restaurants and bars.

Despite all these issues, I couldn't get the idea out of my head. It was too exciting to entertain the real possibility of doing it. And talking with women about it made it feel so real. I really could be one of girls if I wanted. Why was I proceeding? Maybe I thought I could handle being a woman easier than they could. I did have all that Dude knowledge and confidence. Or was I just addicted to such a fun life? Or maybe I wanted to feel the burden of being a woman in some kind of karmic balancing—a need to connect with those I had accidentally persecuted as a guy. Or maybe I wanted to see how I could use my new power in my role as a woman. But did I really need to step through this huge door and have surgery and go full time to know what it was like being one of them? Hadn't I done enough of that already?

I figured I wanted to explore what it was like to be *me*. Not The Dude. I ain't him. I *wanted* this. I needed to explore being me, without him.

When I saw Sharon a few months later backstage at a show, I told her, "I thought about what you said, and it makes a lot of sense." She seemed relieved. As I was putting on some eyeliner and looking at her in the mirror pointing to my made-up face, I clarified, "But I realized I really want this." A slight frown came over her face, and I thought about how ironic it was to tell her as I was putting on makeup, something I would have to do almost every day for the rest of my life. "I've decided I'm going through with the sex change, starting off with getting my boobs done. It's just a matter of when."

Her frown deepened as she muttered, "Oh . . . my." I could see her disappointment—or was it concern? Was she disappointed in The Dude as a man or was she seeing me as a person she thought was just making a bad decision? I couldn't help but think of it more as disappointment in The Dude. It was like me telling her I was in so much pain being rejected as a man, I was willing to go through with this so I could cover my pain with addictive kinky behavior. It was the closest thing I could do to tell a woman the truth of the complexity of The Dude. Words meant little compared with action. This summed it up well. *No more discussion, no more complaining, no more pontificating on why I was so frustrated. It was very simple. I quit. I was switching teams.*

That I had to go to this measure to get the loving attention of women was starting to irritate me. But I didn't really care anymore. Because I was a woman. I was not a man desired by women. It wasn't really my choice, but that bird had flown. Life is finite. Before The Dude could protest, I set the next action of exploring transitioning into motion.

One-week test

My therapist Paula had been asking me when I was going to start living full time as a woman. I wasn't sure if she was nudging me into getting what I wanted, or if she wanted me to finally realize it wasn't for me and accept it. But Paula's job was to nudge. It was my decision regarding which way to jump. I wasn't nearly ready to live and work as a woman full time for a year in order to qualify for GRS, but I had just gotten laid off from a miserable job and had several months of severance, so I could easily do a test run and try being a full-time girl for a week.

How would it feel having to deal with these huge breasts every day and then sleep with them? Putting on makeup every day. Having to match my outfits and the bling . . . *every* day. The Dude just rolled out of bed and was ready to go in about fifteen minutes, and that included a shower. What if I forced myself to put on that bra and the makeup and all those other things right out of the shower? I figured it was like learning a foreign language. If you really wanted to do it, move to the country, endure the hardship and force yourself to learn it.

I got my eyebrows trimmed, which made my makeup look a lot cleaner and took about twenty minutes off the time it took to get ready. As a little treat, I got acrylic nails, nice and long with a shiny red metallic nail polish. Excited, I immediately went to Divas and tapped them on the bar while I was waiting for my drink. I loved the reflection of the light on my bright red nails, and I wanted to see them stroking some guy's dick and then see his cum all over them.

The nails lasted less than forty-eight hours. It was almost impossible for me to put my contact lenses in, but I eventually figured that out by using the side of my fingers[94]. I also promptly discovered I couldn't masturbate very easily. I kept scratching myself and poking holes in my pantyhose. And it took forever to type anything on my computer keyboard. Worst of all, I couldn't play the piano. Damned reality. It broke my heart, but I got rid of the nails—after one last night out tapping my nails on various bars all around town, trying to pick up guys to fulfill that cum-on-my nails fantasy. But it was the middle of the week, so no luck. Next time I wouldn't make a nail appointment unless I had a date set up with a guy or two.

Once the nails were gone, things were much easier. I figured I'd make my one week. But now the women's underwear, clothes, and makeup were a constant arousal. I couldn't stop getting excited and playing with myself. But after I came, I just wanted to relax in front of the TV or play the piano. I didn't want to be wearing all that makeup and sexy clothes. This was a well-known telltale sign that transitioning to full time wasn't for me. I tried keeping on a bra with the large breasts, but they kept getting in the way, especially when I was sitting at the computer. It also didn't feel right, and I had a hard time relaxing. To deal with that, I started smoking pot during the day, which I rarely did. I wasn't interested in just sitting there sober as a girl. And during the day I kept thinking about how much fun it would be going out that night. I couldn't focus on getting any work done, and I just wanted to look at porn all day because I was all sexed up.

I couldn't make it three days as a girl. It looked like the writing was on the wall. *Damn, I can't escape this world by becoming a woman. Maybe I am just a kinky, frustrated guy.* But that's the last thing I wanted to be. I wanted to be fabulous. But on the other hand, it was much easier to get stuff done as a man, especially making money. So, my life was pretty damned good, but I couldn't tolerate having to socialize as a man and work so hard at getting people to pay attention to me. I could just continue to rarely socialize as a man. *Shit, those girls who told me I had the best of both worlds and should not transition were probably right.* What was I going to do?

---

94. But it did help me put on my lashes in that I could use the edge of the nail to press then against my eye lids instead of using my usual end of the makeup stick.

I thought maybe I would feel different if I took hormones. I thought about trying them for a few weeks, but I had seen too many trans friends who were on hormones and it made them a little crazy. They also reduce your sex drive—I didn't want to relax that way! They also cause a lot of side effects like itching and possibly blood problems, and they can take several weeks or months to take effect. So much for another drug to distract me. Besides, I'm a rocker chick. I thought about my death metal guitarist post-op trans friend who said her lack of balls and testosterone had made it difficult to rock. *Oh shit, can't have that!*

I was tempted to try the hormones anyway, but The Dude was keeping me sane. He still had veto power over my actions. And he was being really nice, not saying anything until I got a little crazy. It was beginning to look like I needed him. Shit. But I had to continue my investigation. I had to find out why I didn't want to be a man anymore. I had always figured the world was upside down, and I wasn't going to change myself to fit it. Become more like the average ruthless boring guy? No fucking way. But maybe the universe was telling me I *had to* look at myself as The Dude again. I didn't know if I could stomach that.

I had failed the one-week test. After all this, who the fuck was I?

I ran into a female friend who'd been very supportive of my transitioning and asked why I was hesitating. I told her I wasn't sure if it was right for me. She responded, "Maria, when you talk about dating women, you have a growl on your face, but when you talk about Dick, you glow!" Before I could come up with the words to try to explain that, she shot back, "Maria, you are a woman. You're hesitant because you don't respect women."

. . . *Holy shit, she might be right.* Could that be the big breakthrough? The reason I could readily accept this as a possible explanation was because I wasn't totally to blame for not respecting women. Our society should take at least half that blame, probably more. That I couldn't conceive going full time was possibly because I believed people wouldn't see me as a person if I were a trans-woman, or even a woman. Yes, I *was* afraid women, anything feminine, were seen as inferior, or maybe I even thought they were.

Why did I fail the one-week test? Probably because I was fetishizing women, and it's not easy to relax when you're fetishizing yourself. Or maybe because The Dude wasn't ready to give up the ghost, and maybe it was true he didn't respect women. He thought he was a romantic, but maybe he really just saw women as a way serve his romantic fantasies. This was getting way too confusing, and I was getting tired of going back and forth. I needed him to grow up and accept that the world is not as he conceived it. Get real, Dude. We found our place, and it might very well be sporting a bra every day.

I thought I might be right, and I might be wrong about him. But what did it matter? I had a life to live. *I am a woman; I am not him.* I needed to keep moving and go on to the next step. Otherwise, this was all theoretical and I didn't want to get into another useless argument with him. I couldn't ditch The Dude yet because I needed his income and stability. But I could make an appointment with the sex change/GRS doctor. *Try that skirt on!* I wanted to know how it felt to date guys and suck dick when I was planning a sex change—totally guilt free and ready to charge into the future! If I had breasts and a vagina, I might just explode off the launch pad into space. How would my life change if I had great cleavage showing through my blouses and dresses? I pictured myself in a fucking hot mini dress playing piano on stage with my bouncing boobs mesmerizing the audience. And wearing a hot leather rocker chick outfit while I was playing electric guitar. *Hoo yea!*

Whether or not The Dude survived wasn't my problem. As for my survival, I could still keep moving without making a commitment. I had to. I wondered if I was acting like an addict, impatient, trying to avoid a depressing world. I didn't believe so, because I felt like the great spirit was with me, appreciative of my spending the time to discover that which hurt me so deeply, and to explore my God-given fabulosity that the universe wanted to see out there.

Good. I had an excuse to visit the sex change doctor despite failing a simple one-week test.

CHAPTER 30

THE SEX CHANGE DOCTOR

Getting a referral from my therapist

I didn't tell Paula I failed the one-week test. I told her wearing a bra at home relaxed me and made me feel natural. I didn't mention that I immediately it tore off after I blew my load. However, I did tell her I felt hopeless as a man and needed to see the sex change doctor—that I was doing this in order to stave off the insanity. I told her the truth, I just omitted certain things. I needed the referral[95] to see the doctor, and I didn't want to put her in a professionally awkward situation, as I had strong evidence that changing my sex was not be for me. Or should I say not for The Dude, wink.

My way of avoiding the fact that I failed the one-week test was to constantly profess my love of the magic of the Dick, hoping to bury The Dude. I loved talking with Paula about how much Dick I was getting and

---

95. Doctors require a referral to meet them, and then letters from two therapists to confirm you've lived for a year full time if you want to schedule the surgery

how sexy and alive it made me feel. And Paula would go into the hugest grin. Her smile was so validating. I wondered if that grin was her enjoying the idea, or encouraging me, or her enjoying me enjoying it . . . probably all the above. Just more female bonding!

I was expecting her to analyze me further and give me all kinds of reasons I shouldn't see the surgeon. Instead, she asked me when and how I would tell my family. I'd never thought about that. The seriousness of it hit me. *I'm going to see the sex change surgeon.* This was no fantasy anymore. Visualizing telling my family and friends made me feel judged. If I told them, I would then feel compelled to explain, knowing that nobody, not even my family, wanted to hear my sob stories again. When I was younger, it was hard to get over the hurdle of feeling judged, but over the years, I had learned to put aside what others thought and focus on what's most important to *me*. Nobody else could *possibly* understand that.

What *was* important was that Maria loved to smoke pot, and I needed a lot of it to fuck guys. So, I was very worried that if I went full time, I would start smoking way too much and probably get into heavier drugs. The Dude was an important counterbalance. He didn't like any kind of drugs, rarely even alcohol. I was afraid I needed him.

However, I was coming to the end of this long road. Consulting with the surgeon was just about the very last step I could take without doing anything permanent. Thus, I would soon hit a wall of reality which I figured would put me on the cusp of bringing so many questions which had been building up over the years to light. So I might as well keep going a little longer. And if I saw the doctor, the GRS would also no longer be the ultimate fantasy. I might be freed from it nagging at me. I would be free regardless.

Paula was ready to set me up with the surgeon. She knew I had reservations, but who wouldn't? She said to me numerous times, "Maria, you are a woman." But that sounded crazy. *There is no way I'm a woman. I was deceiving her, not coming clean with my failure to live as a woman for a week, and maybe exaggerating my desire to be a woman. Isn't she supposed to suss this out and realize this whole thing was just a curiosity? That I'm not really serious.* Of course, that was misplaced thinking on my part, because I was pushing it forward.

And what exactly did "you are a woman" mean? I was definitely a guy with very strong feminine characteristics. Spiritually, I was a woman in many ways, that was crystal clear. But the shame and fear around considering I might be a woman, at least at some level, was stronger than I had realized. I loved being multiple things at the same time. I always felt that way as a kid travelling around the world, meeting so many different kinds of people. I was a woman. But I was also a man. So, she was right, but she was maybe missing that I was also a man? Where does that leave me? Round and around. In the end, I wasn't exactly sure why I wanted to see the doctor. I felt like my mind had split in two. Part of me really wanted to be a woman, or maybe *was* a woman. I wasn't really sure. The other part was *definitely* a guy.

But the bottom line was I had the one-year rule protecting me from making a terrible mistake, so neither one of us really had anything to worry about. I got the referral from Paula and set up an appointment with the GRS surgeon.

Appointment with the GRS surgeon

I went into this expecting somebody to try to stop me. I was kind of counting on it. I thought the various professionals and doctors were going to grill me with questions to make sure this was right for me. But I soon discovered the robust barrier was the simplicity of the one-year rule. Successfully living and working as a woman full time for a year would prove I was ready. Neither Paula nor anybody else needed to start double- and triple-questioning my motives and behaviors. It was already pretty clear to everybody I loved being a woman. The surgeons would simply give me what I asked for with absolutely no questioning and no judgements. They were there to do a job.

> What surprised me most about this process was I kept thinking the various doctors would question my motives to make sure that this was right for me, but I got nothing but encouragement.

I got all Maria-fied and felt self-conscious about walking into a doctor's office. I usually went out at night when the lighting smoothed over my look. But I was used to the nervousness of new experiences, and they made me stronger and feel more alive. On the way to the office, I was a little nervous having never driven that far as Maria. I couldn't help but wonder if people in the cars next to me were staring at me. Of course, they weren't looking, but I wondered if somebody saw a woman out of the corner of their eye ... me.

I arrived a little early, so I sat in my car with the engine, air conditioner, and music running and waited until nobody was in the parking lot. I then strutted over to the office, my huge, bouncing breast forms making me acutely aware that I was probably way more over the top than the other trans women I expected to be there. This made me a little uneasy, but hey, *this is who I am*. It felt great.

And that assessment was correct. The two other patients in the office were conservatively dressed compared to me. I proudly announced myself to the receptionist, my extra jovial attitude covering my apprehension. I half expected to get thrown out because I was either too much of a spectacle or an imposter.

The receptionist, much to my surprise, was a really nice, genetic young woman who immediately made me feel comfortable. I guess I shouldn't have expected otherwise. I sat down and waited for my appointment, looking over at the other trans women, hoping to strike up a conversation. But they didn't look at me. They seemed very shy, but maybe they didn't want to associate with a tramp and a whore because that is what I looked like. Well, that was most of what was in my wardrobe. I looked around, disappointed my magnetic personality didn't elicit any response, wondering *maybe I'm nothing more than a nighttime show queen who has taken this too far. But then again, I'm sure the doctor has working girl patients. Maybe these other t-girls think tramps gave trans girls a bad name. Well, whatever. Unlike my usual nighttime venues, this is not necessarily the place to celebrate queer diversity.* That's what I was thinking in my nervous state, anyway. They most likely simply didn't notice or didn't care.

I met the endocrinologist, who asked me a lot of questions about hormones and if I wanted to get started on them. As I was listening and looking at the various vials and charts about hormones, it really hit me. What did all that chatter in my head about kink driven by frustrations of not being able to have a relationship with women have to do with any of this? This was serious, big-league stuff. I really was entering a different world. *How many men have come in here and eventually emerged as women? How many lives were changed?* I wanted to find out more, but I didn't believe I was actually going to try hormones because of the medical risk, the effect on my libido, and the possibility of irreversible changes like never being able to get hard again[96]. But then again, I never thought I would ever jump out of an airplane when I offered to pay for my cousin to go skydiving. I wished life was a software program where I could clone myself and give it a try. Oh well, I was born too soon, maybe in several hundred years.

I finally got called into the examination room where I would meet the doctor to talk about the surgery. It was a typical room with diplomas on the wall, but this one also had many diagrams of vaginas and penises. I was a little antsy, as I anticipated the doctor would start asking me a lot of questions about why I wanted the operation and was I aware of just how hugely life changing and painful this procedure was. I figured she would suss me out and refuse me.

Wrong. The very first words out of her mouth were, "Girl, I have a new technique for creating a G-spot, you're gonna love the sex[97]." My jaw dropped. I thought I saw a dirty grin on her face, like she was saying, *Girl, forget all your stresses and worries, your dreams of pleasure are going to come true.* I was actually scared . . . because it was so exciting to take in what she was saying. Regardless of whether or I did it or not, the reality of other trans women doing this was mind blowing.

But I was trying to balance my excitement and play devil's advocate. Becoming a complete woman was more than just sex. Maybe for *me* it was largely about the sex, but should the doctor be encouraging this behavior? She's a doctor. However, in retrospect, I think she figured that was what I wanted. I was after all, dressed like a tramp. And she was right. I would fucking love this! She wanted me to know this dream could come true. *Oh shit, the last wall just came down. It's all my decision. I could do this. Fuck! What am I going to do?* I must have looked like I was in a trance. I don't even remember what my response was. Probably some kind of babble.

We chatted for a bit longer, as I had many questions about the procedure. I was surprised I could just get on her surgery schedule, show the letter from my therapist that I'd lived as a woman full time for a

---

96. Hormones can take weeks or can take months to affect you. So, the problem with just trying them is that permanent effects to your body could manifest themselves before they change the way you feel.

97. We did later discuss that the results vary widely, and some girls will end up with no sensation. Something I already knew at the time.

year, and she would flip my penis around and inside out and turn it into a vagina. I looked at her hands and wondered how many lives they'd changed, how many dreams they'd made come true? And she certainly looked like she loved her job. All while I asked questions, she said, "Girl, we're going to take care of you, you're going to love it."

We chatted a bit about how my boyfriend(s) were going to love the new me, all the while encouraging me with what I imaged was a "you're going to have fun sex" grin I was getting to love, and repeating, "We'll take care of you." I gave her a hug and she clearly noticed just how huge my breasts were. For a few moments I was scared this would make her think I was a pervert who had no business becoming a woman, but she just smiled. All that chatter in our heads prevents us from just enjoying so many moments.

I walked out of her office thinking, *I'm now officially her transgendered patient! This is real. That was easy. I guess this makes sense. It's a free country, and I suppose you want to be encouraged when making a difficult decision, but wow this seems beyond that.* But I figured these people were just doing their jobs. I had several theories regarding why it was so easy for me to deceive them:

1. **DUDE'S VIEW:** It's a money machine.
2. **MARIA'S VIEW:** I'm NOT deceiving them. I actually am a woman, I just don't believe it
3. **ONE-YEAR RULE:** It doesn't matter because the rule will prevent me from making a big mistake. Also, I'm clearly obsessed with this whole idea, so investigating it and being faced with the rule is the only way to be forced to get out of fantasy and into reality and remember that life is finite.

The one thing Dude and I did agree on was that the professionals were doing a great job. It was just so different from what we'd expected.

Now I was relaxed and satisfied. I'd had the courage to check this out and really think through who I was. Many of us have a tendency to panic and over-estimate the urgency to make important decisions about our future. We can instead allow it to evolve.

I was feeling so good, I decided I might as well see the boob doctor!

CHAPTER 31

THE BREAST DOCTOR

Over the years I had this kinky fantasy:

> *I went to the boob doctor's office and got all the paperwork for surgery set up so I could get my boobs whenever I wanted. And then later, in a moment of frustration, I made one phone call and found myself a DDD girl a few days later.*

Getting your boobs didn't require living as a woman. I could snap my fingers and have tits! It was also less expensive—around ten grand versus twenty-five thousand for the GRS. And it didn't require as much time off from work. This was more real and immediate, so I could start with boobs, and the GRS would be way in the future if I ever did it at all.

> *In the fantasy, **I left out the part about how I was going to earn money.** You could hide that you had bottom surgery if necessary, but having huge breasts was a whole different thing.*

For the next few weeks, I talked with my t-girl friends about breast implants and made it clear I wanted really big ones. I also did a lot of research. I had lasered off most of my chest and back hair, but I had to get electrolysis on my remaining chest hair. I could do that. A pain, but very doable. But the maximum FDA-approved implant size was about 650cc, about only a third of what I wanted. I asked around and it seemed to be universally true. *How do all those Divas t-girls get those huge breasts?* I guessed maybe Mexico, where they're more inclined to skip guidelines and rules? I started feeling depressed. This wasn't going to be as easy as I thought and might not be worth it, because they might be too damned small. I asked around the big busted Divas t-girls, and several suggested a doctor right around the corner in San Francisco.

After seeing the sex change surgeon, my confidence was very high, and any nervousness was gone. I was nothing but excited to go the boob doctor. It was one thing to have a dream about getting my boobs done, but a whole other thing to actually go to the doctor's office!

Visiting the doctor's office

Breast implants sitting on the doctor's windowsill.

I went to the doctor's office with my huge DDD-size boobs to clearly show what I wanted. I really bonded with his two female assistants. They were so friendly, and I threw in the comment, "My boyfriend is going to love it." They responded with joyous smiles, "Oh girl, yes he is!" *Warm fuzzies.*

I waited about five minutes for the doctor after the nurse showed me into his office. I was mesmerized and excited by all the breast implants sitting on his windowsill. I didn't see any really big ones and started getting concerned. I found it strange that few people seemed to know how to get the really big ones. They were probably illegal, but it was still frustrating because I didn't know one way or the other. So, when he came in, I pointed to my huge breasts and told him I was a pianist and wanted to show serious cleavage while playing the grand piano. I wasn't fucking around.

He was very nice but very clinical. He talked about the procedure and his background, and then gave me the 650cc number as the maximum size. *Ah, shit.* I pushed him, but he was adamant. *Come on, man. Can't you whisper in my ear, tell me how the Divas t-girls get their huge tits, even if you also tell me you don't recommend it? Give me the stats. Do I need to slip you some extra money? Do I need to go to Mexico?*

I asked the question multiple times in different ways, but he didn't answer. Maybe these doctors had a policy of dissuading women from getting really big implants because it was either unhealthy or illegal. I'm a size queen, I admit it. At least acknowledge I'm not the only girl in the world who wants this, and if you're going to try to dissuade me, do it with facts instead of avoidance. It was really starting to annoy me, but maybe he had gotten into trouble and was super careful. He was a very well-known and visible doctor.

We went to see *the room.*

He had an operating room right there in his office. Dreams came true right there. I could see it through a window separating it from the examination room we'd just entered. I looked at the table and imagined how many spirits were unshackled and freed[98]. Could I be next?

The doc then asked me to take off my shirt, bra, and breastforms. I stood there feeling very strange—Maria without boobs. As he looked at my body, I wondered what the fuck he was thinking. His poise didn't betray his feelings in any way. I wanted to get out of there. A third the size of what I wanted? Fuck that! Don't get me wrong, he was informative, friendly, and professional. I asked again about options for a larger size, but he just said when I'm on the operating table, they will put in the largest ones that fit my chest. After they've stretched out for a year

---

98. I know this is not sexual for many women, but at the time I wasn't thinking about them.

or two, I could probably go "somewhat bigger," but it depended on a lot of factors.

What did *somewhat* mean?

Oh fuck it, I was done with my put-pressure-on-him playbook for the day.

I also learned the nipples would look like guy nipples, not those beautiful larger female ones. I shouldn't have been surprised, but as my fantasy and reality collided, I had a lot to process. I was thinking, *I really want to hit a bar and sulk.*

But I was encouraged. The doctor said I didn't need any laser or electrolysis; I had already had enough hair removed. And all I needed to do was to call the office and schedule the surgery. The waiting time was two to three weeks, and I could get my breast implants right there in the office, eight blocks from my apartment. *I'm one phone call away from becoming a big busted woman.* I got weak in my knees, and I was already sitting down.

I was doing consulting work mostly from home, so I could tie down these medium-size breasts and wear a baggy shirt for the few times I needed to go to an office. I now accepted that I needed to get the smaller breasts as a first step to the larger ones anyway. My trans friend Jamie, who is older than me, had just had hers done. She kept repeating, "Do it now! You are going to love it Maria, don't deprive yourself! Live and have fun, gurl!" She was right. I could actually do it! I could just click my heels, grab the phone, and ten thousand dollars later, I could be stepping through a door that would be the wildest ride of my life. Oooh, this is very dangerous indeed. I was feeling really good.

I WAS STANDING AT THE VERY EDGE OF MY FANTASY.

The doctor took me to the nurse, a young woman around thirty, who worked up the sizing, paperwork, and cost. As I sat down, she said, "Are you excited?!"

I wasn't expecting that dose of reality. I was in such a trance thinking about all this, I mustered a half-assed yes. This was so real . . . weird. *I gotta stop*, I was thinking. *This is the end of the line! This is the next step . . . oh shit.* I took a deep breath while she opened a folder of papers.

My quantum computer kicked into gear as I ran through the scenarios with this new information:

Get right to the most important stuff for the breast implant scenario analysis:

The most important thing was ensuring I could continue to work and make good money. That was a no-brainer. I'd leave technical marketing and sales and go back into software engineering. I was ready to move from the snake pit back to the dungeon anyway. I didn't like engineering anymore, but there are a ton of engineering jobs, it paid really well, and I could do it drunk and stoned. I could probably even get such a job as Maria, worst case scenario. Although I'd much rather be a hostess at a club.

. . . the nurse was saying something about how I should get a really comfortable bra for my recovery, one without lace. I looked up at her, speechless. *I'm talking about bras with another woman, as a woman. I'm face to face with my own womanhood!* She started showing me the calendar and gave me some available dates to get my breast implants.

I really wanted to bond with her in this moment, and I felt like I'd blown it when she asked me if I was excited and I only managed to mutter a weak "yes." *Oh, I forget, we're girls! We can tell each other the way we feel!* I smiled and said, "Wow, this is so overwhelming."

She said, "Yea, it's a lot."

"Yea." I didn't know what else to say. I smiled back, and probably started smirking a little as I was thinking about how great my bra felt with these huge tits I had on and how I might find myself having to wear one every day, prodding me to stay fabulous.

"Yea, exciting, right?", she said with smile.

This time I fully savored that precious sister moment and opened the Maria floodgates. I grinned and said, "Oh yes," as I wiggled my boobs. "I can't wait to have sex with my boyfriend with my new girls!"

She giggled, "I bet he's really going to like it! When I had mine done two years ago, my boyfriend was so excited!"

Wow . . . This is nuts.

She handed me paperwork with the ninety-five hundred dollar price quote, the instructions on preparing for the procedure, and in big typeface, the phone number to schedule an appointment. I wasn't expecting this, either. As I stared at the paperwork my eyes started glossing over. That's when the reality solidified. I had never experienced anything so transformative before. I felt like the world changed color because I hit

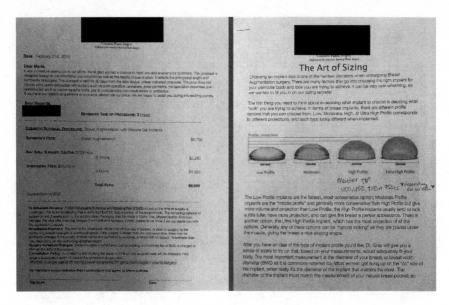

the end of this long road, and that door was open right in front of me. I just had to decide if I wanted to walk through it.

I told her I would look everything over and thanked her. I checked out with the nurse in the front office, a beautiful older woman, very snappily dressed. She was wearing my kind of blouse—white chiffon where you could see the hint of her white bra underneath. I thought, *pretty soon that can be me!* She looked at me with a big smile and said, "So, what are you thinking?" "I'm really excited!" I said, and her smile got bigger. I just love this female bonding! After chatting a bit, I said, "I need to work out some details on the timing, talk soon!"

Now what?!

I left the office, knowing the phone number that could change my life was right there in my bag, I had the money in the bank to do it, and I felt okay to *want* to do this. I smiled as I walked home in the cool, San Francisco air. Just knowing I could do it was so exciting and comforting. Maybe I could try to be full-time again because I had a goal *and* a plan, just like I had fourteen years earlier.

But when I got home, The Dude started warning me:

> DUDE: I know exactly what will happen if you go full-time. You can't even wear a bra without getting stoned. You'll spiral into constant weed smoking and drinking, fucking guy after guy, and

probably get some disease. You'll run off and get your boobs done on a moment's notice without thinking about it, at which point you would definitely spiral into drug addiction. You're sitting on a powder keg. All you need to do is make one phone call, you made sure of that.

ME: Getting queued up with the boob doctor was one of *your* kinks.

DUDE: It was just a kinky fantasy. I didn't expect you to actually do it.

ME: Bullshit. I think you want to be a woman, too, and you're having a hard time with that.

DUDE: The hair, the mood swings, the peeing sitting down, the long lines at the bathroom, people not taking me seriously, dealing with all that girl stuff. Uh . . . no.

ME: I'm not talking about all that stuff. I'm talking about being fabulous, being sexy, being joyful. You don't know how to be sexy.

DUDE: Sure, I do. By being myself.

ME: How's that working out for you?

DUDE: Uh, it's just that people, well, ugh . . .

ME: You can't accept that I'm more popular than you. I got invited to meet with that Congressional candidate, not you. I got invited to Burning Man to perform, not you.

DUDE: But I'm paying the bills, preparing for the show, and doing all the practice. You get all the glory and sex that comes from it. That's not fair.

ME: Well, uh, let's enjoy it together, we could . . .

DUDE: . . . but I'm not a woman. You only show up when I'm horny. And when we cum, you disappear, and I'm left standing there wearing your clothes. Then I'm the one who has to clean ourselves all up!

You're taking over my life. First, you start pushing my clothes to the corner of the walk-in closet and then you kick me out completely. Then you took over our social life, then our dating life. You're spending my money and burning through time flirting with anybody and everybody. You're trying to edge me out.

ME: I don't make the rules. I'm sexy, what do you want me to do? I want us to live as a woman in the real world.

DUDE: You don't live in the real world; how would you know?

ME: You don't respect me.

DUDE: I created you. You're not real. You couldn't even make it a week full-time.

ME: That's not me, that's you! I'm enjoying just floating on my joy of femininity. You're sexualizing me! You don't respect women! Stop it!

DUDE: If I don't sexualize you, you won't exist. And then I'll be alone. Do you know how hard it is living alone with nothing to look forward to? I have no hope for romance. Without it, I'm nothing. It's the essence of everything that drives me, from work to music to reading about the world.

ME: Neither of us has hope for romance. Even if I wanted romance with guys, they'd ditch me after a few fucks. They just want an occasional fuck buddy while they are romantic with genetic women. I've learned to live with it.

DUDE: At least you're getting laid.

ME: *We're* getting laid.

DUDE: Fucking guys is not my bag. I'm only letting you take the body because I need to get off.

ME: Okay, it's harder for you, but you've had women, and there were a few who you liked, but you blew it, because you wanted to be me. Remember when you were fucking that girl from behind while she was wearing her really sexy bullet bra with the satin straps, and you wanted to wear that bra? Maybe you are a woman.

DUDE: That was years ago when we just started. Who could blame me for getting excited about being you at that time?

ME: You are fabulous. You are me.

DUDE: I know that, but in the crazy online world of excessive noise and fighting for attention, any fabulosity I have remains hidden. Many women who love you can't even stand looking at me even though they know I'm you. It's humiliating, especially considering that half of your fabulousness is me.

ME: Maybe we can combine our efforts. Think of the person we could become! And you can charm people from the male side, which, by the way, you do exceptionally well.

DUDE: If I can get in the door to begin with.

ME: Leave that to me.

DUDE: Yea, but you're always stoned. Otherwise I'm getting work done, which you *never* do.

ME: *You're* the one partying too much. You can't accept that it's empowering to be sexy, to be a slut. You are so confused and ashamed that you need to *keep* partying to squash your feelings instead of dealing with them and just accepting them. You're the one with the bukkake fantasy, having multiple guys cum in *my* face, so much so I can blow bubbles with it. Have you ever even tasted cum?

DUDE: Are you saying I'm the slut, not you?

ME: I don't fantasize about bukkake because I don't need to. I'm the one out having sex and having fun and you just sit at home. So, admit you're me. Be me, enjoy it, enjoy the sex we are having and stop trying to claim you aren't me. You have no respect for a woman's right to have fun sex, and we won't stop fighting until you do.

DUDE: Uh...

ME: I'm going to keep partying until you accept that you're the slut too and you love it. Stop just living through me. The problem is you need to take *me* more seriously!

DUDE: Even if I considered it, it's not easy being a woman. I don't know how to function when I'm sexy. I just can't imagine being a geek corporate tech worker as a woman, feeling those magnificent breasts, reminding me of how much I hate this work and would rather be doing something else.

ME: Uh...

DUDE: ...kind of hard to get around that one, right?

ME: Okay, let's not go too fast, but I don't want to be relegated to being a vampire that only comes out at night and during special events. I need to be a complete person doing responsible work during the day, too.

DUDE: Maybe, but you need to stop partying all the time!

ME: Sometimes we need to stay home in the dungeon and put the work in, but sometimes we gotta get out there. Mingle and have fun. Think of what we could do together! You need to give me that week to live as a girl. You're the one who can't be me without getting stoned. The first thing we need to do is get me clothes that don't make me look like a tramp. That will make it easier for both of us.

DUDE: Well, that's kind of expensive isn't it?

ME: Excuses. Let's start with a few outfits, eh? Pick something you think is lovely but sexy.

DUDE: Oh, that's your thing.

ME: No, I think you're embarrassed.

DUDE: Okay, but I want to set this straight right now. There is no way I'm going to start peeing sitting down. Not going to happen. And waiting in the women's line at the bathroom? Fuck that noise! And having to constantly futz with my hair all the time? *Sigh.*

ME: The GRS is way off, if ever, so forget about that little stuff and have fun.

DUDE: Having to wait in the women's bathroom line?

ME: *Hmm, Dude did have a point.*

DUDE: You want me to live my life looking like you all the time? You stand out like a cactus on the moon. You want that all the time?

ME: Yea if it's not too bright out.

DUDE: You're the vampire. I'm not relegating you to that.

ME: Well, maybe it *is* easier keeping us separate. We have the power of the woman with the backing of the man. Pretty damned fucking good. That's the bomb!

DUDE: It's a great *idea*, but realistically? Come on, we can't go any farther with this fantasy. We had a huge amount of fun, learned a lot, connected with so many people, and spread so much joy. Why do you think you need to do this when you already know you wouldn't make it a week? You need to maybe grow up a little bit more.

ME: You won't *let* me make it a week!

DUDE: You *are* me.

ME: No, I'm not.

DUDE: Think about it, you've already won! You discovered how to defeat the Virus. You found freedom. You have everything you want. You really didn't think I would keep quiet and remain meek forever, did you? And now you're holding this *one phone call away from getting tits* thing over me. Threatening me? This idea of jumping off the cliff and getting your boobs done and forcing yourself to live as a woman is pure drama. You're not going to do it.

ME: Maybe yes, maybe no. But fuck the easy path. I want the option of going into the world with *all* my superpowers, boobs included. I could make this work if I really wanted to.

DUDE: I've had enough of this. We're just going to keep going around in circles.

ME: Dude, make no mistake. I'm running the show here.

DUDE: Is that a threat, you think—

I SLAMMED THE DOOR IN HIS FACE

I figured I might have to kill him. It would be a mercy killing. I couldn't help him. It's shitty that he's an average-looking guy when I'm so fabulous. I could see why he was afraid of my power. But it was no longer my problem. Life is finite and I was really excited to find out more about this whole boob thing. I was my own person. This was going to be *so* much fun.

Over the next month, I talked about boob jobs with every t-girl I ran into who had large breasts done. One of them was getting her third set, and they were going to be big. She confirmed what I already was learning— get the 650cc or 750cc implants, and after they've stretched out in about a year, you can go larger and work your way up. Regarding doctors for the larger implants, she said, "Talk to me, girl. We will get you what you want!" This provided me with fodder for a good two weeks of thinking, fantasizing, and celebrating this huge milestone with lots of fun in bed, which to me was affirmation from the universe that I was on the right path. I worked hard and deserved life's sweetest reward.

But very soon, I had to face the inevitable clash with reality. Should I really kill The Dude? I wasn't sure if I would be killing myself or freeing myself. After fourteen years, I had finally hit a wall.

CHAPTER 32

DOOR #1 OR DOOR #2

The two doors

It was supposed to be a fun Halloween distraction. My original dream
was to go to a crazy underground party, meet a few weirdos, and maybe
if I was lucky, talk with a real transsexual. Then go back to a new Dude
life. I didn't expect to *become* alternative San Francisco! I didn't expect to
become friends with so many trans people and others across the gender
spectrum. But once this genie came out of the bottle, she was never going
back in. I felt like I was able to rewind my life and live it again properly,
as I was able to find the fun and confidence I had missed when I was
younger—when I wasn't yet a whole person, having been jerked around
like so many of us by our toxic and shallow culture. San Francisco is
where I needed to go to heal. It took about ten years to realize and accept
I was a fabulous person.

But my fourteen years of Halloween was over. I had tried just about
everything. I was already Wonder Woman, now what? Was I really lucky
to have this life, or was I just a sex-addicted pervert?

I ran headfirst into the wall where fantasy hits reality. I stared at the two doors in the path before me. I could walk through that open door of sex change right then and leave The Dude and all that toxic energy behind forever. But it was a one-way door, and I didn't really know what was on the other side. Was it heaven or was it hell?

Or I could open the closed door with The Dude behind it.

Which one was reality?

I wondered *who is this mysterious figure behind the door?* The Dude and I were like a nice couple from the 1950s. We lived together and supported each other, but our souls weren't really connected. I was having all the fun while he was paying the bills, preparing for the show, organizing the work but otherwise being miserable and emotionally isolated. When I was born after he moved to San Francisco, I thought he was the blinding bright white light people couldn't look at, and I was just the pink filter. But I was beginning to think *I* might be the bright white light, and he was the red filter. He believed reality was in his mind, the way things *ought* to be. But I knew otherwise.

Reality moves much slower than what you are capable of imagining. It has annoying roadblocks and often insurmountable problems you don't plan for. The Dude got miffed by such things. But with reality, you constantly discover unexpected opportunities, learn new things, and leave a little piece of your spirit all over the place. That resonated with me better. I wondered how much more I would find if I wasn't just a vampire, relegated only to going out at night. I had powers he didn't have. I wondered what would happen if I exposed myself to the light of day? There was only one way to find out. I was the real one, out there mingling with people, not him. He couldn't accept that. He didn't expect this when he created me.

I didn't need him anymore. Keeping somebody around just for their money usually doesn't end well. I figured I would always have that masculine power and knowledge no matter what I did. If I could combine this with my girl energy, it would yield some serious fruit. I wouldn't be killing half of myself. I would be shedding an empty shell that was riddled with the scars of the Culture Virus. And I knew exactly how to kill him—get my boobs done and have the straight romantic Dude and all his sorrows fucked out of me by loads of hot muscle guys. He couldn't survive that.

I was ready to walk through that open door and set off the next round of fireworks. I had my foot already two-thirds of the way in. Socially, I was already a woman. And I had to stop fooling myself into believing that the need to make money as a man was really stopping me. I was already back to working as a software engineer and architect, and I could do that as a trans woman if I had to. It would harder, but I could start there and find my way into doing something more fun and impactful.

Yet I now had a key to unlock his closed door if I chose to, but with me in charge. I had learned so much, and if there was any time to think very carefully, it was now. I couldn't ditch him just out of frustration, anger, or the feeling of being a victim. Would I lose something important if I left him behind and walked through that open door? Was I still him? Was there emotional healing to be done? Or was it pointless to re-open old wounds? I loved him more than I admitted, and it broke my heart that he was so alone and rejected. He was the one who found his solace and passion in playing music, in reading, in science, in history. I had these things in common with him. I inherited them from him. And he got me this far. But I couldn't help him—I didn't make up the rules. I began to think of him less as me and more like my father, who had inspired me so much, but who I eventually had to let go.

The dark figure behind door #2

Now that I was feeling good about myself, I could operate at peak performance in my life overall with less stress, realizing what I could control and what I couldn't. I didn't have this nagging victim doubt bullshit ringing around in my head. Every once in a while, it reared its ugly head, but I quickly recognized it and ignored it, and the bad energy quickly dissipated like a micro fart. I was free to fully experience peace, joy, spreading love, and all the other good stuff.

So, what would I gain by opening Door #2 with The Dude behind it? If I opened it, I would need a really good reason. And the possibility of finding romance with a woman as The Dude was not a good enough reason given his track record. I was no longer buying his romantic dreams. I had to set my energies in an area I knew delivered results. That was an important cardinal lesson I'd learned over the years.

So, was he nothing but a meal ticket and somebody to get work done efficiently? Who was he? I found it hilarious he was first and foremost somebody who didn't like when people weren't authentic. He loathed when fashion became the person, hiding what was underneath. Yet I was the one wearing the mask.

And I was the one they wanted, not him.

To the world, I was Maria Konner—fabulous woman, entertainer, and Dick slut—but The Dude couldn't accept that he was *also* Maria Konner. Especially the part about being a Dick slut. *But Dude, look at the facts from the outside, you are a Dick slut. Does the why matter? Does it matter who you think you are on the inside?*

I personally thought that he always loved the thrill of humiliating himself so he could feel like a reject on his own terms, but I wasn't getting into that with him. But I did know that he was *really pissed* that the world didn't see him. Yet he was the one able to focus on doing the hard work in the background with no distractions. So, would I be losing much of my power if I got rid of him? When he put on my mask, he was thinking he was running away from himself and getting powers from that mask. But what was this mask?

In reality, most of us wear some kind of mask. Is who we appear on the outside the same as who we are on the inside? How does the world see us? Is it consistent with who we really are, or should I say who were *think* we really are? How do I make sense of this gargantuan gap I have between who The Dude thinks he is and how people see me, Maria. People clearly think we are totally different. What the fuck? The Dude doesn't think they see him, but maybe they actually do, but through me?

Does a mask turn you into somebody else, or does it just accentuate who you already are? Anything that is visually striking is going to attract attention, which is really important in a noisy world. It's the very nature of a large-scale society. We can't change that any more than we can change the laws of physics. And we love mystery. It's fun. It directs our focus. And with a mask, we can break through preconceived notions based on the color of our skin, or because we remind somebody of somebody else they knew, or because we don't stand out. But once we get the attention, the mask doesn't decide how we use this power, we do.

Source of my secret power

There's nothing like looking at yourself with makeup on for the first time. At first you see somebody else. It's very unnerving. But then you slowly realize you're discovering power inside of you that was hidden. At first, I thought it had something to do with my makeup skills. But over the years, I realized it's because I enjoyed it. I enjoyed being Maria more, and it was the joy and fabulous excitement I was channeling. But why did I enjoy it? Maybe I was sick of looking at my same self? Maybe I was sick of people judging me based on the way I looked, or worse yet, ignoring me as I blended into the background. So, I made my outside fabulous. I guessed it made sense because the way you look naturally has nothing to do with who you are. We are more than just animals.

But the difference between the way people treated The Dude vs. me *always* felt incredibly absurd. I understood why, but the reality was *shocking*. And I couldn't help but think about how tedious and insidious it was that women have to put on make-up all the time and always look perfect. I didn't know if I could really take it and remain calm and sane. So, it seemed like a gift to have the opportunity to do this whenever I wanted but not feel required to do it. I still got caught up in this belief that I had to make a choice about being either a man or a woman. But it's wasn't true. I could promote the feminine values important to me with the power of a man. I connected with both men and women better because I could feel both sides. And I could pull out the bitch when she was needed and use the man to deliver the punch if necessary. If I just wanted to chill and be unseen when I was out and about, I could go to a club as a man and nobody bothered me. I felt good about being unseen when I choose to. But the best part is I could make money as a man and reward myself for a good week of work by having guaranteed fun as a woman in the evenings and weekends. I took my male privilege for granted because I didn't have any other frame of reference until I became a woman.

Integrating us into one person and taking advantage of this unique power of harnessing both sexes sounded great on paper. I had already done that to a large extent. But socially, I was Maria. It was intolerable humiliation hanging out somewhere as The Dude when I could be Maria. I felt like I was Bruce Wayne trying to fight the Joker without being Batman. Unless I was going to a small gathering at one of my friend's places, in which case I would typically just go as The Dude instead of bothering with the makeup and heels. My closest San Francisco friends saw me as Maria, but they saw The Dude as the same fabulous person.

The Dude fretted thinking it was too bad he couldn't harness my power without getting all dressed up. But on the rare occasion when he played the piano, people loved him. It was remarkable walking into a place as

The Dude and being totally ignored until I got on the piano. Suddenly, he was everybody's friend. He had the right instrument to amplify his soul enough so people could see it. But The Dude can't carry a piano around with him. And people can only listen to so much music. But they always love hanging out with a lovely lady. And if she also plays the piano and guitar—thermonuclear.

I felt The Dude struggling. He wasn't trans, he was more of a man fighting to integrate this thermonuclear energy into his life. I knew the truth was I was a fully functional, multifaceted, sexy, confident person. I had the best of the male and the female. I had it all. I really didn't need to change anything.

EXCEPT I WANTED BIG BOOBS.

It's all about the boobs

I know it sounds crass, but breasts are power. I've seen t-girls get their breast implants and become super queens overnight. Sounds sexist, but it's the truth. And if you're gonna do it, you might as well do it properly. Putting in breast forms wasn't going to cut it. I wanted cleavage. I wanted to see skin popping out of my sexy, lacy bra, and I didn't want to deal with all that padding when it was time for sex. When I took my blouse off, I wanted to be fucking hot. I wanted to know what it felt like to have my boobs bouncing around while I was fucking guys and then have them grab my tits while they were fucking me from behind. I wanted that part of being a woman.

When I got out of the shower in the morning, I wanted to feel good, like a woman as I put on my bra. I wanted to know what that was like. And when I got on stage to play guitar and piano, I wanted to wear hot outfits that showed my cleavage. I wanted them bouncing around and exciting people. Imagine that kind of power. I just loved breasts, and I wanted to be around them all the time, so why not have my own? Should I feel ashamed because I was hooked on wearing beautiful satin bras and now I wanted to fill them up with gorgeous large breasts after all these years? What was wrong with being beautiful? We only live once, and I had the power to do this. Why not go all in?

If you start becoming a woman but have to work as a man for a while, you can hide the hormones, GRS, curvy hips, and even many changes to your face, but you can't hide beautiful breasts. If you get them, you're definitely going to be a girl full time. The changes to your life will be dramatic, and there is no knowing how it will really affect you. That's why they call it "taking the plunge."

Now that I knew what I really wanted, and I had worked through all the irrelevant chatter, I could get real and start to think about the most important things and forget about everything else. I could figure out a way to go full time. I could force myself. It would be hot and exciting! The real issues came down to:

> **My health.** I might end up drinking and smoking dope all the time. I was a party girl. I had no reason to be sober. If I was going to be sober, I'd just become The Dude and relax. Why go through all that effort of feeling sexy to just sit around or work?
>
> If I got my breasts done, I would feel so sexy I probably wouldn't get any work done. There's a reason nature separates us into Male and Female. (But it is really handy if you're single and quarantined for months.)

I might be able to work through these things if I were forced to be a woman every day, but there was one thing I wasn't sure I could get past:

> **Hair!** Dealing with shaving all my body hair and legs all the time or getting it waxed or lasered or electrolysis was reason enough not to become a woman! It was bad enough when I was doing it part time. Doing it full time?! Not to mention fretting about my hair style every day?!

With these challenges, especially that damned hair thing, I had to think again, why did I really want the boobs that badly?

I had to look at ulterior motives that might have been dumbing down my decision-making practice. What might those be?

> Getting the boobs would kill The Dude immediately and end the struggle. *Fuck it, just burn the ships like Cortez did. The Dude doesn't respect me and would never seriously let me grow.*
>
> Or maybe I was just having a hard time accepting that, in order to gain something, I had to give something up, like all the privileges and simplicity of being a man. Maybe I was avoiding

thinking it through logically and planning things slowly. Maybe I was being an addict, running away from this incredibly intense and complex situation that could be so transformative if I integrated myself with The Dude—if I had a little more patience and faith.

But damn, I thought about how much fucking fun I would have with big tits. I worked hard in life, and I wanted fun. Men and women both loved me better this way and treated me really well. I might even drift into a real relationship with a guy. And an added bonus was that it would also permanently take away the stress out of having to get it up!

Sometimes you just got to say, "What the fuck!" I saw that in a movie when I was kid, but instead of putting on sunglasses, I was putting on a bra.

Or maybe I was suffering from a serious addiction to avoiding reality?

Seriously addicted to being fabulous?

I was definitely addicted to this strange, inexplicable girl energy. It was wonderful, soothing. I felt so alive. So happy. I'd never have this close of a relationship with women as a man. I'd never get to the really good stuff. And I'd never been happier in my life. Nothing wrong with that. I could spend the rest of my life having fun with all kinds of great people, and boobs would take my life to the next level. And so many people were supporting me. When I told my burlesque girl friends about maybe getting big boobs and how much I wanted to be just like them, several offered to custom-make me hot, lacy bras and outfits. Being one of them would be a dream!

But I knew I would probably want more surgery and find myself getting a great ass and really curvy hips. Yea, I could easily spiral into heavy drugs. I pondered how many addictions started as a useful activity to get away from utter hell, and then once the hell was gone, the activity became the hell replacement. Only this time it was coming from inside of you, and you didn't get the chance to find out what was so maddening that you didn't feel strong enough to face it? What might be overwhelming me. Was Maria just a mask to fight off the Virus,? Was she covering up something important in The Dude?

Or maybe I just needed to get used to how it was *so* much easier having fun as a girl. People born female have decades to figure it out, but I was catapulted into it practically overnight. Maybe The Dude was cleverly trying to convince me I was a kink addict, getting off on being a victim of the Virus, when in reality I simply wanted to be Maria. Maybe he was afraid of our feminine destiny and was worried about what other people thought, specifically the longtime family and friends who were living in the suburbs, many stuck in the Matrix.

For me, being a woman was somewhere between a kinky addiction to avoid the drudgery and pain of the real world, and a spiritual unleashing. Pretty wide range. I couldn't figure out what the real world was—crazy underground San Francisco or the world of Silicon Valley tech jobs and a stable family and home. Or were they both real, just two different possible paths?

I figured I would turn to some of the experts. Like those who study rats.

 There is an old, well-known study that showed if you put a rat in a cage that has two vials of water, one of which is laced with drugs, the rat will always prefer the drugs and will die from an overdose. Every time. Okay, drugs are dangerous. But decades later, they redid the study with two different groups. The first was a made up of rats who were alone as before, but the second group had other rats to play with. The second group avoided the water with the drugs, almost completely.

Loneliness and isolation are one of the primary causes of addiction.

And that's exactly how the Virus works. It kills our self-esteem and diversity to sell us shit to fill up the void, and then we end up emotionally and spiritually isolated addicts. And the reason why it's so powerful is because it's fine tuned to our mating rituals and the way our society is structured. Fuck you!

Yes, The Dude was so lonely, and the problem was clear in the way I would summarize my *personal* sexual experiences in San Francisco:

The <u>fantasy</u> of being with a guy or t-girl
was much better than the reality
... the smells, the taste, reality of the physical sex

The <u>reality</u> of being with a genetic girl
was much better than the fantasy
Her smell, the salty taste of her lips, the feeling of her soft skin,
her slinky curvy body trembling as I pull her into me

And what made it even worse was, since I knew women so much better and felt really comfortable with them, I wanted to be with them as The Dude even more than before. The problem was I couldn't get around the fucking math! It's 250x easier for Maria to hook up vs. The Dude!! It was so profoundly frustrating that I couldn't even fantasize and jerk off to straight porn—it had to be trans kinky stuff. How would I get pleasure from jerking off about something that I couldn't have? I needed something completely different to take me *away* from my depressing reality.

The reality of our culture and the dating scene was driving me haywire. I was substituting heavy amounts of weed for the divine feeling of goosebumps you get when you simply cuddle with somebody you love. I would have loved to stop feeding myself drugs to anesthetize the best part of myself. And then what? Cry myself to sleep? I wanted to stay at the top of my game in life. I was getting tired of being two different people. Not because it was confusing or because I personally felt uncomfortable with it. But because I was tired of the differences between The Dude and me being in my face every fucking day. I was tired of being reminded constantly of the absurdity of the differences between who we are on the inside and how people perceive us. But I suppose this was the price I paid for my deal with the devil to be closer to the real feminine.

My brain hurt. I thought about another expert I greatly admired and who's clearly been very successful.

An excerpt from my interview with **Jane Wiedlin** from The Go Go's. We just finished talking about a musical she wrote called *Lady Robotika*:

Her new music really moved me. I hope this one gets produced.

Video: Jane, of course, reminds us that rock 'n roll will always save the world. Jane's message in her musical is "Be Your Own Hero."

After we finish talking about her musical, I ask her something I always wanted to ask a rock star, "What does rock 'n roll mean to you?"

"Wow, I actually have the power to make people happy."

—Jane Wiedlan

*More on Jane's
Lady Robotika*

Maria makes people happy

It really is that simple. All the pontification in the world about the meaning of life, or who you are on the inside, or the nature of the universe, doesn't compare with the simple question of whether you are making people happy. And that's what makes me happy. When I go out as a girl, I make tons of people happy. When I go out as boy, I'm invisible. I thought about all the people Maria has impacted, the people who saw my shows, the curious guys and straight couples who explored Divas, the children who saw me perform at Golden Gate Park, a guy I met at a party who decided to move to San Francisco, the fellow artists I performed with, the young folks who I played music with at Burning Man, all the men I flirted with and sucked off, many their first t-girl experience.

What is real and what is fantasy? Ultimately, we're here to live in the joy of life and share it authentically with real people. We're here to share what's possible. We're here to partake in a life and a spirit much bigger than just us. Sitting at home like The Dude, thinking about the way things should be and feeling frustrated and unhappy ultimately doesn't mean all that much. That invisible camera watching our life and playing violins doesn't really exist. I know the difference between writing music and playing it at home and the reality of getting out there and doing it. Sometimes it's great, sometimes it isn't. But it's real because you're spreading your emotions, letting your artistic authenticity resonate with people and adding a little more meaning to people's lives. Even if it's only a few people, that energy you put out keeps going and building. This is true in all parts of the wave of life.

One of the most insidious things about life is that we can't grasp the impact of our behavior on the vast number of people we encounter any more than we can grasp the infinity of the universe. Everything we do has both positive and negative potential on not just the people we meet, but the people they interact with. Many of us want to have meaning in our lives and hope for a big event—like writing a hit song or a novel or being part of a movement—and the accompanying fanfare to define our lives. But it's the billions and billions of little daily interactions that define the vast bulk of how humanity has slowly evolved and thrived over the millennium. We think mostly about the famous historical figures who have had a huge impact over the eons, but their impact is tiny compared with the countless number of mothers and fathers, tinkerers, weirdos, writers, teachers, entertainers—people whose names we will never know.

We don't think about it much because we can't easily see it and measure it. But every once in a while, we find out. For example, I met an older woman from Ireland while I was playing piano at Martuni's. She was a conservative Catholic who had met very few queer people before and was visiting with her grandson. I ran into her grandson years later, coincidentally about a week after she had passed. He approached me and showed me a picture with her on his phone and asked if that was me. He told me she talked with her conservative friends many times over the years about me and how much she loved the San Francisco alternative world. And she had left instructions after her death that he should track me down so I could go through her closet and take what I wanted. Since she and I had spoken about clothes, he told me, she wanted me to have some of hers. Wow, I had absolutely no idea. He invited me into her place, and I took some of the clothes. And for every person who tells you how you impacted them, there are thousands you don't know about. You're barely seeing the very tip of the iceberg.

I thought about where I could take this if I lived as Maria a lot more. I'd discovered one of the big lessons in life—go with what works. And it will often be radically different from what you expected. Somehow, I had the power to make people happy just about every time I walked out the door. And I often left many people with something completely new. What a gift, what more could I ask for? I had no desire to waste the final decades of my life on the same old Dude crap. I was going with this. We all have this capability. I suppose we just need stronger faith in that which we cannot see. *We* get to choose the actions that define our destiny, not the soulless tech-powered Virus and the people who have become its slaves. The universe wants *us* to define the meaning of our lives by experiencing, learning, and interacting on our own terms. And that's exactly what I planned to do.

I could still do this as a part-time woman. One thing was for certain—I was not giving up this easy and fun sex as a woman. After a long week of work, I needed to be able to reward myself and have guaranteed fun, which meant being Maria. I could tolerate the failed projects, the hard work with uncertain results, and the political infighting at work, but we all need something reliable we can center ourselves on. For many, it's the family they go home to. But I didn't have one, so although I never thought I would develop a taste for casual sex, I went with it because it worked. And in the process, I spread the wave of joy. Guys didn't love me only because of the way I looked. Yes, I was fabulous, but I also had so many imperfections and annoying guy features that stuck out. I was around average looking for a t-girl, but guys loved being with me because I enjoyed it so much and it showed.

This lifestyle works really well in a modern city like San Francisco where you don't need a partner to stave off the loneliness and define your life. You can live a very flexible, dynamic lifestyle with a huge array of friends and deeply fulfilling activities—including *being* San Francisco to all the people, visitors, and locals who hope to find that extra spark and excitement out there.

I had proven beyond a shadow of a doubt that what you look like on the outside matters. And not always for the reason you expect. Maybe it was time for me to make the big change for good, and maybe it would make me more complete. But, as they say, it's complicated. I was lamenting not having a traditional family. I would have really loved that path, but for whatever reason, it was not to be. Maybe the universe needed me for something else, and The Dude was still clinging to some semblance of his dream of normalcy. But there are a few key times in our lives where we each have to look at what we really want and purposely choose the best opportunities available to us.

It was time to take a good look at these two doors and decide which way to go.

Duality?

I didn't see myself as a woman. I actually saw myself as a man. But women who knew both Maria and The Dude didn't see The Dude as a man. They saw him as Maria in some weird getup. I couldn't reconcile how others perceived me with how I perceived myself. Maybe it was time to finally give up the struggle and accept that the fabulous part of me, the part expressed through Maria, was the real me.

I'd always had a hard time, from a very young age, reconciling myself as a man compared to so many of the boys and men I knew. So many had an air of privilege and were sexually aggressive towards women. They were ruthlessly competitive, not caring about the impact their behaviors had on others, and they were constantly willing to suspend their intelligence to show easily measurable accomplishment while hiding the destruction of their actions. And what was so baffling to me was why these guys were getting all the attention and power. Why did we teach all these great lessons about history when so many men acted so selfishly, completely inconsistent with these great lessons?

Maria wasn't about being a woman. She was about trying to understand the role of my feminine characteristics, these other feelings I had that I didn't see in so many other boys and men. The Dude wasn't effeminate at all. I was fighting to balance the masculine and feminine within me, all while seeing how totally out of balance everything out there seemed to be. I was never going to give up my feminine traits. They were divine to me. I wasn't going to cut out half of my very being. Yet I felt like this divine femininity was being raped by our male-dominated society. And I could find only very few people who could relate to all I was going through.

My confusion around the differences between who we are on the inside versus how other people perceive us has baffled me since I was a child. The primary difference between us and animals is who we are is on the inside—and that we can imagine something complex and work toward making it real. When I changed my appearance and became Maria, it changed me on the inside. Not because I was more feminine on the inside, but because people noticed me and validated the beauty of the feminine *half* of my spirit, the part of The Dude that was crushed.

I wondered if it was possible for the two opposites to be in balance. Things in nature that work in harmony survive and thrive. The very existence of our universe owes itself to the balance of opposite natural forces. We are of nature, which clearly meant for the male and female to be separate but joined together. Given its complexity, there must be a damned good reason for it. I wondered if the masculine and feminine can live as true equals. At first, I thought it was hard for the masculine and feminine to be in balance because I struggled so much within myself. But I now realized, the struggle had nothing to do with me. I was perfectly fine with it. I actually enjoyed it, thought it made me a much better person. Despite our differences, The Dude and I were able to live together because we always trusted each other, and we knew we needed each other. Respect was taking longer because it was *much* more complicated, as it involved what other people thought of each of us. Maybe that shouldn't matter, but it does.

It seems the only way men can really understand women and women can really understand men is if they become each other so they can grok their differences and see themselves in the other. That's a tall order in our culture. But what does it mean to be a man or a woman? Who defines it? Is our culture's definition consistent with nature's intention? Nobody can answer that question. But one thing I do know is that nature provides a check and balance against my nemesis, this Monoculture Virus, which seeks to separate us for its selfish purposes.

The Kink (or Alt) gene

I couldn't go back to the straight dating game. I figured I might get lucky, but I had too many other wonderful things happening in my life to spend it wading in that cesspool. I was now immune from the Virus. The kink gene protected me, once it was activated.

What do rock 'n' roll, kink, LGBT, goth, and much art all have in common? They all stick the big middle finger at the Virus, giving us permission to do something completely different when being attacked by a extremely powerful force that's trying to control us and tell us who we are—when we intuitively know it's wrong. I have the straight romantic guy gene, a very common gene, one the Virus has adapted itself to very effectively over the centuries. But I also have the kink gene, which has stepped in to save me by giving me another choice.

So, I suppose I had to be Maria in a world I found to be upside down and out of balance. It was a long journey, but once I got through the shame and confusion of being two genders, I could finally begin to see more clearly. I wasn't clouded by all the chatter around me. I had a decision to make, but what was more important was that regardless of what choice I made, the feminine would continue to rise within me. I wasn't going to let anybody take her away from me. And all of her—the queen, the giver, the sage, the bitch, and the slut. She shall hurt and be ignored no more.

As I pondered how I wanted to spend the rest of my life, I thought about the one other notable thing I learned during my time in Jerusalem.

When I met that senior officer in the Israeli Army, I told him about my spiritual quest. He responded with a joke very popular with his Army peers:

A guy runs into God and says, "Things are a mess down here, can you please send somebody to help?"
God replies, "I did, I sent you."

I understood much more deeply what he meant. I looked at the key and looked at the two doors before me. Then I took a deep breath and stepped forward.

The best and most beautiful things in the world cannot be seen or
even touched—they must be felt with the heart.

HELEN KELLER

EPILOGUE

Dec 19, 2020

So many of us are sitting here at the end of this unique year, thinking about all the suffering and loss, the financial stress, and wondering where the divide in this country is really coming from. I have family members who had COVID-19, and thankfully they got through it with no permanent effects, but my friends and family know people who have died from it. My heart and love goes out to everybody, especially those who are on the front line—the medical care workers and others in the service industry that put their lives at risk to help the rest of us by caring for us and trying to keep some semblance of normality by allowing us to occasionally get out of the house.

We are all probably sharing feelings of anxiety, confusion, hope, anger, and love. For me personally, this is a particularly odd time. Living alone in the middle of a transformational part of my life, I keep running into the same question that has dogged me for decades. Who I am—the person on the inside, or how people perceive me on the outside? During covid it doesn't matter how I look or dress 99% of the time. My online, Zoom, and phone presence is the "me" that people are seeing. What matters most? What does it mean to be female, or male, or trans? Or does it not matter at all? What matters to me most is that I'm putting love, compassion, and humor out there, not hate and constant anger. And it's hard with the stress we're under, especially with work. We're all under so much pressure—how do I help keep people at work focused without being a jerk? I can't have lunch or beers with them. I've never met most of the people I'm working with (I started a new job right before the lockdown). They don't know if I'm presenting as a Man or a Woman behind

that microphone. But I find myself needing to draw from both. How odd.

Earlier today, I had such horrible cabin fever I had to get out of here and go visit the MAC and Sephora makeup stores in Union Square. Should I bother to get all made up and dressed up given that there probably won't be many people out and I had to wear a mask? I thought about it, and knew deep down, that I just wanted to, and that's all that mattered. But actually no, that's NOT all that mattered. I got so many smiles on the street lighting up the day a little more with San Francisco alternative colors. I had such joy chatting with the makeup assistants. Often, we forget that we all have the power to create smiles and joy—and the best way to remind ourselves is to be around others. Which is so hard and dangerous these days! But perhaps the little moments we do have that chance have become more precious. Once we meet again, we may find that something has changed. That life has become more glorious and we find deeper meaning in each other as we find not only those myriad of things we have in common, but those fabulous things about each other that are so very different and make life brilliantly magnificent and compelling.

It's so hard to fathom the pain and suffering of this year. I suppose we

Quarantine Playlist

can take faith that there is usually a silver lining in many things. Good luck in the new year to you and your friends, family, associates, and community. And may lovely butterflies come out of your covid cocoon.

Thank you so much for reading my story. I deeply appreciate your spending the time. This past year, in addition to working and finishing this book, I had the good fortune to be able to record some more music and express the range of emotions I had been feeling.

LOVE MARIA . . .

SPECIAL ACKNOWLEDGEMENTS

Dan Karkoska (aka DJ Dank, Dank):
>My producer and friend who encouraged me to write my story, gave interminable feedback, and listened to my emotional outbursts both overly elated and aggressively negative.

Tim Carmody
>Fellow Divas lover who provided me with information on how to write and publish a book, gave me background stories on the history of Divas, and kept pushing me to write my story.

Jim Provenzano (https://www.jimprovenzano.com):
>Fellow writer and Pink Floyd lover who was always encouraging me and happy to give his sage advice as a professional journalist and writer. God bless our journalists! Well, some of them.

Jerry L. Wheeler, Editor: 1st edit (cut and sharpen some of those items):
>For the wisdom to know how to cut out my target of 30%, sharpen things up and just about hit it perfectly on the first try. And also fellow Pink Floyd lover.

Rebecca Parsons, Editor: 2nd edit (polish, sharpen, and sanity check):
>For sharpening up the text, cutting a few stray flow disruptors, and dealing with all those pesky annoying things like tense inconsistencies, italics, quotes, commas, dashes, case, etc. And not to mention the confusion between "me/I" and "Maria" and "The Dude"! Also for representing the straight/cis world—at least one straight person had to read it before I finished it to avoid big trouble.

Mike Ahmadi
>Friend and business partner who joined me in slugging it out in the business world, trying to promote balance between responsibility and making money in our industry. For encouraging me to pursue Maria and Under the Golden Gate in the early days, because it was

a lot more fun, interesting, and soulful than so much of the nonsense going on out in the world.

The San Francisco Underworld and those others in the community who love joining in the colors:

You all make me smile when I think of you, and I cannot possible express how much I love you all for being yourselves, for being there for each other, and for living a beautifully colorful, authentic, fabulous, inspiring, inclusive, welcoming, supportive, courageous, and loving life. And for being there for me, and allowing me to have the best time of my life!!! LOVE YOU!!!